DATE DUE

NO 7 '96			
NO 7 '05			
DE 19 05			
JE 6 06			
DE 17 07			

DEMCO 38-296

Ivory Power

SUNY Series in the Psychology of Women

Michele A. Paludi, Editor

Ivory Power

Sexual Harassment on Campus

Edited by

Michele A. Paludi

State University of New York Press

Published by
State University of New York Press, Albany

© 1990 State University of New York

For information, address State University of New York
Press, State University Plaza, Albany, N.Y., 12246

Library of Congress Cataloging in Publication Data

Ivory power : sexual harassment on campus / edited by Michele A.
    Paludi.
        p.   cm. — (SUNY series in the psychology of women)
    Includes bibliographical references.
    ISBN 0-7914-0457-9 (alk. paper). — ISBN 0-7914-0458-7
(pbk. : alk. paper)
    1. Sexual harassment in universities and colleges—United States.
I. Paludi, Michele Antoinette. II. Series.
LC212.862.I95   1990
370.19'345—dc20   90-9478
                                                                   CIP

10 9 8 7 6 5 4 3

I dedicate this volume to my friends
who understood my need
to have this book written:

Mary P. Koss
Ron Towne
Sandy Shullman
Louise Fitzgerald
Darlene C. DeFour
Dorothy O. Helly
Sue Rosenberg Zalk
Richard Barickman

Contents

Forewords

An Ecological Perspective to Understanding Sexual Harassment

Richard Barickman, Sam Korn, Bernice Sandler, Yael Gold, Alayne Ormerod, and *Lauren M. Weitzman*

Recently a college student wrote this about her experiences with informal, collaborative methods of composing essays:

> The anxiety of writing a paper used to destroy me. (I know I'm not alone here). Writing my first draft for this class, I didn't cry, I didn't despair, I didn't consider dropping the course (nor did I think of dropping out of school altogether). I didn't conclude that I'm some sort of fake and a totally useless human being. I simply sat down and wrote and wrote and wrote. That's the idea, isn't it?

Maria's account of her anxieties is not bizarre, not even atypical—just unusually candid. Whenever students write informally, in a comfortable environment, about their experience of writing for courses, the great majority reveal similar anxieties about the self-exposure involved in writing essays and submitting them for evaluations. And almost all feel alone as well as vulnerable: "This is *my* special problem, my weakness, my shame." Simply hearing other students read similar "confessions" is a revelation and an immediate relief of tension.

Now, writing is a particularly exacting, complex, and personal process. But Maria's classmate Andrew had similar apprehensions about the prospect of studying poetry (even though he is a fiction writer, majoring in English): "I must confess that this course marks my very first course in poetry and that starting with Whitman and Dickinson terrifies me...." We also know that many students get quite anxious about courses in mathematics and science, anxious when facing any sort of examination, afraid of speaking in class, and so forth. In fact, most colleges offer special programs for overcoming or coping with such anxieties. The problem is, our knowledge often remains abstract, general, not brought to bear on the day-to-day experiences students actually live through in their courses. We are even likely to insulate ourselves from our own memories of emotions like Maria's and Andrew's, when we were panic-stricken students handing in a paper at arm's length, face turned away, gasping, "Oh, don't read it *now!*" as the professor casually flips the title page and glances at the opening paragraph.

The fact is—a fact manifest in virtually every college classroom but obscured by our academic routines and proprieties—the classroom is a place of power and vulnerability as well as a place of open inquiry and invigorating discussion. When all goes well—and it often does—the power in the classroom is shared, decentralized, truly empowering for students and teachers. It energizes a process of collaborative investigations and responses that, apart from their intellectual content, give students a sense of sharing in a cultural inheritance, connecting the privacy of the self with the great currents of common, public tradition.

To often, though, power in the classroom is abused, and the vulnerable become victims. Unfortunately, its destructive impact is likely to be directly proportional to the trust the academy encourages its students to have in an ideal of education. Whatever their ages, sexes, or backgrounds, students—through their very status as students and through the very autonomy of the classroom that we prize in college education—are in an unusual position of vulnerability. The greater the eagerness to learn, the greater the implicit trust in the college's professions of a community of shared values, the greater the shock and pain when that trust is violated. And, as our whole society should realize through our increasing awareness of the extent and nature of incest, sexual abuse of children, rape, battery of women, pornography, and prostitution, power is often most cruelly abused when it is directed against an individual's sexuality or sex.

Inevitably, if we are teachers or counselors or administrators in a college—or if we are custodians, security guards, electricians, cafeteria workers—we deal with the complexities of these power relations. For the college community exists in its corridors, offices, and cafeterias, as well as in its classrooms. Its members include all employees and all students. It is—and should be—a protected and privileged environment, where people can speak their minds without risking loss of face or job, or the often violent retaliation of the streets. It must be, if this special environment is to be a reality, a community that protects and nurtures its members. Not, perhaps, standing in *loco parentis*, but always as a *locus humanitatis*.

Inevitably, also, given the predatory and discriminatory behavior rife in U.S. society, a great majority of women students, a very significant percentage of women staff and faculty, and—in all probability—a great many gay students, faculty, and staff will be victimized by sexual or gender harassment. The most reliable studies indicate that 30 percent of women students are sexually harassed by at least one instructor in college. When we consider gender harassment as well (the sort of sexist behavior comparable to racist treatment of non-Whites), the incidence rate is close to 70 percent. These figures—especially when we come to know the individuals whose lives are damaged by sexual harassment—should in themselves help explain why those of us who become organizers and members of college panels on sexual harassment persist in the demanding and delicate interactions they require—and why we advocate similar panels for every college in the country.

The Panel on Sexual Harassment at Hunter College of the City University of New York has, since 1982, served as a resource for students, faculty, and staff where they can find information about sexual and gender harassment, counseling, and redress for harassment they have experienced in the college community. The Panel, and others like it across the nation, necessarily deals with abuses of power within the college community; but it also has another primary role: to help the entire college community recognize the existence, nature, and extent of sexual and gender harassment so that we may work together toward eliminating these pervasive, but often hidden abuses. In my experience as a founding member and, for the past few years, co-coordinator of the Panel, a group such as this learns as it seeks to establish procedures, to investigate complaints, and to share information and insights with others. As we deal with the complexities of actual personalities and circumstances, the reality of the term "abuse" becomes apparent and this awareness, we hope, fosters the sensitivity needed to help the person who feels victimized. At the same time, we must investigate the complaint without prejudging circumstances and events. Although such panels deal with a particular issue, their methods almost necessarily intersect other approaches to the nature and problems of traditional academic structures and methodologies. Research in ethnic and racial diversity, challenges to an exclusive Eurocentric college curriculum and feminist scholarship in every field are natural allies and primary resources. The collaborative nature of our Panel, composed of faculty, staff, and students, in itself suggests ways that the classroom and college environment can be something better than a traditional hierarchy, deeply split between professor and student.

Finally, we work against the complicity of ignorance. I still hear colleagues say, with a laugh or smirk, when I tell them I'm off to a meeting of the Panel, "Oh, are you going to harass someone?" or, "Can I volunteer to be harassed?" I suspect that if the meeting were on rape counseling, AIDS, or racism, the response would be different. We still lack public recognition that the problem of sexual harassment in the academy is a problem, one of major importance and shared responsibility. Whatever covert biases continue—as they will—public recognition is a necessary precondition for significant change. Those who have fought, with significant success, for decent treatment of the victims of rape and racial abuse know the importance of public debate.

The chapters in this collection are very important contributions to the growing, collective effort to inform the college community about the sexual harassment that affects at least a third of its members. The authors of the chapters have all been engaged in direct action to remedy the abuses caused by sexual harassment. They offer no abstract theories; they present results of practical research and experience that can serve as models for individual and collective action.

—*Richard Barickman*

*   *   *

In viewing this volume there are a number of separate issues that converge as the chapters unfold. My experience as the College Ombudsman at Hunter College, and as one who became a part of the Sexual Harassment Panel even before it was formalized, may shape my focus on this volume. Each reader may bring to this material a different perspective. The strength of this volume is that it provides ample opportunity, information, and guidance along a wide range of concerns in this area. Sexual harassment is a crime, and it is a shame that it has not received appropriate consideration in the work place and in the academic halls until relatively recently.

From my vantage point, the data on the relative frequency of the occurrence of sexual harassment is not a genuine concern. Frequency does not identify the importance of horrendous events. The action taken with regard to the events identifies its importance to the victims, the potential victims, *and* to those who intentionally or inadvertently engage in these practices. This is true of lynchings, restrictive covenants, racist acts, and racism and sexism in general. Again, it is not the frequency of these events that make them horrible acts, it is the very nature of the acts themselves. The measure of a civilized society is how it protects the less powerful, and how it reacts to the victimization of the less powerful.

Sexual harassment in the academic community is most often the victimization of the less powerful. It involves coercion and potential retaliation in a system in which advancement is based on subjective evaluations. The victim's helplessness is exaggerated by the dependency that is fostered by the powerful agents in the university—the teacher, the thesis sponsor, the faculty member who is expected to provide letters of recommendation, etc. The junior faculty member, like the student, is equally dependent, and is just as likely to be victimized as long as these issues are ignored. The fact that the system is based on subjective criteria—for grades, for promotion—makes the victim even more helpless.

The problems of encouraging reports or complaints of sexual harassment are further exacerbated by the fact that the victims may not suspect that harassment actually occured, or may even feel guilty that they may have been at least partially responsible for the harassment. The victims blaming themselves! Thus the problem of encouraging and investigating complaints of sexual harassment become very difficult. Following the initial act of harassment to its final impact requires very careful examination of the information provided. The review of the complaint must be very sensitively handled. This is well outlined in this volume.

Anyone who has tried to adjudicate complaints of sexual harassment finds this particularly troublesome. It is most often a private event. The victim is often left hurt and confused, and the victimizer has denial immediately available as a defense. The investigation of such complaints is very demanding—the fragile rights of both the accused and the accusor must be carefully protected.

Prevention of sexual harassment is our most important goal. Even if retaliation is prevented, even if justice finally triumphs, the personal impact of sexual harassment cannot be undone for the victims. The history of the event persists and the victims need help beyond simple adjudication. A very troubling matter indeed.

What are we left to do? We must put everyone in the community—the university—on guard. We must sensitize potential victims and warn potential victimizers by raising the awareness of the kinds of behavior that fall within the category of sexual harassment. We have to make clear the sources of help for the victims of sexual harassment—how to report the incident, where to go for help, and what protections are available. We have to emphasize the victims' responsibilities to their peers and to the institution to report sexual harassment whenever it occurs. In order to provide "power equality" judicial review must be thorough and swift. We must have sanctions that are commensurate with the degree of harassment and damage done, and we must have sanctions that will be imposed. The responsible administrative officers must demonstrate their readiness to impose penalties that reflect the seriousness of the violation involved. Without the latter, the whole matter falls like a house of cards.

As the chapters of this volume unfold, we see that these issues, and other related matters, are given the thorough attention that they merit.

—*Sam Korn*

*   *   *

Our Project on the Status and Education of Women at the Association of American Colleges wrote the first nationally distributed report on sexual harassment in 1979. Pandora's box opened in 1977 when 5 students, claiming sexual harassment by faculty, sued Yale University under Title IX, which prohibits sexual discrimination in institutions receiving federal assistance. Subsequently, in the early 1980s, many institutions developed policies and educational programs to deal with sexual harassment. These institutions are now reevaluating those policies and programs in light of their experiences over the last few years. Other institutions are just developing their policies and making critical decisions as to just what that policy ought to be. Clearly this book comes at a good time.

Although a lot has been written about sexual harassment on campus, less has been written about policies and policy implementation. Often each institution has had to reinvent its own wheel as it shaped and implemented its policy because there has been no place to get information about what options to consider and what other institutions have found successful.

Sexual harassment on campus is not a rare occurrence. Between 20 to 30 percent of all female undergraduates experience some form of sexual harassment behaviors such as leering, sexual innuendos and comments, obscene gestures, humor and jokes about sex or women in general, unwanted touching or other physical contact, and direct or indirect threats or bribes for unwanted sexual activity.

About two percent of undergraduate women report that they have received specific threats, coercion or offers of bribes for unwanted sexual activity. Two percent may sound like a small number but it represents over 130,000 women students. Using the lower figure of 20 percent as an estimate for all forms of sexual harassment—subtle and overt—by faculty and staff means that over 1,300,000 women students experience harassment. For graduate women, the percentage is higher, somewhere between

30 and 40 percent experience sexual harassment. Additionally, between 70 and 90 percent of women students report having been harassed by their fellow male students; indeed, a new campus issue is student peer harassment.

A small percentage of cases—perhaps three or five percent—involve male students being harassed by either men or women faculty or staff. Only a few studies have examined harassment of faculty and staff. These figures vary more widely than those of student harassment and in most incidences are higher; one study suggests that as many as 50 percent of untenured women faculty may experience some form of harassment. For staff the figures may even be higher. It is increasingly clear that for a large number of students, faculty, and staff the college environment is not one of learning and support but one of stress and exploitation. Most men are not harassers. Usually it is a small number of men who are harassing a larger number of women, either sequentially or simultaneously or both. It is quite rare for a person to harass only once; it is typically a pattern of behavior that is repeated again and again.

Sexual harassment continues to be a troublesome issue on campus. Certainly more research is needed to analyze the causes, extent and efficacy of remedies. The problem will not go away, nor are there easy answers. The issues are complex and not readily resolved. This book is a step in the right direction and will provide institutions with much of the help they need to provide a climate where men and women can learn and work in an environment that is free of harassment.

—*Bernice Sandler*

*   *   *

Writing the foreword to this volume on sexual harassment in academia has given us the opportunity to look at our individual and collective commitment to feminism and our expressions of this commitment through our research. We have each come to recognize that it is important to actively express our dedication to issues affecting women. As a result, we have chosen to combine personal aspirations with this commitment and to develop a career that seeks to contribute substantively to women's empowerment.

As graduate students, we were interested in obtaining hands-on research experience; as feminists, we were fascinated with the topic of sexual harassment. These combined interests prompted us to individually approach Louise Fitzgerald with the desire to participate in her project examining sexual harassment in academia. Through our inclusion in Louise's work, we have evolved into a strong collaborative feminist research team that has been active in presenting and publishing for the last three years.

It has been professionally satisfying and personally exciting to be involved in this research group. We have also experienced a dual role conflict given the area that we investigate, and our status as graduate students. Our research has increased our awareness by sensitizing us to the range of sexual harassment behaviors that often exist in the university environment (*e.g.*, sexist innuendos and comments, a general sexist atmosphere, and offensive behaviors). This increased awareness has allowed us to empathize with the experience of our research subjects, and has resulted in an increased motivation to address issues of sexual harassment in our empirical work. It has also presented us with the dilemma of how to resolve or address harassment that we may notice or experience as students. We are placed in the position of needing to assess the benefits and repercussions that any possible action would have on our academic careers. This can at times cause us to remain silent when we feel outrage, or to question our very involvement in this sometimes unpopular, and always controversial, area.

In studying sexual harassment, we have discovered that its origin and many of its expressions stem from the sexism that persists in our society. We are reminded of the feminist slogan that "the personal is political," and we have come to view our research efforts as our vehicle for social change. One obvious drawback in using research to achieve this goal is that the effectiveness of the research is not always immediately visible. There is often a substantial time lag between the discovery of new information and the use of it. The process of doing research can be abstract and necessarily removes the investigator's subjective feelings from the area under investigation, so that the phenomena may be examined in an unbiased manner.

The positive aspects in doing this type of research are many. If an idea is substantiated, it can lead to reliable and accurate information that can be used for positive changes that benefit women students. Our own knowledge of harassment and its effects has increased. Our identities and abilities as professionals have been greatly enhanced by our empirical experience, as well as by our exposure to collegial relationships with other professionals. In learning the process of research, we gain a tool for channeling idealism and outrage into knowledge that can be used for creating an educational system beneficial to all.

In looking forward to the future we anticipate the day when one group will not dominate another and sexual harassment will no longer be an issue. We believe that any real change must begin with increased awareness at all levels. A majority of students and faculty must recognize that sexual harassment is an imposition inflicted by a person in a position of power over a person with lower status. Development of workshops for students and faculty, panel discussions related to this topic, support for victims, and sound institutional guidelines for dealing with sexual harassment are possible concerete actions toward obtaining this goal. We hope that both the subtle forms of sexual harassment and its more blatant manifestations will disappear. The university environment is one where all persons have the right to seek education in a harassment-free setting, and is one that can set guidelines for social change. This volume is an important step in this process. We hope that other students and professionals, women and men, will follow their passions and hopes for a more equitable world and seek to realize this in their personal and professional lives.

—*Yael Gold, Alayne Ormerod,* and *Lauren M. Weitzman*

Preface

The career psychology of women continues to be an active area of research and theory, as evidenced by the recent textbook in this area by Nancy Betz and Louise Fitzgerald (1987). In an attempt to understand why women do not attain levels of success frequently attained by men, why traditional measures of achievement motivation and behavior are unrelated for women, and how to motivate women to enter previously all-male occupations and careers, research has focused on the following socio-psychological factors: child rearing and socialization patterns (Horner, 1968), women's attributions for success and failure (Deaux and Emswiller, 1974), as well as how women define success (Stein and Bailey, 1973).

In recent years, research on the career psychology of women has included structural or institutional factors involved, including performance evaluation and discrimination against women. Recently, a considerable amount of evaluation and controversy has been devoted to the operation of mentors on women's career development. Arguments in favor of mentors (preferably female) for women have stressed the importance of women's identification with female models, the importance of the information provided by the mentor's behavior, and the positive incentive through illustrative success. Women have been advised to find a female mentor and to be one to other women. This appeal is most likely a response to the numerous research findings that suggest that women do not receive as much mentoring as do men. Explanations for this finding have concerned the paucity of women who are in positions of power to serve as mentors.

Thus, several researchers have commented on the crucial part played by mentors in promoting their protégés' professional growth (Gilbert, Gallessich, and Evans, 1983; Rawles, 1980; Wallston, Cheronis, Czirr, Edwards, and Russo, 1978). Research has typically indicated that mentoring influences are related to individuals' level of career development (Farylo, Jerome, Hicks, and Paludi, 1985; Farylo and Paludi, 1985; McNeer, Haynes, and Paludi, 1983). Undergraduate women appear to benefit from having the opportunity to observe a female professor. Professional women, on the other hand, are more interested in determining how to pursue their career goals. Furthermore, the sex of the mentor relates to women's self-assessment of competency, aspirations, and self-worth

(Farylo and Paludi, 1985; Gilbert, Gallessich, and Evans, 1983).

For the last several years I have been conducting research into the sociopsychological and structural factors affecting women's achievement and the career pathways they follow. Key sociopsychological factors I have investigated included fear of success, achievement orientation, causal attributions for success and failure, and gender-role identity. Structural factors have included the influence of social policy on achievement potential, performance evaluation, employed mothers and the family context, and attitudes and attributions about women's abilities and roles. In 1982 I began conducting research on another structural factor, the availability of role models and mentors on women's career development. With the assistance of several graduate and undergraduate students in my women's career development research collective at Kent State University and Hunter College, I have investigated the impact of mentors on women's perceptions of competency, aspirations, and self-worth. These studies were done using several cohorts: undergraduate women, graduate women, women faculty and administrators. A great deal of information was obtained from these studies that failed to support the enthusiasm of a woman having a mentor that other authors were suggesting. Instead of the positive influences being discussed, women in our studies were telling us about the drawbacks of having a mentor—especially if the mentor was a man. My research collective and I learned from these women that they were typically perceived by their male mentors as needing assistance, as requiring help with their studies or work. The male mentors from whom we obtained responses described their male protégés as having a long-term commitment to their careers. The same mentors described their female protégés as needing their help to get through school or their job. Similar results were being reported around the same time by Marianne LaFrance (1987), who commented on the paradox of mentoring for women: As women continue to get the mentoring they need, they will be seen as needing the mentoring they get.

And Phyllis Bronstein and her colleagues (1986) found that male mentors, in their letters of recommendations of female protégés for faculty positions, described the woman's family responsibilities as a burden. For men, a family life was presented as an asset. None of the female protégés mentioned lifestyle/family status in their vitae; male mentors, however, mentioned it. Furthermore, Marilyn Haring-Hildore and Linda Brooks (1986) reported that approximately half of the protégés they studied reported having problems with their mentors. Thus, data was beginning to accumulate that suggested that having a mentor did not ensure a successful mentoring relationship in which the protégé receives the sponsorship, coaching, encouragement, and criticism that enables them to accomplish their career goals.

In addition, the women in our research described their experiences with being trivialized, ignored, and omitted from important meetings that would further their careers. They described their battles with being called "girl" in class and on the job; their being touched, patted, looked at, and propositioned backed by the threat of a lowered grade or failure to get a promotion. Our research on mentoring and being mentored thus led us to investigate another structural factor involved in women's achievement: sexual harassment.

At about the same time two colleagues, Louise Fitzgerald and Sandy Shullman, obtained a research grant from the U.S. Department of Education to develop an instrument that would enable them to get a national profile of the incidence of sexual harassment in undergraduate, graduate, faculty, administrative, and staff women. Furthermore, it was also at this time that Mary Koss and I were involved in sex discrimination cases ourselves. We thus found ourselves totally immersed in research on women's victimization (Mary's research is on date rape; mine on mentoring and harassment), as well as immersed in the struggle to understand emotionally as well as intellectually what was happening to us in our own professional lives. The women participants in our research and in the studies being conducted by Louise Fitzgerald and Sandy Shullman were most helpful to us in this process. As feminist education suggests, we entered into dialogues with individual colleagues, family, friends, students, and research participants about the experience of harassment on women's professional careers, health, relationships, self-esteem, and sense of trust. This volume is one of the outgrowths of these dialogues.

A great many individuals deserve recognition for their participation in these dialogues. I would like to express my appreciation to them in this book: Paul Koss, John Koss, and Paul S. Koss, Ron Towne, Linda Guran, Virginia Harvey, Laurel Wilcox, Jan Litwack, MaryAnn Kinney, Sandy Shullman, Louise Fitzgerald, Margaret Richards, Nancy Bailey, Pat Louka, Janet Dix, Cathy Kane, Debbie Plummer, Barb Watts, Nancy Betz, Louise Douse, Marilee Niehoff, William Dember, Richard Melton, John Allensworth, Sandy Christman, and John Marino.

The participants in our Hunter College Women's Career Development Research Collective also deserve recognition for their willingness to research harassment and for their wonderful ability to share the information on harassment with women and men in a variety of disciplines: Carole Ann Scott, Joni Kindermann, Marc Grossman, Susan Matula, Judi Dovan, Lisa Goldstein, Pam Schneider, Don Grimm, Lorraine McKenney, Meryl Zacker, Dolly Soto, and Elizabeth Wilson-Ansley.

The Sexual Harassment Panel at Hunter College also deserves my appreciation for inviting me to share the research and personal expertise with them. Dorothy O. Helly and Richard Barickman have been most supportive and encouraging and I have learned a great deal by working with them. Sam Korn, Jean Rieper, Ruth Smallberg, Vernell Daniels, Marc Grossman, Carole Ann Scott, Mary Lefkarities, Kathy Katzman, Michael Carrera, Carolyn Somerville, Sally Polakoff, and Sue Rosenberg Zalk also deserve my thanks.

And I thank Jacquelynne Eccles, Virginia O'Leary, Dona Alpert, Hannah Lerman, and Lenore Walker for inviting me to speak to them in Washington at the Division of the Psychology of Women's Executive Committee Meeting in 1986. As a result of this discussion, the Task Force on Sexism and Ethics was formed. I also thank Lenore Walker, Hannah Lerman, and Ellen Kimmel for inviting me to co-chair this Task Force with Hannah Lerman.

Anthony Mazzella and his staff at the Employee Assistance Program at Hunter College made it possible for me to offer workshops on sexual and gender harassment for faculty and staff.

And, I thank Sue Rosenberg Zalk for inviting me to apply for a position as Visiting Associate Professor of Women's Studies at Hunter College in 1986. It was at Hunter College I completed this volume, met many of its contributors, made dear friends, and understood myself once again. Sue's invitation led me to meet and work with Florence Denmark, Florence Howe, Donna Shalala, Dorothy O. Helly, Joan Tronto, Darlene DeFour, Fina Bathrick, Nancy Dean, Mary Lefkarities, Marcia Darling, Rosalind Petchesky, Mary Brown Parlee, Sue Riemer Sacks, Sarah Pomeroy, Susan Lees, and K.C. Wagner.

I especially thank Richard Barickman, with whom I am co-coordinating the Sexual Harassment Panel at Hunter College. Richard's generosity, caring, and support have been gifts to cherish.

I finally thank the person whose name appears first on the dedication page, Mary P. Koss. We both knew the struggle was worth it all along. We both knew we would be survivors. We got to be close friends—something many male colleagues of ours never wanted to happen. We really did win, Mary.

—*Michele A. Paludi*
Manhattan, January, 1990

References

Betz, N., and Fitzgerald, L.F. (1987). *The career psychology of women.* New York: Academic Press.

Bronstein, P., Black, L., Pfennig, J., and White, A. (1986). Getting academic jobs: Are women equally qualified and equally successful? *American Psychologist, 41*, 318-322.

Deaux, K., and Emswiller, T. (1974). Explanations of successful performance on sex-linked tasks: What is skill for the male is luck for the female. *Journal of Personality and Social Psychology, 29*, 80-85.

Farylo, B., Jerome, L., Hicks, J., and Paludi, M.A. (1985, March). *College women's role models: Relationships to academic advisor and college major.* Paper presented at the Association for Women in Psychology, New York, NY.

Farylo, B., and Paludi, M.A. (1985). Developmental discontinuities in mentor choice by male students. *Journal of Social Psychology, 125*, 521-522.

Gilbert, L., Gallessich, J., and Evans, S. (1983). Sex of faculty role model and students' self-perceptions of competency. *Sex Roles, 9*, 597-607.

Haring-Hidore, M., and Brooks, L. (1986). *Learning from problems mentors in academe have perceived in relationships with protégés.* Paper presented at the American Educational Research Association, Special Interest Group on Research on Women and Education, Washington, D.C.

Horner, M.S. (1968). *Sex differences in achievement motivation and performance in competitive and noncompetitive situations.* Unpublished doctoral dissertation, University of Michigan. Ann Arbor: University Microfilms.

LaFrance, M. (1987, July). *The paradox of mentoring.* Paper presented at the International Interdisciplinary Congress on Women, Dublin, IR.

McNeer, A., Haynes, B., and Paludi, M.A. (1983, May). *Developmental discontinuities in women's role model choice.* Paper presented at the Midwestern Psychological Association, Chicago, IL.

Rawles, B.A. (1980). *The influence of a mentor on the level of self-actualization of American scientists.* Unpublished doctoral dissertation, The Ohio State University.

Stein, A.H., and Bailey, M.M. (1973). The socialization of achievement orientation in females. *Psychological Bulletin, 80*, 345-366.

Wallston, B.S., Cheronis, J., Czirr, R., Edwards, S., and Russo, A. (1978, March). *Role models for professional women.* Paper presented at the Association for Women in Psychology, Pittsburgh, PA.

Introduction

Myths and Realities:
Sexual Harassment on Campus

*Michele A. Paludi, Marc Grossman, Carole Ann Scott,
Joni Kindermann, Susan Matula, Julie Ostwald, Judi Dovan,
and Donna Mulcahy*

> Dr. ----- asked me to come to his office to help him rearrange his books.
> Maybe it was my fault for going in the first place. He has these high bookcases,
> and the only way you can reach them is to stand on this little stool. I
> remember I had on this blue tight skirt that made it hard for me to step off and
> on that stool, but the skirt was pretty long. After a while, he got up and walked
> over and started bumping the stool. At first I thought he was just kidding
> around and I laughed. Then I got sort of scared because he almost knocked me
> over. I told him to be careful and that I didn't think he knew I was really
> scared. "I know you are, but the only way to keep from falling is for you to go
> about your business while I lay down on the floor here and watch you." I
> think that's exactly how he said it. I didn't know what else to do. I was afraid
> to leave, so I just kept on taking books down while he laid on the floor and
> looked up my dress at my underpants. Then I left, and he said, "thank you,"
> and never mentioned anything about it again. I guess I should have reported
> him to somebody, but I didn't know who. No one would have believed it
> anyway.
>
> (Dziech and Weiner, 1984, 10)

This statement by a woman college student illustrates several issues
about sexual harassment that will be addressed in this book:

First, *sexual victimization of women is not limited to cases of rape.* Many
women have experienced incidents of degrees of sexual harassment from
blatant statements (*e.g.*, making it clear that sexual activity is a prerequisite
to a good grade or to being promoted) to more subtle verbal and physical

gestures (leering, ogling, brushing up against one's body, squeezing or pinching).

Second, *traditional thinking blames the victim*, suggesting that the woman behaves and/or dresses provocatively or explicitly initiates sexual activity in the hope of getting a good grade, raise, promotion, etc.

Third, *because incidents of sexual harassment differ in the degree of coercion, they are difficult to define both legally and personally.* Sexual harassment trades on women's uncertainty about how to define and self-validate their experiences. Consequently, women self-impose silence (as with cases of rape, incest, and battering) which, in turn, contributes to the continued invisibility of harassment.

Fourth, *victims of sexual harassment may experience a lack of control over their own lives.* They fear that protesting will call attention to them and fear reprisals by the harasser and his colleagues.

Fifth, *women who experience sexual harassment are in a powerless position relative to the harasser* (e.g., student versus professor; employee versus employer). Women believe that *they* themselves need to deal with harassment, that there is no point in public protest, for no one would believe them. And, it is precisely because men are more often in positions of greater power at work and in the academy that sexual harassment becomes both a possibility and a reality.

Although this college woman's statement illustrates an experience of a college student, harassment is experienced by women of all ages, races, ethnic backgrounds, socioeconomic class, occupation, physical appearance, sexual orientations, and relationship statuses. Sexual harassment is not simply an annoyance or flirtation. It can mean the difference between passing a college course or failing one, between being given a raise or being fired. For women who are supporting themselves and/or children, being fired to dismissed from work or leaving school for sexual noncompliance is disastrous. Thus, the potential for harassing women is enormous. Sexual harassment, like rape, incest, and battering, represent male expressions of power and dominance over women.

SEXUAL HARASSMENT ON CAMPUS:
DEFINITIONS AND INCIDENCE

The *Project on the Status and Education of Women* (1978) referred to sexual harassment as a "hidden issue." Although sexual harassment has only recently been labeled, it has been an issue women have always faced. Franklin, Moglen, Zatling-Boring, and Angress (1981) pointed out that:

> On occasion, in certain forms, it appeared as romance: the naive student swept into bed by her brilliant professor. . . . Charlotte Brontë wrote about it more than a hundred years ago; in the popular confessions magazines, authors write about it still, in fictional form, it remains the stuff that fantasies are made of, fantasies that reflect and reinforce the tendency of our society to limit the definition of women to the sexual and domestic spheres and to soften . . . the linking of sexual dominance with the powerful and sexual submission with the powerless. (3)

Franklin et al. further distinguished between sexual and gender harassment. Gender harassment, a form of sexual harassment, consists principally of verbal behavior, i.e., remarks, jokes, and innuendos, which are directed at women because they are women. These behaviors may or may not be aimed at eliciting sexual cooperation from women. They are directed at individuals whom the initiator deems inferior. Therefore, gender harassment resembles racial and ethnic slurs and epithets.

In recent years, research has provided compelling evidence that sexual and gender harassment of students can result in serious psychological, emotional, physical, and economic consequences. Such harassment often forces students to forfeit research, work, and even their career plans. Research by Adams, Kottke, and Padgitt (1983) reported that 13 percent of the women students they surveyed said they had avoided taking a class or working with certain professors because of the risk of being subjected to sexual advances. Furthermore, a 1983 study conducted at Harvard University indicated that 15 percent of the graduate students and 12 percent of the undergraduate students who had been harassed by their professors changed their major or educational program because of the harassment. Wilson and Kraus (1983) reported that 8.9 percent of the female undergraduates in their study had been pinched, touched, or patted to the point of personal discomfort, while 17 percent of the women in the Adams et al. survey received verbal sexual advances, 13.6 percent received sexual invitations, 6.4 percent had been subjected to physical advances, and 2 percent received direct sexual bribes.

Bailey and Richards (1985) reported that of 246 women graduate students in their sample, 12.7 percent indicated they had been sexually harassed, 21 percent had not enrolled in a course to avoid such behavior, 11.3 percent tried to report the behavior, 2.6 percent dropped a course because of it, and 15.9 percent indicated they had been directly assaulted.

In one of the first comprehensive studies, Dziech and Weiner (1984) suggested that 30 percent of women students are harassed by at least one professor during their four years in college. When definitions of sexual harassment include gender harassment, the incidence rate in student populations reaches close to 70 percent. Dzeich and Weiner reported that sexual harassment often "forces a student to forfeit work, research, educational comfort, or even career. Professors withhold legitimate opportunities from those who resist, or students withdraw rather than pay certain prices" (10). As Crocker and Simon (1981) suggested, "formal education is, in the United States, an important factor in an individual's career possibilities and personal development, therefore stunting or obstructing that person's educational accomplishment can have severe consequences" (542). To the extent that sexual and gender harassment exists in the academy, it constitutes a serious structural or institutional barrier to women's career development.

SEXUAL AND GENDER HARASSMENT ON CAMPUS: LEGAL ISSUES

Title IX of the 1972 Education Amendments, administered by the Office for Civil Rights (OCR) is the law prohibiting sex discrimination against students. OCR's definition of sexual harassment is the following:

Sexual harassment consists of verbal or physical conduct of a sexual nature, imposed on the basis of sex, by an employee or agent of a recipient (of federal funds) that denies limits, provides different, or conditions the provision of aid, benefits, services, or treatment protected under Title IX.

No guidelines on sexual harassment have been issued for the Title IX. However, the parallels between Title VII (prohibition of sex discrimination in the workplace) and Title IX secure that harassment of students is a form of sex discrimination. Title IX has had a limited enforcement history, however. To date, the sole Title IX ruling directly dealing with the sexual harassment of students is *Alexander v. Yale*, filed in 1977 by a graduate of Yale University, Ronni Alexander, who stated that she "found it impossible to continue playing the flute and abandoned her study of the instrument, thus aborting her desired professional career," because of her professor's repeated sexual advances, "including coerced sexual intercourse." In addition, Alexander stated that although she complained to Yale officials about the harassment, she "was discouraged and intimidated by unresponsive administrators and complex and *ad hoc* methods." Ronni Alexander was joined in her legal action by four students, Margery Reifler, Pamela Price, Lisa Stone, and Ann Olivarius, who claimed that Yale

University's tolerance of sexual harassment created an intimidating atmosphere that was conducive to neither teaching nor learning. These claims were dismissed by the court on the grounds that the charges were "untenable," "moot," or "inadequate." Ronni Alexander's original complaint was dismissed by the United States Court of Appeals, which maintained that she had failed to prove her case and that Yale University had adequately addressed her concern by setting up a sexual harassment grievance procedure.

A major significance of *Alexander v. Yale* is that the District Court decision upheld that if sexual harassment does occur, it may constitute sex discrimination. The ruling maintained that:

> It is perfectly reasonable to maintain that academic advancement conditioned upon submission to sexual demands constitutes sex discrimination in education, just as questions of job retention or promotion tied to sexual demands from supervisors have become increasingly recognized as potential violations of Title VII's ban against sex discrimination in employment.

During the litigation of *Alexander v. Yale*, the Report of the Dean's Advisory Committee on Grievance Procedure at Yale was published. It claimed that the effects of harassment on students may endure past their graduation:

> Though sexual harassment in any situation is reprehensible, it must be a matter of particularly deep concern to an academic community in which students and faculty are related by strong bonds of intellectual dependence and trust. Further, the vulnerability of undergraduates to such harassment is particularly great and the potential impact upon them is particularly severe. Not only does sexual harassment betray the special bond between teacher and student, but it also exploits unfairly the power inherent in an instructor's relationship to his or her student. Through grades, recommendations, research appointments, or job referrals an instructor can have a decisive influence on a student's academic success and future career. If this influence should be used overtly or implicitly in an attempt to exact sexual favors, a situation is created that may have devastating implications for individual students and for the academic community as a whole. Through fear of academic reprisal, a student may be forced to comply with sexual demands at the price of a debilitating personal anguish, or to withdraw from a course, a major, or even a career, and thus is forced to change plans for a life's work.

IN THEIR OWN VOICES:
WOMEN DISCUSS HARASSMENT ON CAMPUS

Identical sentiments were obtained from undergraduate women in a
recent study by Dovan, Grossman, Kindermann, Matula, Paludi, and Scott
(1987). Women reported, when describing a college woman's experience
with sexual harassment:

> The professor violated her right to privacy and overstepped the
> boundaries of his authority as a professor.

> It seems clear that the professor was taking advantage of this student
> as a professor. He probably felt secure that the student would not say
> anything, and if she did, would not be believed.

> Psychologically, the fact that he is a professor with power over your
> grades and other stuff can't be underestimated. Otherwise he
> wouldn't have been able to get her to his office. Students are used to
> taking orders from professors.

> Men are socialized to be the sexual aggressor and to believe that
> women should be the object of that aggression.

> Male dominance is apparent in most every aspect of our society. It is
> so ingrained in our culture that often it goes unrecognized.

The following accounts all illustrate the extent and negative consequences of being in an environment conducive to harassment:

> Dr. P. gave me the creeps. Whenever we took a test, I'd look up from
> my paper, and there he would be staring at me. He was always looking
> at my top or my legs. I quit wearing skirts to that class because I was so
> uncomfortable around him. I felt like I was some kind of freak in a
> zoo. (Dziech and Weiner, 1984, 92)

> One of my professors had singled me out in the classroom and would
> detain me after the class—always to talk. I was brief but polite. But
> one day he saw me on campus and stopped me. He made some very
> suggestive comments, off-color remarks. Then he proceeded to tell
> me how he would like to come in my room with me at the dorm. At
> first I ignored the comment, but he repeated it. I shook my head no
> and tried to laugh it off. After that I tried to ignore him and make it
> quite obvious my intentions as a student. I was very angry and

disgusted and shocked. I also felt very helpless and trapped. I talked about it with people—women police, etc.—but it didn't really seem to resolve the situation. As far as grades go, I made sure that I got good grades in class so he couldn't possibly flunk me. (Dziech and Weiner, 1984, 94)

SEXUAL AND GENDER HARASSMENT: EXPLANATORY MODELS

Many of the explanations of the extent of sexual and gender harassment have tended to be satisfied with results that pinpoint this issue within the individual rather than in the situation or social structure. This explanation may be seen as a rationale for maintaining the *status quo* and permits women who complain about harassment to remain isolated. This isolation in turn leaves women at a disadvantage. Tangri, Burt, and Johnson (1982) identified this explanation as the *natural/biological model* of harassment. They have also identified two additional models: *organizational* and *sociocultural*, which have recently been used as theoretical models for understanding sexual harassment.

The natural/biological model interprets sexual and gender harassment as natural sexual attraction between people. This model maintains that harassing behavior is a natural expression of men's stronger sex drive and/or any person may be attracted to another individual and pursue that attraction without intent to harass. The natural/biological model has been used in court by universities as well as corporations seeking to avoid charges of sex discrimination for allowing sexual harassment to exist. This model continues to be the interpretation of sexual harassment most in need of modification in order to bring sexual harassment under the purview of sex discrimination statutes. The model rests on several assumptions about sexual and gender harassment and in the workplace that deny that it is illegal and discriminatory. This model denies the consequences of sexual and gender harassment on women's educational and physical health, career aspirations, and job security. Tangri *et al.* pointed out that if the natural/biological model was adequate in explaining sexual harassment, then certain conditions should be the norm, *e.g.*, women recipients should be similar to their male harassers in age, race, and occupational status, they should be unmarried; the behaviors should resemble courtship behaviors, and should stop once the woman shows disinterest. In addition, women should report feeling flattered by the behavior, not offended.

Tangri *et al.* tested this model with data from the U.S. Merit Board Study; it was not supported:

The consistent negative reactions of female victims to incidents they consider harassing, plus the tendency of individuals with greater degrees of personal vulnerability and dependence on their job to experience more harassment constitute the strongest evidence available in these data against the natural model. (52)

They found more support for the organizational and sociocultural models. The organizational model asserts that sexual and gender harassment results from the opportunities presented by power and authority relations which derive from the hierarchical structure of organizations. Thus, sexual harassment is seen as an issue of organizational power. As Tangri *et al.* claimed:

Since work organizations are characterized by vertical stratification, individuals can use their power and position to extort sexual gratification from their subordinates. Although typically males harass females, in principle, it is possible for females to sexually harass males. It is less likely only because women tend to be employed in occupations subordinate to men. (37)

Thus, the organizational model holds that institutions provide the opportunity structure that makes sexual and gender harassment possible. This model also explains why women may feel less comfortable, receive less professional support, and fewer intellectual challenges from male colleagues. Women are viewed by this model as being vulnerable to the economic, psychological, social, and physical consequences of sexual and gender harassment. This model thus relates sexual and gender harassment to aspects of the structure of academia and the workplace that provide asymmetrical relations between supervisors (*e.g.*, male professors) and subordinates (*e.g.*, female students).

The sociocultural model posits that sexual and gender harassment is only one manifestation of the much larger patriarchal system in which men are the dominant group. Therefore, harassment is an example of men asserting their personal power, based on sex. According to this model, sex would be a better predictor of both recipient and initiator status than would organizational position. Thus, women should be much more likely to be victims of sexual harassment, especially when they are in male-populated college majors. As Tangri *et al.* noted:

If sexual harassment is as widespread as the results of the MSPB survey indicate, it may approximate a random event in women's working lives—something that is highly likely to happen at some time with just when, where, and how being so multidetermined that prediction is difficult. This very fact supports the cultural model in some ways, but it also implies that finding empirical support for the cultural model will not be easy, if only because few, if any, circumstances exist where the dominant culture does not exert its influence. (52-53)

Gutek and Morasch (1982) have proposed an additional explanatory model of harassment: *sex-role spillover*. This is the carry over into the workplace of gender role based expectations of behavior. The spillover, predicated on skewed sex ratios in the workplace, is of two types. First, women who are employed in non-traditional occupations or are in non-traditional college majors, where they operate under a "token" status, will be treated as role deviates; they will be particularly salient as women (because of their singularity) and they will be treated different from their male colleagues. Second, women in female-populated careers will experience sex-role spillover, but of a different nature because their work parallels gender-role expectations. The former group of women are treated differently from their male colleagues and are more likely to report incidences of harassment than the latter group, who are relatively unaware that their treatment is based on their sex. In sum, the first kind of sex-role spillover is to the *women*, while the second kind of sex-role spillover is to the *field* (*i.e.*, sex-typing of the occupation of major) *per se*.

The sex-role spillover explanation is compatible with the sociocultural model of harassment discussed by Tangri *et al.* (1982). As Gutek and Morasch pointed out, "according to the power differential hypothesis, sexual harassment will always be perceived as sexual harassment" (72). Support for this explanation is available from several sources (Shullman and Fitzgerald, 1985; Till, 1980). Researchers have found evidence of greater incidence of sexual and gender harassment of women in non-traditional areas.

IVORY POWER REVISITED: IMPLICATIONS FOR TRAINING PROGRAMS

Recently, Dovan, Grossman, Kindermann, Matula, Paludi, and Scott (1987) reported that college women were more likely to label a faculty member's harassment of a woman student in terms of his abusing his power as a professor over the student instead of abusing his power as a man. They recognized sexual harassment as allowing professors to undermine students' positions in higher education. This finding supports the organizational model of harassment: women were able to explain harassment as resulting from the opportunities presented by power and authority relations which derive from the hierarchical structure of the academy. This adherence to the organizational model promoted more of a sense of empowerment for women students: they reported seeking redress for the victimization. Such response would not be predicted from adherence to the sociocultural model: women would not be likely to take interpersonally assertive action or to act on an expectation that the organization will help them resolve the issue.

These findings have implications for training programs for raising consciousness about harassment, especially about sexual jokes, requests for sexual favors and how images of women may affect individuals' perceptions of women's career commitment. This is especially important for training programs dealing with re-entry women as students and the unique issues they, as a group, raise as well as the harassment of women of color.

Another focus of such training lies in the politics involved in the mentor-protégé relationship. Typically, this relationship is not clearly conceptualized. Consequently, students and faculty do not share similar definitions of mentor and protégé (Haring-Hidore and Brooks, 1986; Paludi, 1987). Mentors are seen as essential because they generate power. Training of faculty about students' perceptions of power would be useful, especially given the recent results by Fitzgerald, Gold, Ormerod, and Weitzman (1988). Male faculty members who participated in this study typically denied that there exists an inherent power differential between students and faculty. Thus, educational programs are needed to deal with women's and men's understanding of the concept of harassment and the social meanings attributed to behaviors that legally constitute harassment. Truax (cited in Fitzgerald, 1986) claimed "men's perceptions of what their behavior means are vastly different from women's. . . . We find, in working with victims of sexual harassment that there is often little disagreement with what has happened between student and professor, but rather, with what the conduct means. Professors will try to justify their behavior on the grounds that they are just friendly and trying to make a student feel welcome, or they thought that the student would be flattered by the attention" (24). However, the interpretation given to the professor's behavior by women students is not flattery or friendliness. The consequences of being harassed to undergraduate and graduate women have been devastating to their physical well-being, emotional health, and vocational development, including depression, insomnia, headaches, helplessness, decreased motivation (Whitmore, 1983). The behaviors that legally constitute harassment are just that, despite what the professor's intentions may be. It is the power differential and/or the woman's reaction to the behavior that are the critical variables.

And it is this misuse of the power or authority by male faculty members that this book addresses. *Ivory Power* discusses sexual and gender harassment as the confluence of power relations and sexism in an institution stratified by sex. The contributors to this volume are all actively involved with sexual harassment cases as attorneys, researchers, clinicians, training consultants, and members of sexual harassment task forces on campuses in the United States. For example, Mary Koss and Kathryn Quina describe the interrelationships among rape and sexual harassment in terms of the consequences to women survivors. Louise Fitzgerald offers psychometric work to the measurement of sexual harassment, which has led to a more refined definition of the construct. She and Lauren Weitzman, in addition to Sue Rosenberg Zalk, discuss harassment in terms of male faculty members' views of women students and faculty members. Sandra Shullman and Barbara Watts address legal issues involved in harassment of students and workers. Darlene DeFour discusses the incidence and dimensions of sexual and gender harassment of women of color on campus and how this victimization contributes to the attrition rate in graduate training programs. Donna Stringer and her colleagues discuss clinical interventions with women survivors of harassment. Discussions of the establishment and maintenance of task forces are presented by Dorothy O. Helly, K.C. Wagner, and Mary Kay Biaggio and her colleagues. Louise Fitzgerald also discusses developmental issues involved in sexual and gender harassment: how women faculty, administrators, and staff experience harassment and their individual, legal, and institutional methods of seeking redress for harassment.

All contributors to this volume are committed to generating a feminist agenda for research, theorizing, education, and practice concerning these key issues in academic sexual and gender harassment. All have made specific recommendations to guide instructors, practitioners, and researchers in the continuing search for improved knowledge and practice in this barrier to women's career development. All contributors have, in their roles as professor, dean, student, and counselor, transformed the way the campus views sexual and gender harassment.

References

Adams, J.W., Kottke, J.L., and Padgitt, J.S. (1983). Sexual harassment of university students. *Journal of College Student Personnel, 24,* 484-490.

Bailey, N., and Richards, M. (1985, August). *Tarnishing the ivory tower: Sexual harassment in graduate training programs in psychology.* Paper presented at the American Psychological Association, Los Angeles, CA.

Crocker, P., and Simon, A. (1981). Sexual harassment in education. *Capitol University Law Review*, 10, 541-584.

Dovan, J., Grossman, M., Kindermann, J., Matula, S., Paludi, M.A., and Scott, C.A. (1987, March). *College women's attitudes and attributions about sexual and gender harassment*. Symposium presented at the Association for Women in Psychology, Bethesda, MD.

Dziech, B., and Weiner, L. (1984). *The lecherous professor: Sexual harassment on campus*. Boston: Beacon Press.

Fitzgerald, L.F. (1986, August). *The lecherous professor: A study in power relations*. Paper presented at the American Psychological Association, Washington, D.C.

Fitzgerald, L.F., Gold, Y., Ormerod, M., and Weitzman, L. (1988). Academic harassment: Sex and denial in scholarly garb. *Psychology of Women Quarterly*, 12, 329-340.

Franklin, P., Moglin, J., Zatling-Boring, P., and Angress, R. (1981). *Sexual and gender harassment in the academy*. New York: Modern Languages Association.

Gutek, B., and Morasch, B. (1982). Sex-ratios, sex-role spillover, and sexual harassment of women at work. *Journal of Social Issues*, 38, 55-74.

Haring-Hidore, M., and Brooks, L. (1986, November). *Learning from the problems mentors in academe have perceived in relationships with protégés*. Paper presented at the American Educational Research Association, Washington, D.C.

Paludi, M.A. (1987, July). *Women and the mentor-protégé relationship: A feminist critique for the inadequacy of old solutions*. Paper presented at the Interdisciplinary Congress on Women, Dublin, IR.

Project on the Statuys and Education of Women (1978). *Sexual harassment: A hidden issue*. Washington, D.C.: Association of American Colleges.

Shullman, S., and Fitzgerald, L. (1985, August). *The development and validation of an objectively scored measure of sexual harassment*. Paper presented at the American Psychological Association, Los Angeles, CA.

Tangri, S., Burt, M., and Johnson, L. (1982). Sexual harassment at work: Three explanatory models. *Journal of Social Issues*, 38, 33-54.

Till, F. (1980). *Sexual harassment: A report on the sexual harassment of students.* Washington, D.C.: National Advisory Council on Women's Education Programs.

Whitmore, R.L. (1983). *Sexual harassment at UC Davis.* Davis, CA: Women's Resources and Research Center, University of California.

Wilson, K., and Krauss, L. (1983). Sexual harassment in the university. *Journal of College Student Personnel, 24,* 219-224.

I

Sexual Harassment

Conceptual and Methodological Issues

Editor's Notes

> My impression (and belief) is that most professors do not know that they
> behave differently towards women (in class, in conference, and in administra-
> tive affairs).

> I have not encountered discrimination by faculty with regard to classroom
> and academic activities. I have, however, consciously chosen not to take
> particular courses with faculty who have reputations concerning sexual
> discrimination. In this way, my scope of available coursework was limited.

> Many professors, while admitting awareness of sex stereotyping language,
> often justify their continued use of these labels. Frequently, they joke about
> their continued male chauvinism, as though their admission serves as an
> exoneration for a continuation of sexism.

> Women who asked questions are not answered, so women have stopped
> asking questions.
>
> (Taken from Hall and Sandler, 1982)

What is sexual harassment? Are the experiences of the women cited above illustrative of sexual harassment? A great deal of confusion has resulted from the lack of a clear, concise, widely accepted definition of academic sexual harassment. Definitions of sexual harassment are important because they can educate the college campus and promote discussion and conscientious evaluation of experiences (Crocker, 1983). While definitions of sexual harassment (as well as policies prohibiting sexual harassment) vary from campus to campus, there are some common aspects and conclusions. For example, the definitions include some concept of the misuse of differential power, concern for the academic environment, and include a range of behaviors from sexist language to physical assault (Somers, 1982).

Louise Fitzgerald, in "Sexual harassment: The definition and measurement of a construct," describes the persistent problem that has existed in defining sexual harassment. She reviews the most influential definitions that have been used and critiques them from a feminist methodological perspective. Dr. Fitzgerald also discusses the development and initial psychometric studies using the *Sexual Experiences Surveys*, developed by herself and Dr. Sandra Shullman in 1985. These surveys, designed for students, faculty, and administrators, measure five levels of sexual harassment: gender harassment, seductive behavior, sexual bribery, sexual coercion, and sexual imposition. Based on a program of research with the *Sexual Experiences Surveys*, Dr. Fitzgerald offers the following definition of sexual harassment:

> Sexual harassment consists of the sexualization of an instrumental relationship through the introduction or imposition of sexist or sexual remarks, requests or requirements, in the context of a formal power differential. Harassment can also occur where no such formal differential exists, if the behavior is unwanted by or offensive to the woman. Instances of harassment can be classified into the following general categories: gender harassment, seductive behavior, solicitation of sexual activity by promise of reward or threat of punishment, and sexual imposition or assault.

As Crocker (1983) argued, ". . . the effectiveness of any definition will depend not only on the grievance procedure that enforces it but also on the commitment of the university administration and faculty to creating a truly nondiscriminatory environment for all students" (707). The definition offered by Dr. Fitzgerald has assisted college campuses with meeting Crocker's goals. It has also been of enormous value for alerting sexual harassment task forces about the failure of many victims of harassment to label their experiences as sexual harassment. Appropriate educational and psychotherapeutic interventions can be implemented to assist women in this cognitive appraisal. Examples of interventions are discussed throughout this book.

Darlene DeFour, in "The interface of racism and sexism on college campuses," refines Dr. Fitzgerald's definition and conceptualization of sexual harassment by including a sociocultural perspective. Dr. DeFour's discussion centers on the need to develop research paradigms on sexual harassment as well as sexual harassment task forces that are not Eurocentric in their focus. She currently is working on obtaining incidence rates of the levels of sexual harassment for women of color. Dr. DeFour notes, based on research conducted by the Hunter College Women's Career Development Research Collective, that women of color report sexual harassment that has racist overtones. Balancing the sexual harassment task force for racial and ethnic issues is a major call for action by Dr. DeFour. Her own research in the area of sexual harassment has stimulated (1) task forces to include individuals of color on harassment investigative teams, and (2) campus counseling centers to have on staff individuals of color who are trained in issues involved in sexual harassment and who are of color and who speak languages in addition to English.

Dr. DeFour alerts us to the ways in which images of women of color increase their vulnerability to harassment. One form of this discrimination concerns the establishment of a "null environment" (Betz, 1987) for women of color in which they are ignored and kept at a distance from faculty, administrators, and other students who may be potential collaborators. This form of interpersonal discrimination is also addressed by Bernice Lott in "The perils and promise of studying sexist discrimination in face-to-face situations." Dr. Lott describes a series of laboratory experiments she designed to investigate how women students and faculty on college campuses are silenced by those in power in the academic settings. Viewing this distancing behavior as a form of gender harassment, Dr. Lott calls for campus task forces to include programs on feelings, cognitions, and actions involved in this type of sexist behavior. She offers additional suggestions for eliminating the "chilly climate" (Hall and Sandler, 1982) for women on campuses.

Drs. Fitzgerald, DeFour, and Lott express concern that a campus environment that fosters sexual harassment interferes with the educational process and career development of women. Many women students' career options may be foreclosed and the campus community may lose women students, faculty, and administrators of great potential if the campus reinforces the chilly climate (Hall and Sandler, 1982). The Hunter College Sexual Harassment Panel publishes "The student in the back row," which describes techniques for fostering an egalitarian campus climate. This brochure is presented in the appendix. It concludes with a sentiment expressed by all three authors in this section:

> Greater understanding and awareness can lead to important changes in behavior. The long-term professional rewards of these changes include better communication with students, improved teaching effectiveness, and eventual realization of equal educational opportunity for all students.

References

Betz, N. (1987, May). *The null environment for women*. Paper presented at the First Biennial Meeting of the Midwestern Society for Feminist Studies, Akron, OH.

Crocker, P. (1983). An analysis of university definitions of sexual harassment. *Signs, 8,* 696-707.

Hall, R.M., and Sandler, B.R. (1982). *The classroom climate: A chilly one for women?* Washington, D.C.: Project on the Status and Education of Women.

Somers, A. (1982). Sexual harassment in academe: Legal issues and definitions. *The Journal of Social Issues, 38,* 23-32.

1

Sexual Harassment:
The Definition and Measurement of a Construct

Louise F. Fitzgerald

The unnamed should not be taken for the nonexistent.

(MacKinnon, 1979, 28)

One of the most persistent and troubling problems in the sexual harassment literature has been the lack of a widely agreed upon definition of the concept, one that was both broad enough to comprehend the variety of experiences to which the construct refers, and yet specific enough to be of practical use. As MacKinnon (1979) notes "It is not surprising . . . that women would not complain of an experience for which there has been no name. Until 1976, lacking a term to express it, sexual harassment was literally unspeakable, which made a generalized, shared and social definition of it inaccessible" (27). She notes that Working Women United Institute appear to have been the first to use the term, in connection with the case of Carmita Wood, one of the first women to seek unemployment compensation after leaving a job due to the sexual advances of her superior (*In re Carmita Wood*, 1975). It was also advanced at about the same time by the Cambridge-based Alliance Against Sexual Coercion (1976) and by Brodsky (1976). Over a decade later, a decade marked by an explosion of interest, research and litigation, MacKinnon's "generalized, shared and social definition" remains inaccessible.

Separate from this problem, but related to it, is the lack of a generally agreed upon *operational* definition, one that can be used in research and theory building in this area. Although many studies have been conducted, each has tended to develop its own methodology, a practice yielding conflicting estimates of incidence rates and behaviors. This not only leads to disarray in the literature, but also has the unfortunate "real world" effect of diminishing the credibility of such reports within the legal system and the opportunity for social science to contribute to social change in this important area of women's rights.

The present chapter begins by analyzing the most influential of the various sexual harassment definitions that have been proposed, both those that are *a priori* (theoretical) in nature, and those that have been developed empirically, particularly through investigation of what various groups of people perceive sexual harassment to be under different circumstances and in different contexts. We then move to a consideration of *operational definitions*, that is, to the instruments that have been developed to measure sexual harassment, and conclude with a discussion of theoretical and practical issues in the definition and measurement of harassment in higher education as well as the workplace.

DEFINITIONS

A Priori Definitions

Although likely based to some degree on previously, informally observed phenomena, most definitions of sexual harassment are *a priori* in nature; that is, rather than being explicitly data-based, they are derived from theoretical propositions concerning the nature of the construct. Such *a priori* definitions take one of two forms, the first (Type 1) of which consists of a general statement describing the *nature* of the behavior and (sometimes) the status relationship of the persons involved. Such statements generally do not, however, define or list any particular behaviors or classes of behavior. The second type (Type 2) take a quite different, and in some ways opposite form, consisting as they do of a list of specific actions, with no formal explication of the theoretical framework from which such a list is derived, with the general exception that the behavior is usually described as unwanted by the recipient. It is sometimes the case that the first type of definition is followed by examples, and the second occasionally the basis of some later generalization; thus we appear to have instances of what is generally comprehended by the terms *deductive* and *inductive*. However, a closer examination reveals both forms to be examples of deductive reasoning, with the distinction being that the original theory statement is sometimes explicit and sometimes not. (Since the list of behaviors found in Type 2 definitions are not preceded by or based on any data collection activity, it is logically necessary that they derive from the writer's theoretical perspective, however implicit that may be.)

Definitions of the first type include all legal and regulatory constructions, as well as other, more explicitly theoretical statements. For example, the Equal Employment Opportunity Commission states in its Interim Interpretive Guidelines on Sex Discrimination:

> Unwelcome sexual advances, requests for sexual favors, and other verbal or physical conduct of a sexual nature constitute sexual harassment when (1) submission to such conduct is made either explicitly or implicitly a term or condition of an individual's employment, (2) submission to or rejection of such conduct by an individual is used as the basis for employment decisions affecting such individual, or (3) such conduct has the purpose or effect of substantially interfering with an individual's work performance or creating an intimidating, hostile, or offensive working environment." (33)

Similarly, the National Advisory Council on Women's Educational Programs developed the following working definition of sexual harassment in an educational context:

> Academic sexual harassment is the use of authority to emphasize the sexuality or sexual identity of the student in a manner which prevents or impairs that student's full enjoyment of educational benefits, climate, or opportunities. (Till, 1980, 7)

Probably the most influential nonregulatory definition (and one by which all others were, to some degre, influenced) is that of MacKinnon (1979) who states "Sexual harassment . . . refers to the unwanted imposition of sexual requirements in the context of a relationship of unequal power. Central to the concept is the use of power derived from one social sphere to lever benefits or impose deprivations in another.... When one is sexual, the other material, the cumulative sanction is particularly potent" (1979, p. 1). A conceptually similar definition is offered by Benson (1979): "Sexual harassment is broader than sexual coercion . . . (and) can only be understood as the confluence of authority relations *and* sexual interest in a society stratified by gender" (quoted in Till, 1980). And, LaFontaine and Tredeau (1986) suggest ". . . sexual harassment is defined as any action occurring within the workplace whereby women are treated as objects of the male sexual prerogative. Furthermore, given that women are invariably oppressed by these actions, all such treatment is seen to constitute harassment, irregardless of whether the victim labels it as problematic" (435). Farley (1978) asserts "Sexual harassment is . . . unsolicited nonreciprocal male behavior that asserts a woman's sex role over her function as worker" (14). These statements constitute the most well known and influential examples of the first type of a priori definitions described above. Type 2 definitions, on the other hand, take quite a different form, being much more concrete and "point-at-able" in nature. Betts and Newman (1982), for example, state "A good definition of sexual harassment . . . includes the following behaviors:

1. Verbal harassment or abuse;
2. Subtle pressure for sexual activity;
3. Unnecessary patting or pinching;
4. Constant brushing against another person's body;
5. Demanding sexual favors accompanied by implied or overt threats concerning an individual's employment status;
6. Demanding sexual favors accompanied by implied or overt promise of preferential treatment with regard to an individual's employment status" (48).

Similarly, Working Women United Institute (WWUI, 1978) note "Sexual harassment can be any or all of the following: verbal sexual suggestions or jokes, constant leering or ogling, 'accidentally' brushing against your body, a 'friendly' pat, squeeze, pinch or arm around you, catching you alone for a quick kiss, the explicit proposition backed by threat of losing your job, and forced sexual relations" (1). Finally, the Project on the Status and Education of Women (1978) stated that sexual harassment may take the form of "verbal harassment or abuse, subtle pressure for sexual activity, sexist remarks about a woman's clothing, body, or sexual activities, unnecessary touching, patting, or pinching, leering or ogling of a woman's body, demanding sexual favors accompanied by implied or overt threats concerning one's job, grades, letters of recommendation, etc., physical assault" (2).

Empirical Definitions

A more inductive, data-based definitional strategy, one generally employed more by researchers than by legal theorists, regulatory agencies, or women's political or professional organizations is to ask women directly if they have ever been harassed, and if so, to describe their experiences. These qualitative data are then content analyzed, and a classification scheme developed, the categories of which serve as the general elements of the definition. (Ideally, such a system would then be validated with data from an independent sample, using raters trained in the classification scheme. To date, however, this has not occurred.) The most complete effort of this sort is that of Till (1980), who classified the responses of a national sample of college women into five general categories, covering a wide spectrum of behaviors from sexist comments to rape. The first of these categories, or types, was labeled *generalized sexist remarks and behavior*—similar in appearance to racial harassment, such behavior is not necessarily designed to elicit sexual cooperation, but rather to convey insulting, degrading, or sexist attitudes about women. Category 2 consists of *inappropriate and offensive, but essentially sanction-free sexual advances.* Although such behavior is unwanted and offensive, there is no penalty attached to the woman's negative response. The third category includes *solicitation of sexual activity or other sex-related behavior by promise of reward,* while the fourth covers *coercion of sexual activity by threat of punishment.* (It is these "contingency," or *quid prop quo* situations that appear to be what most people mean when they refer to sexual harassment.) Finally, Till reports instances of *sexual crimes and misdemeanors,* including rape and sexual assault. He notes in his discussion that "categories are not sharply delineated, although they are arranged in a roughly hierarchical continuum. Many of the reported incidents involve several categories, as when a student is promised something in exchange for sexual favors and simultaneously threatened about noncooperation" (8). Despite such classificatory difficulties, Till's work has been extremely influential, and provides the basis for much of the research described below, and in other chapters of this book. A slightly different, but conceptually related definitional strategy has been to present a series of behaviors, varying in severity, type, and context, and ask subjects whether or not, in their opinion, the situation constituted sexual harassment. Such a strategy thus shifts the definitional locus (*i.e.*, from victim to "observer") and attempts to develop the construct through consensual validation. Gutek, Morasch, and Cohen (1983) reported one of the earliest and most influential studies of this type. In this study, subjects (218 undergraduate psychology majors) were presented with a series of vignettes portraying "socio-sexual behavior" in a workplace setting. The vignettes systematically varied the sex of the initiator, the status of the initiator (supervisor, coworker, subordinate) and his/her behavior (sexually suggestive touching was depicted in some vignettes and accompanied by either a personal or a work-related comment). A typical vignette read "Jane is walking down the hall at work. Mr. Davidson, Jane's boss, walks up from behind. As Mr. Davidson passes Jane, he pats her on the fanny and says "Hurry up, you'll never get everything done today" (35). Subjects rated the incident on 19 Likert-type items that were factor analyzed to produce five dimensions: The quality of the relationship between the two, (*e.g.*, the extent to which they were friends, liked each other, etc.); the qualitative aspects of the incident itself, (was it friendly, insulting, welcome, and so forth); the appropriateness of the initiator's behavior; the probability of the incident; and, finally, the probability of such an incident occurring with the roles reversed. In general, women viewed the incidents much more negatively, particularly when they involved touching combined with a work-related comment (as in the example above). In addition, the women assessed the general quality of the relationship between the participants somewhat more negatively (p < .08). The relationship was also viewed more negatively by the subjects when the initiator was male, or of higher status. This was particularly true if a high status initiator was portrayed as touching and making work-related comments.

The results reported in this study identified many of the important variables that have since been shown to influence perceptions of sexual harassment: sex of rater, status of initiator, explicitness of behavior, and degree of connection to work situation. The finding of gender differences in perceptions of sexually harassing behaviors is the most robust of all that have been examined to date, having been reported in almost every investigation so far completed (see, for example, Collins and Blodgett, 1981; Ormerod, 1987; Padgitt and Padgitt, 1986; Powell, 1986; and others. For one of the few exceptions, see Terpstra and Baker, 1986). Not surprisingly, women are consistently more likely to view such behaviors as harassment (Koenig and Ryan, 1986; Ormerod, 1987), as offensive (Padgitt and Padgitt, 1986), or both. While various attempts have been made to "explain" such differences, such as gender role (Powell, 1986) or organizational variables (Konrad and Gutek, 1986), they have been relatively unsuccessful and are probably unnecessary. As Powell (1986) points out, "women as a group have consistently been demonstrated to experience more unwanted sexual attention than men . . . further explanation may be unnecessary and inappropriate" (18).

A similarly consistent finding has been that behaviors initiated by supervisors or others with a substantial power advantage are more likely to be judged as harassment. In her investigation of perceptions of sexual harassment on a college campus, Ormerod (1987) reported that several forms of sexual behavior were rated more severely when the faculty member was portrayed as having some formal responsibility for evaluating a student. This parallels Gutek et al.'s (1983) report that subjects viewed incidents more negatively when they were initiated by a supervisor.

A variably closely related to initiator status is the degree of coercion represented by the behavior. Subjects overwhelmingly agree that requests for sex linked to threats of retaliation for noncompliance constitute sexual harassment; to a slightly lesser degree, the same is true of behaviors that link sex to promises of reward. For example, 94 percent of the men and 98 percent of the women in Konrad and Gutek's (1986) sample agreed that "Being asked to have sexual relations with the understanding that it would hurt your job situation if you refused or help if you accepted" was sexual harassment. In Adams, Kottke, and Padgitt's (1983) sample of college students, sexual bribery was defined as harassment by over 97 percent of the men and 99 percent of the women. Eliciting sexual cooperation by threats (either direct or subtle) received the highest sexual harassment ratings from the students and faculty in Ormerod's (1987) sample (6.95 and 6.92, respectively, on a 7-point scale). Thus, both *a priori* and empirical definitions clearly agree that such *quid pro quo* behaviors constitute sexual harassment of the most basic, unambiguous sort.

At the opposite end of the spectrum lie the more ambiguous behaviors and those that are more sexist (as opposed to sexual) in nature. Behaviors drawn from Till's gender harassment category received the lowest sexual harassment ratings from Ormerod's sample, while only 30 percent of the male (but 47 percent of the female) students surveyed by Adams, et al. (1983) defined sexist comments as sexual harassment. Similarly, Padgitt and Padgitt (1986) found that their original data (perceptions of eight sexually harassing behaviors) did not form a Guttman scale, using standard criteria for scalability and reproducibility. They noted that three items seemed to account for many of the inconsistent answers: sexist comments, body language (such as leering at one's body or standing too close) and invitations (*e.g.*, for dates) in which sexual expectations are not stated. When these items were removed, the five remaining behaviors demonstrated sufficient pattern to approximate a reasonable Guttman scale for both male and female subjects.

Review of these and similar studies would seem to suggest that the more coercive *quid pro quo* behaviors are always seen as harassment, whereas *gender harassment*, and *seductive behavior* (the first and second categories in Till's, 1980, typology) elicit much less agreement. Although this is generally the case, it is also true that contextual variables moderate such perceptions in even the most seemingly clear cut cases. A study by Reilly, Carpenter, Dull, and Bartlett (1982) makes this point. These researchers utilized a "factorial survey" methodology (Rossi and Anderson, 1982) as a means of assessing what factors are of importance in judgements of sexual harassment. Briefly, this methodology involves presenting respondents with a series of brief stories or vignettes that vary along the various dimensions of interest. Using a computer program to generate vignettes of faculty-student interaction, several factors were systematically varied including (a) the instructor's status (graduate student or professor), age, and marital status; (b) the class standing of the female student; (c) the setting of the interaction; (d) the nature of any past relationship between the instructor and student; (e) behavior of the student; (f) verbal behavior of the instruction; (g) physical behavior of the instructor; and (h) presence or absence of threat or coercion. The authors offer the following illustrative vignette: "Andrea G., a senior, after being asked had declined to go out with Donald L., a 30-year old professor. While at the library they ran into each other and started talking. She asked about her grades. He said that he looked forward to working with her while he playfully poked her in the ribs" (103). The subjects (faculty and undergraduate students) read each vignette and then judged, on a nine-point scale, the extent to which the incident did or did not constitute an instance of sexual harassment. These ratings were then analyzed using multiple regression. Table 1 summarizes the relevant results, and presents unstandardized regression coefficients that provide an estimate of how much overall impact, on the average, any particular factor had on the dependent variable. For example, if the woman was portrayed as saying she would "do anything" for a grade, or brushing up against the instructor as

TABLE 1

Factors that Affect Perceptions of Whether a Particular Student
Interaction Constitutes Sexual Harassment (Reilly et al., 1982)

Factors that Lowered Rating	Regression Coefficient[1]
1. Nature of Past Relationship	
— They were close friends	-0.27
— They had gone out several times	-0.41
— They had been dating regularly.	-0.99
2. Female Student Action	
— She said she would do anything for a grade.	-0.93
— She used suggestive language.	-0.86
— She touched his arm.	-0.49
— She brushed up against him.	-0.93
Factors that Raised Rating	
1. Nature of Past Relationship	
She had previously declined a date.	0.21
2. Female Student Action	
— She said she was concerned about her grades.	0.27
3. Instructor Verbal Behavior	
— He asked about her courses.	0.28
— He remarked on her progress in class.	0.40
— He said he looked forward to working together.	0.71
— He said he wanted to speak more privately.	0.84
— He admired her hair.	0.94
— He commented on her personality.	0.67

— He said she reminded him of an old girlfriend.	0.98
— He suggested dinner and a movie.	0.97
— He asked her home.	1.33
— He told a dirty joke.	0.99
— He said she would be good in bed.	1.98
4. Instructor Action	
— He straightened her hair.	0.72
— He held her hand.	0.43
— He put his hand on her shoulder.	0.47
— He moved closer to her.	0.59
— He poked her in the ribs.	0.63
— He squeezed her waist.	1.13
— He fondled and kissed her.	1.82
— He attempted sex.	3.13
— He forced her down.	3.16

[1]All results are significant at or beyond the .05 level of probability.

they talked, the average rating of the vignette decreased by almost one point on the nine-point scale (-0.93, to be exact), whereas if the faculty member admired the student's hair, or suggested dinner and a movie, the rating was correspondingly increased (0.94 and 0.97, respectfully). What seems clear from Table 1 is that any prior social relationship between the pair or any "suggestive" behavior on the part of the student predictably lowered the rating, while faculty suggestive or coercive behavior had the opposite effect. Predictably, faculty coercive (*quid pro quo*) behaviors or forceful ones (*e.g.*, attempted sex, forced her down, and so forth) had the most powerful effect on subject responses. No student behavior, however seductive, had an equivalent effect. Unfortunately, this study reports only main effects and does not evaluate any possible interaction effect of various combinations of variables. This presents a difficulty as the various factors undoubtedly combine in ways that affect the meaning assigned to a particular interaction. For example, "he touched her hair" and "suggested dinner and a movie" projects a different image when the two people "have been dating regularly" than when they had merely "talked on occasion." Despite this shortcoming, the Reilly *et al.* (1982) research remains one of the most sophisticated attempts to date to develop an empirical definition of sexual harassment (see Rossi and Weber-Burdin, 1982, for a replication and extension, and Rossi and Weber-Burdin, 1983, for a discussion and integration of both studies).

A somewhat different approach to this problem was taken by Terpstra and Baker (1986). Rather than varying the contextual components of interactions, these researchers used a standard stimulus list and examined the effect on perceptions of individual differences in subjects' attitudes, attributes, and behaviors (gender, attitudes toward women, religiosity, self esteem, and locus of control). The results of this study are complex and somewhat difficult to interpret, consisting as they do of a series of interaction effects, for example, "nonreligious subjects with liberal attitudes toward women perceived a relatively high number of incidents as harassment, whereas religious liberal subjects perceived fewer examples as harassment. The opposite relationship was found for subjects with conservative attitudes toward women" (468). Discussing the complexity of their results, these authors offer a model of perceptions of sexual harassment that includes individual difference variables with respect to the perceiver (e.g., sex, age, attitudes, and so forth), situational variables (including characteristics of the offender), the actual behavior exhibited, and variables involved in the cognitive appraisal process (e.g., causal attributions).

MEASUREMENT

Not surprisingly, a satisfactory operational definition of harassment has proven even more difficult to achieve than a linguistic one. Although numerous surveys and studies have appeared, each has typically constructed its own data collection instrument, a situation that has resulted in much confusion in the literature.

In their discussion of the progression of research in new fields, Edwards and Cronbach (1952) describe the initial phase as one of *survey* research, in which investigators attempt to identify and isolate variables of importance. This stage is typically followed by that of *technique* research, where the focus is on operationalizing the variables in a reliable manner, a process that is necessary before research can proceed to the more advanced *experimental* and *applied* stages. Even the most cursory review of the sexual harassment literature makes clear that the field is only now beginning to make the transition from survey to technique investigations.

As Edwards and Cronbach (1952) suggest, initial efforts were open-ended in nature, as investigators attempted to isolate and define the variables of interest. Thus, Crull (1979) reported on the experiences of 92 women, self-identified as victims of sexual harassment, and identified types of behaviors and experiences that appeared to typify the phenomenon, while Till (1980) classified responses to his open-ended survey of harassment in higher education into five types or levels, each of progressively greater severity. Similarly, Benson and Thomson (1982) presented their subjects (senior women at the University of California-Berkeley) with the definition of sexual harassment developed by the Working Women

United Institute (WWUI, 1978) and then asked them, among other things, whether they had ever been sexually harassed, and if so, to describe the incident. Responses were classified into seven categories, ranging from body language and undue attention to sexual bribery. Somewhat more structured approaches included that of Wilson and Kraus (1983), who presented their subjects with the seven types of harassment identified by the Project on the Status and Education of Women (1978) and asked them to report the numbers of professors who had engaged in each. Adams, Kottke, and Padgitt (1983) took a similar approach, albeit with a slightly different list, while Maihoff and Forrest (1983) asked subjects about only four behaviors, three of which were extremely severe. Finally, in an extensive examination of harassment at the University of Rhode Island, Lott, Reilly, and Howard (1982) asked respondents not only about sexual insults (both verbal and nonverbal), threats or bribery, or sexual assault that they themselves had experienced, but also if they had ever heard of such incidents happening to others, and present figures for both types of data.

The investigations reviewed to this point have all (with the exception of Crull, 1979) taken place within the university environment; examinations of the workplace, however, reveal similar methodologies. In the largest investigation undertaken to date, the United States Merit Systems Production Board asked a stratified probability sample of the federal work force whether they had experienced any of seven sexually harassing behaviors during the previous 24 months. At about the same time, in a large scale study of the private sector, Gutek (1985) used a structured interview conducted by telephone to elicit information about six behaviors (sexual comments, sexual looks or gestures, sexual and nonsexual touching, and coerced dating and sexual relations).

As a review of these studies makes clear, the objective measurement of sexual harassment remains at a somewhat rudimentary level. As important as these investigations are, they contain several problems from a measurement perspective, suggesting that researchers have seriously neglected (or thought unnecessary) the *technique* research requirement outlined by Edwards and Cronbach (1952). These problems center on the very basic issues of reliability and validity, the *sine qua non* of any data collection technique. To examine the latter first, let us consider for a moment the issue of validity. Of the three facets of validity generally contemplated by measurement theorists, content validity is probably the most relevant here. According to commonly accepted definitions, content validity requires, at a minimum, an adequate specification of the domain of interest, and the generation of a set of items that adequately sample this domain. Each facet of the domain should be represented and appropriately weighed, and care must be taken to construct the items in such a way that they are interpreted similarly by all respondents. This last consideration brings us to the concept of reliability; that is, whether or not the instrument consistently measures what it is supposed to measure, both across subjects, and within subjects across time.

In reviewing the studies considered so far, it is apparent that these issues have not been sufficiently addressed. With respect to stability, no study reports a test-retest correlation coefficient (nor an internal consistency coefficient, for that matter, although that is a separate issue). We have no assurance that the subjects' responses are stable; that is, would they answer the same way if asked again. Equally important, there are logical grounds upon which to suspect that the subjects may not have interpreted the items in the same manner. For example, some studies have utilized the term "sexual harassment" and asked women whether or not they have been harassed (e.g., Till, 1980); others label their intentions in cover letters or survey titles and then present women with a list of behaviors to consider (U.S. Merit Systems Protection Board, 1981); finally, some do not use the term harassment, but ask women to determine whether the touching was meant to be sexual, or the comments were meant to be insulting (e.g., Gutek, 1985). Such procedures introduce a large element of error into the measurement. It has been widely demonstrated that substantial individual differences exist in the perceptions of what constitutes sexual harassment (see, for example, Gutek and Morasch, 1983; Ormerod, 1987), therefore, asking respondents whether they have been harassed, or labeling behaviors as harassment and asking whether a respondent has experienced them, introduces systematic as well as random error into the procedure (random because of idiosyncratic definitions of harassment; systematic because most women have been socialized to accept many forms of sexual exploitation under the guise of joking or compliments, thus systematically reducing their rate of response). A conceptually similar problem is introduced when a researcher asks a subject to make a subjective determination of the intent of a behavior (e.g., was it meant to be insulting?) before they can say whether or not they have experienced it. Although this may be feasible when examining person perception or attribution, it is likely not appropriate for collecting incidence data. The likely result, again, is a lowering of true incidence rates, given that women are less likely to label a behavior as sexual than are men, and are socialized not to recognize many sexually insulting behaviors as being just that.

Finally, it appears that investigators have not paid sufficient attention to the concept of content validity. Many studies give no rationale for the behaviors they have chosen to include while others include a statement to the effect that these items were chosen because they had been used in previous research. Examination of the studies suggest that several tap a rather narrow spectrum of behavior (e.g., Maihoff and Forrest, 1983) while others list what might be considered the major facets of the domain but do not include multiple items to measure each facet (*e.g.*, Reilly, *et al.*, 1982; USMSPB, 1981), suggesting that they may not have been adequately sampled and measured.

It was in an effort to address these considerations and others of a similar nature that the Sexual Experiences Questionnaire (SEQ) was constructed. First reported in Fitzgerald and Shullman (1985) and elaborated in a more extensive study by Fitzgerald, Shullman, Bailey, Richards, Swecker, Gold, Ormerod, and Weitzman (1988) the SEQ represents, to our knowledge, the only inventory of sexual harassment that attempts to meet standard psychometric criteria. To define the domain of interest, we began with Till's (1980) five levels of sexual harassment, identified by him through content analysis of responses to his national open-ended survey of college women. This classification has the advantage of being derived from a broadly based sample and of appearing to encompass all types of sexual harassment that had previously been identified in the literature (MacKinnon's, 1979, distinction between *quid pro quo* situations, where a distinct reward or punishment is contingent on sexual cooperation, and *conditions of work*, a somewhat more subtle situation where the woman is the target of sexually charged behavior but no explicit demand is made; and Franklin, Moglen, Zatlin-Boring, and Angress', 1981, concept of *gender harassment*). Once this theoretical framework had been identified, the first step in instrument development was the generation of an item pool; thus, items were identified from the literature or written to measure the five general areas:

1. *Gender harassment:* Generalized sexist remarks and behavior not necessarily designed to elicit sexual cooperation, but to convey insulting, degrading or sexist attitudes about women;
2. *Seductive behavior:* Inappropriate and offensive sexual advances. Although such behavior is unwanted and offensive, there is no penalty explicitly attached to the woman's negative response; nor does this category include sexual bribery;
3. *Sexual bribery:* Solicitation of sexual activity or other sex-linked behavior (*e.g.*, dating) by promise of rewards;
4. *Sexual coercion:* Coercion of sexual activity, or other sex-linked behavior by threat of punishment;
5. *Sexual imposition:*[1] Sexual imposition (*e.g.*, attempts to fondle, touch, kiss or grab) or sexual assault.

All items were written strictly in behavioral terms, and took the form of "Have you ever been in a situation where a professor or instructor . . . (*e.g.*, made crudely sexual remarks, either publicly in class, or to you privately?).'' The words "sexual harassment" did not appear anywhere on the instrument until the final item ("Have you ever been sexually harassed by a professor or instructor?"). Every attempt was made to avoid ambiguity in terminology, and to develop a full range of items measuring each area. The five scales and representative items from each appear in Table 2. The items were piloted on 468 students (both male and female, graduate and undergraduate) enrolled at a medium-sized state university in the midwest, who were instructed to respond to the items in terms of their clarity, wording, ambiguity, and so forth, and to suggest additional items where necessary. The instrument was then revised with their feedback, and scoring options developed.

TABLE 2

Definitions of and Representative Items from the Five Levels of the SEQ

Level 1: Gender Harassment

Definition: Generalized sexist remarks and behavior.
Sample Item: "Have you ever been in a situation where a professor or instructor habitually told suggestive stories or offensive jokes?"

Level 2: Seductive Behavior

Definition: Inappropriate and offensive, but essentially sanction-free sexual advances.
Sample Item: "Have you ever been in a situation where a professor or instructor made unwanted attempts to draw you into a discussion of personal or sexual matters (*e.g.*, attempted to discuss or comment on your sex life)?"

Level 3: Sexual Bribery

Definition: Solicitation of sexual activity or other sex-linked behavior by promise of rewards.
Sample Item: "Have you ever felt that you were being subtly bribed with some sort of *reward* (*e.g.*, good grades, preferential treatment) to engage in sexual behavior with a professor or instructor?"

Level 4: Sexual Coercion

Definition: Coercion of sexual activity by threat of punishment.
Sample Item: "Have you ever been *directly* threatened or pressured to engage in sexual activity by threats of punishment or retaliation?"

Level 5: Sexual Imposition

Definition: Gross sexual imposition or assault.
Sample Item: "Have you ever been in a situation where a professor or instruction made *forceful* attempts to touch, fondle, kiss, or grab you?"

For each item, the instructions direct the respondent to circle the response most closely describing their own experiences. The options include (1) Never; (2) Once; and (3) More Than Once. If the subject circles (2) or (3), she is further instructed to indicate whether the person involved was a man or a woman (or both, if it happened more than once) by circling M, F, or B. Since the SEQ is designed primarily to identify the frequency of various types of harassment, it is scored simply by counting the number of subjects who endorse the *Once* or *More Than Once* response options for each item. (This distinction was introduced to control for the possible tendency of subjects who had experienced a low-level or non-traumatic harassment behavior on a single occasion to dismiss that experience because "It only happened once." The distinction is, however, typically not used in scoring.) Initial psychometric analysis using Cronbach's coefficient *alpha* yielded an internal consistency coefficient of .92 for the entire 28-item inventory on a new sample of 1395 university students (again, both male and female, graduate and undergraduate) enrolled at the same university where the pilot was conducted. Test-retest stability on a small subsample of graduate students ($N = 46$) yielded a stability coefficient of .86 over a two-week period. Corrected split-half reliability coefficients for the five "scales" of the SEQ ranged from .62 to .86, and averaged .75, reasonable for scales of this length.

As described above, content validity was built into the SEQ through basing item construction on Till's (1980) empirically derived categories. In addition, an attempt was made to evaluate the criterion-related validity of the inventory. Thus, the final item ("I have been sexually harassed") was treated as a criterion, and correlated with each of the other items. With the exception of two items measuring sexual bribery (that showed very little variance) and one item measuring gender harassment, all items were significantly positively correlated with the criterion item. In addition, if the five areas of harassment are considered as levels, we would expect the average item-criterion correlations to increase systematically from Level 1 to Level 5. With one exception, the correlations conformed to theoretical expectation, ranging from $r = .15$ for Level 1 (gender harassment) to $r = .37$ for Level 4 (sexual coercion). The coefficient for Level 5 (sexual imposition) was lower than expected, most likely because several items showed very little variance.

With respect to construct validity, three relevant investigations have been completed. First, Fitzgerald and Shullman (1985) factor-analyzed the original SEQ, as well as a second version designed for employed women, the SEQ2 (Shullman and Fitzgerald, 1985). Their results failed to confirm the hypothesized five level structure; rather, a three-factor solution, in which bribery and coercion collapse into one factor, seduction and sexual imposition group together as another, and gender harassment stands along as a separate factor, appeared to more accurately account for the data. This structure was further supported through a complete link cluster analysis of the original SEQ conducted by Fitzgerald (1986) that yielded three clusters conforming to the original three factors.

However, as Fitzgerald, et al. (1988) point out, such solutions must be considered tentative, due to the unstable nature of the correlations computed on the items showing very little variance. Thus, although the SEQ may yield a three factor solution in all samples tested to date, this does not clearly speak to the dimensionality of the construct itself, but to the methodological constraints inherent in attempts to measure critical but relatively low frequency behaviors. This interpretation is supported by Fitzgerald (1987). Using ratings of the SEQ items developed by Ormerod (1987) to develop a complete inter-item correlation matrix, with data from all subjects on all items, a five-factor solution was reported that conformed quite closely to the five levels suggested by Till (1980).

Finally, Ormerod's (1987) data itself provides support for the construct validity of the SEQ. Briefly, Ormerod presented faculty members and students at two west coast universities with items from the SEQ and requested them to rate the items on a seven-point, Likert-type scale, anchored at one pole by "Definitely is not harassment" and at the other by "Definitely is harassment." If a mean rating for each level is developed by averaging over the items within each level, and these mean ratings examined, they arrange themselves according to theoretical expectation, ranging from a mean score of 4.37 for Level 1 to 6.40 for Level 5.

In summary, then, although more research is obviously necessary, it appears that the SEQ (and its companion instrument for working women, the SEQ2) possess acceptable psychometric characteristics of reliability and validity for research use at this time.

ANALYSIS, INTEGRATION AND RECOMMENDATIONS

In reviewing the definitions described above, it becomes apparent that none of those so far articulated are completely satisfactory; similarly, although progress has been made toward the development of adequate measurement devices, several problems, both theoretical and practical, remain to be solved. This section of the chapter will address these issues in an attempt to integrate the literature and recommend directions for future research in the area.

Definitions

As outlined above, the discussion of definitions began with the basic distinction between those that are *a priori* in nature, and those that have been developed in a more empirical manner. (The measurement-minded reader will note the resemblance to the *rational* and *empirical* modesl of test construction.) Although each is informative, neither is completely satisfactory; for example, while many behaviors are clearly harassing no matter the relational context within which they occur, this is not always the case. Thus, simple "lists" of behaviors can not serve as adequate definitions of harassment, and are generally less useful than formulations in which the *principles* or *elements* of harassment are articulated (*e.g.*, power, authority, sexuality, gender stratification, lack of consent, and so forth). Without such statements of essential elements and the necessary relations among them, there is no basis for identifying and classifying novel instances of behavior as harassment.

Similarly, although social consensus is important (and a worthwhile subject for investigation in its own right), it cannot serve as the sole definitional basis for the construct. The reasons for this are twofold: first, the perceptions of observers, influenced as they are by various demographic and attitudinal factors, likely differ in important ways from those of the recipient of the behaviors in question. MacKinnon (1987) makes this point when she notes that the laws against sexual harassment mark the first time in legal history that injuries to women have been defined *by* women, and from their point of view. Thus, a woman's experience of harassment is definitionally valid whatever the perceptions of observers may be; her perception of an interaction as harassing is definitionally sufficient. It is not, however, necessary. As LaFontaine and Tredeau (1987) point out, "given that women are invariably oppressed by (sexual harassment) all such treatment is seen to constitute harassment, *irregardless of whether the victim labels it as problematic*" (435, emphasis added). It is this premise that gives rise to the assertion that perceptions alone (whether those of observers or victims) are not adequate for a valid definition. Women are, after all, socialized to accept many nonconsensual or even offensive sexual interactions as being nonremarkable, a fact of life. One has only to peruse the literature on acquaintance or marital rape to see that this is so. That it is also true of sexual harassment can be seen from the data reported by Fitzgerald *et al.* (1988), in which women students indicated experiencing many behaviors clearly qualifying as harassment (*e.g.*, propositions, fondling, etc.), yet often did not label those as such. This still widespread acceptance of what LaFontaine and Tredeau (1987) label the "male sexual prerogative" is at the heart of the assertion that victim perceptions are sufficient but not necessary for a definition of harassment.

It would appear that, before a definition can be attempted, it is necessary to outline the premises upon which it is to be based. First, to paraphrase Benson (1979), sexual harassment involves the confluence of authority (power) relations and sexuality (or sexism) in a society stratified by gender. Second, it is important to remember that power or authority can be either *formal* or *informal* in nature; that is, it can be either achieved or ascribed. Formal, or achieved, power is derived from a formal role, such as that of supervisor, employer, professor, and so forth. Informal power, on the other hand, arises from the male sexual prerogative, which implies that men have the unfettered right to initiate sexual interactions or to assert the primacy of woman's gender role over her role as worker or student. It is this prerogative, a sort of psychological *droit de seigneuer*, that accounts for the mystification that often leads women to misperceive and mislabel their experiences of harassment. Based on these premises, the following definition is suggested:

> Sexual harassment consists of the sexualization of an instrumental relationship through the introduction or imposition of sexist or sexual remarks, requests or requirements, in the context of a formal power differential. Harassment can also occur where no such formal differential exists, if the behavior is unwanted by or offensive to the woman. Instances of harassment can be classified into the following general categories: gender harassment, seductive behavior, solicitation of sexual activity by promise of reward or threat of punishment, and sexual imposition or assault.

Such a linguistic definition appears to have several advantages. It combines both a rational and an empirical component, thus providing both the theoretical elements necessary to define a given interaction as harassment, as well as a framework within which to classify such interactions. The nature and elements of harassment are drawn from theory, whereas the classificatory framework is essentially data-based. Finally, the concept of intent is not addressed; rather, it is the power differential and/or the woman's reaction that are considered to be the critical variables. Thus, when a formal power differential exists, all sexist or sexual behavior is seen as harassment, since the woman is not considered to be in a position to object, resist, or give fully free consent; when no such differential exists, it is the recipient's experience and perception of the behavior as offensive that constitutes the defining factor.

One of the more controversial implications of such a definition is that, within this framework, so-called consensual relationships between persons of formally different statuses (*e.g.*, professor/student) would be, strictly speaking, impossible. This leads to a difficult and very complicated issue. On the one hand, Hoffman (1986) argues eloquently against the position suggested above, at least in the educational setting. Beginning with

MacKinnon's (1979) statement that "women wish to choose whether, when, where, and with whom to have sexual relationships, as one important part of exercising control over their lives" (25), she argues that an absolute prohibition against faculty-student amorous relationships assumes that "the relatively powerless group—students—is incapable of empowerment and, in seeking to prevent its victimization, reinforce(s) and perpetuate(s) its powerlessness and vulnerability" (113). Arguing the opposing view, Mead (1980) suggested some years ago that society should institute taboos proscribing sex among people who work together, to ensure that women are not victimized by sexual advances from the men with whom they work.

The present definition does not address this problem explicitly, but does clearly imply that truly consensual relationships are probably not possible within the context of unequal power, and thus may be generally inappropriate (a point with which Hoffman, 1986, agrees). As noted elsewhere, "while not always unethical, such relationships are almost always unwise" (Fitzgerald, Gold, Ormerod, and Weitzman, 1988).

Measurement

Operational definitions are, to some degree, more easily addressed directly than linguistic ones. Given that a sufficiently articulated framework exists, it becomes a merely technical (as opposed to philosophical) problem to generate a reasonably adequate measurement device, to test it, refine it, and so forth. Possibly because such a framework has only recently become available, and further complicated by the fact that research has proceeded in two parallel but different domains (academic and the workplace), it is only lately that such efforts have been undertaken. The SEQ represents a promising beginning, but much more remains to be done. In addition to the need for more validity studies on this instrument, and the development of other, alternative devices, several additional problems require attention, possibly the most pressing of which is to insure sampling adequacy.

One of the more salient criticisms of current research is that it is women who have been harassed, or who are sensitive to the issue of harassment, who are most likely to return surveys on this topic, thus possibly inflating estimates of the phenomenon. Although the collection of data from intact groups (e.g., classrooms, professional meetings) avoids this problem, it also risks rendering the obtained data setting-specific, or, in the latter case, nonrandom. Many studies of sexual harassment report unacceptably low response rates [for example, Till received only 259 responses to the 8,000 calls for information he sent out, and our own return rate for mail out questionnaires has averaged only about 30 percent, compared to the nearly 100 percent we obtained from intact classes (Fitzgerald et al., 1988)]. Although appropriate (but expensive) follow-up techniques can raise this to a more acceptable level, and some studies have had success with these (Lott, Reilly, and Howard, 1983; USMSPB, 1981) it is unlikely that mail surveys will ever approximate the desired precision. A more promising approach may be that of Gutek (1985) who utilized standardized telephone interviews to achieve a random sample of the Los Angeles work force, with only a 23 percent refusal rate. It is imperative that adequate samples be obtained if such data are to be useful within either a scientific or practical context.

A more basic issue may simply be the acceptability of self-report data in this extremely sensitive area. There is still, unfortunately, a tendency to disbelieve women's reports of sexually exploitive experiences. That this is so can be seen from policy statements (such as that of one university) that have more extensive discussions of the penalties for false accusations of harassment than for harassment itself! MacKinnon (1987) addresses this issue when she notes "In 1982 the EEOC held that if a victim was sexually harassed without a corroborating witness, proof was inadequate as a matter of law. . . . To say a woman's word is no proof amounts to saying a woman's word is worthless. Usually all the man has is his denial. In 1983, the EEOC found sexual harassment on a woman's word alone. It said it was enough, without distinguishing or overruling the prior case. Perhaps they recognized that women don't choose to be harassed in front of witnesses" (113). She could just as easily have said that men don't choose to harass in front of witnesses.

It is possible that this is a legal issue, more than it is a scientific one. After all, the great majority of data in many fields of psychology is based on self-report, and, given the usual qualifiers concerning response bias and response set, is none the less acceptable for that. Still, if the data are to be useful as a basis for social policy and legal change, the issue must be attended to. Possibly the best way of doing so is to address the sampling issues raised above. After all, if 40-70 percent of a rigorously selected random sample of women endorse items indicating that they have been sexually harassed, it is only the most unreconstructed misogyny that could respond (as a student once did, after a two-hour lecture on harassment) "How do you know they're not just making it all up?"

Conclusions and Recommendations

Although the measurement of sexual harassment is still in its infancy, it seems possible to make some recommendations based on what has been learned so far. First, instruments attempting to measure harassment must demonstrate, at a minimum, the same characteristics of reliability that are required of any other psychometric technique. Secondly, at least some validity data should be reported. Evidence of content validity is probably the most appropriate at this time, as well as the most practical, given the criterion problem. Third, researchers should avoid the term *sexual harassment* in either the title or body of their instrument, as well as in their instructions or cover letter. To do otherwise introduces an unknown amount of error into the data. Fourth, it appears that asking respondents about the *intent* of a behavior they have experienced (*e.g.*, was it meant to be playful, complimentary, insulting, etc.) is useful for examining attributions or perceptions; it is, however, quite problematic when collecting incidence data. Similarly, asking respondents if they know of anyone who has been harassed or has experienced a certain behavior is a useful way to document awareness of the problem. Such data should not, however, be used to support inferences about incidence rates, if only because multiple respondents may report the same incident. This is particularly true as episodes of sexual harassment received wider publicity and media coverage. Finally, the traditional techniques for sampling and criteria for response rates should be adhered to.

As Boring (1950) once said of psychology, sexual harassment has a long past, but a short history. The phrase itself is barely a decade old, its definition is still a matter of controversy, and its measurement is only a beginning. The present chapter has attempted to summarize what is known concerning these issues and to contribute to the dialogue by developing a rational-empirical definition and recommending guidelines for research.

Notes

1. Till's original system used the term "sexual crimes and misdemeanors" for this category. We used the more inclusive term to enable reference to less severe behaviors.

References

Adams, J.W., Kottke, J.L., and Padgitt, J.S. (1983). Sexual harassment of university students. *Journal of College Student Personnel*, 24, 484-490.

Alliance Against Sexual Coercion (1976). *Fighting against sexual harassment: An advocacy handbook.* Cambridge, MA: Alliance Against Sexual Coercion.

Benson, D.J., and Thompson, G.E. (1982). Sexual harassment on a university campus: The confluence of authority relations, sexual interest and gender stratification. *Social Problems, 29,* 236-251.

Betts, N.D., and Newman, G.C. (1982). Defining the issue: Sexual harassment in college and university life. *Contemporary Education, 54,* 48-52.

Brodsky, C.M. (1976). *The harassed worker.* Lexington, MA: Lexington Books.

Collins, E.G., and Blodgett, T.B. (1981). Sexual harassment: Some see it . . . some won't. *Harvard Business Review, 59,* 76-95.

Crull, P. (1979). *The impact of sexual harassment on the job: A profile of the experiences of 92 women.* Working Women's Research Series, Report No. 3.

Edwards, A.L., and Cronbach, L.J. (1952). Experimental design for research in psychotherapy. *Journal of Clinical Psychology, 8,* 51-59.

Equal Employment Opportunity Commission (1980). Guidelines on discrimination because of sex. *Federal Register, 45,* 74676-74677.

Farley, L. (1978). *Sexual shakedown: The sexual harassment of women on the job.* New York: McGraw-Hill.

Fitzgerald, L.F. (1987). *Sexual harassment: The structure of a social phenomenon.* Paper presented to the Annual Meeting of the American Psychological Association, New York, August.

Fitzgerald, L.F., and Hesson-McInnis, M. (1988). The structure of sexual harassment. *Journal of Vocational Behavior (In press, to appear December, 1988).*

Fitzgerald, L.F., and Shullman, S.L. (1985). *The development and validation of an objectively scored measure of sexual harassment.* Paper presented to the annual meeting of the American Psychological Association, Los Angelos.

Fitzgerald, L.F., Shullman, S.L., Bailey, N., Richards, M., Swecker, J., Gold, Y., Ormerod, A.J., and Weitzman, L. (1988). The incidence and dimensions of sexual harassment in academia and the workplace. *Journal of Vocational Behavior, 32,* 152-175.

Fitzgerald, L.F., Weitzman, L.M., Gold, Y., and Ormerod, A.J. (1988). Academic harassment: Sex and denial in scholarly garb. *Psychology of Women Quarterly, 12,* 329-340.

Franklin, P., Moglin, H., Zatling-Boring, P., and Angress, R. (1981). *Sexual and gender harassment in the academy.* New York: Modern Language Association.

In re Carmita Wood (1975). App. No. 207, 958. New York State Department of Labor, Unemployment Appeals Board (October 6, 1975).

Gutek, B.A. (1985). *Sex and the workplace.* San Francisco: Jossey-Bass.

Gutek, B.A., Morasch, B., and Cohen, A.G. (1983). Interpreting social-sexual behavior in a work setting. *Journal of Vocational Behavior, 22,* 30-48.

Hoffman, F.L. (1986). Sexual harassment in academia: Feminist theory and institutional practice. *Harvard Educational Review, 56,* 105-121.

Kenig, S., and Ryan, J. (1986). Sex differences in levels of tolerance and attribution of blame for sexual harassment on a university campus. *Sex Roles, 15,* 535-549.

Konrad, A.M., and Gutek, B.A. (1986). Impact of work experiences on attitudes toward sexual harassment. *Administrative Science Quarterly, 31,* 422-438.

Lafontaine, E., and Tredeau, L. (1986). The frequency, sources, and correlates of sexual harassment among women in traditional male occupations. *Sex Roles, 15,* 433-432.

Lott, B., Reilly, M.E., and Howard, D.R. (1982). Sexual assault and harassment: A campus community case study. *Signs: A Journal of Women in Culture and Society, 8,* 296-319.

MacKinnon, C.A. (1979). *Sexual harassment of working women.* New Haven, CN: Yale.

————. (1987). *Feminism unmodified.* Cambridge, MA: Harvard University Press.

Maihoff, N., and Forrest, L. (1983). Sexual harassment in higher education: An assessment study. *Journal of the NAWDAC, 46,* 3-8.

Mead, M. (1980). A proposal: We need taboos on sex at work. In D.A. Neugarten and J. Shafritz (Eds.), *Sexuality in organizations.* Oak park, IL: Moore.

Ormerod, A.J. (1987). *Perceptions of sexual harassment.* Paper presented to the annual meeting of the American Psychological Association, New York, August.

Padgitt, S.C., and Padgitt, J.S. (1986). Cognitive structure of sexual harassment: Implications for university policy. *Journal of College Student Personnel, 27,* 34-39.

Powell, G.N. (1986). Effects of sex role identity and sex on definitions of sexual harassment. *Sex Roles, 14,* 9-19.

Project on the Status and Education of Women (1978). *Sexual harassment: A hidden issue.* Washington, D.C.: Association of American Colleges.

Reilly, T., Sandra, S., Dull, V., and Bartlett, K. (1982). The factorial survey technique: An approach to defining sexual harassment on campus. *Journal of Social Issues, 38,* 99-110.

Rossi, P.H., and Anderson, A.B. (1982). The factorial survey approach: An introduction. In P. Rossi and S. Nock (Eds.), *Measuring social judgements: The factorial survey approach.* Beverly Hills, CA: Sage.

Rossi, P.H., and Weber-Burdin, E. (1983). Sexual harassment on campus. *Social Science Research, 12,* 131-158.

Till, F. (1980). *Sexual harassment: A report on the sexual harassment of students.* Washington, D.C.: National Advisory Council on Women's Educational Programs.

Terpstra, D.E., and Baker, D.D. (1986). A framework for the study of sexual harassment. *Basic and Applied Social Psychology, 7,* 17-34.

Weber-Burdin, E., and Rossi, P.H. (1982). Defining sexual harassment on campus: A replication and extension. *Journal of Social Issues, 38,* 111-120.

Wilson, K.R., and Kraus, L.A. (1983). Sexual harassment in the university. *Journal of College Student Personnel, 24,* 219-224.

Working Women's Institute. (1978). *Responses of fair employment practices agencies to sexual harassment complaints: A report and recommendations.* New York: Working Women's Institute, Research Series Report No. 2.

U.S. Merit Systems Protection Board. (1981). *Sexual harassment in the federal workplace: Is it a problem?* Washington, D.C.: U.S. Government Printing Office.

2

The Interface of Racism and Sexism on College Campuses

Darlene C. DeFour

In each of the chapters in this volume there is a plea to the academy to establish a new taboo with respect to sexual and gender harassment. The academy needs to offer models which define the academy in modes which do not have a masculine bias. There is also a need to develop models which are less Eurocentric. An example of this can be seen in what are considered to be appropriate standards for research and publication. Sue (1983) pointed out the difficulty in getting work published using within-group designs when people of color are the study participants. It is considered "bad" design if the people of color are not compared to white participants. The same demand is not required in studies with white samples. Thus, the experience of the white samples is considered the norm.

The necessity for models which are less Eurocentric can also be seen in the sexual harassment literature. Researchers have indicated the high rate of the different levels of sexual harassment which has plagued women in academic settings. These studies have paid some attention to the women's stage of career development when reporting incidence rates. In all or most of the studies, the investigators were careful to report whether they were studying undergraduates, graduates or professional women (*e.g.*, Bond, 1988; Dziech and Weiner, 1984; Gutek and Morasch, 1982). However, in the majority of the studies the researchers have failed to look at the impact of sexual harassment on women of color. In most of the studies the researchers have not asked the respondents to indicate their race or ethnicity (DeFour, 1988). As a result of this omission, we do not have a knowledge of the level of victimization of women of color in the academy. Thus, not only have there been androcentric and Eurocentric biases in the academy, there has also been a Eurocentric bias in the sexual harassment literature in regard to women of color.

In this chapter I will talk about types of power and how they intersect with the levels of harassment. I would first like to provide a general definition of power. "Power, specifically social or interpersonal power, refers to the ability to achieve ends through influence" (Huston, 1983, 170). Social psychologists have studied power and it bases extensively (e.g., French and Raven, 1959; Raven, 1965; Raven, Centers, and Rodrigues, 1975). French and Raven (1959) identified six types of power. They are: (a) reward power, (b) coercive power, (c) referent power, (d) legitimate power, (e) expert power, and (f) informational power.

Reward power involves the ability to give positive reinforcement to influence behavior. Coercive power involves the use of threats to remove a reward or threats of punishment to influence behavior. Under "referent power" the individual complies with requests because they like or admire the powerholder. Legitimate power is based on the authority that the powerholder derives as a result of in a particular social role. Expert power describes an individual who is perceived to have superior knowledge or skill in an area. A person can exert "informational power" when they have access to information that other individuals want or need.

I would now like to illustrate how I think that the types of power can manifest themselves within the following levels of harassment: gender harassment, seductive behavior, sexual bribery, sexual coercion, and sexual assault.

Gender harassment. Women of color have reported being victims of gender harassment which also have racist overtones (see Demby, this volume). For example, a student in an American literature course wants to do her paper on Maya Angelou's work. She is told by her instructor that this is not an author which can be studied in his course. He doesn't consider Maya Angelou's work to be "important." In this example, both legitimate and expert power are being exerted. On the one hand he is indicating that in his role as professor he has the right to set up what is acceptable in his course (legitimate power). His standard excludes the work of women of color. In addition, the instructor could also be perceived as having expert power. "He has a Ph.D. in this field; he should know." Statements such as "it is my experience that Asian women usually do not do well in this course" fall into this category of harassment. All of these remarks are both sexist and racist and can seriously affect women of color's sense of competency and self-worth.

Seductive behavior. Unwanted inappropriate and offensive sexual advances can also have both racist and sexist components. Here both referent power and reward power could be at its base. An untenured Hispanic faculty member has an appointment with her department chair in his office to request travel funds. When she enters the room the lights are dim. There is soft music playing in the background. The chair which she is asked to sit in reclines. He indicates that there is an excellent chance that she will receive the travel funds which she is seeking. He goes on to discuss how bright and attractive she is. He states that although minorities in the past haven't done well in the department she will. He will see to it. Here reward and legitimate power are being used. There is a suggestion that her cooperation will lead to concrete resources (reward power). The chairperson is also using the power of his role (legitimate power).

Sexual bribery. Obviously one power base which underlies sexual bribery is reward power. An example of this would be a male faculty member who offers rewards such as authorship on papers, work on grants, or fellowships appointments to students in return for sexual favors, dates, etc. The flip side to this is the use of coercive power which underlies *sexual coercion.* A student is told that she will not be granted authorship or recognition for work she has performed. Another example is receiving threats of the withdrawal of fellowship money and sponsorship if she will not date him. Coercion is also being used when a woman is told that her professional reputation will be damaged if she does not comply with the wishes of a male who is well known in her field. Referent power can also be the basis of both sexual bribery and sexual coercion. A woman complies with her harasser because she admires him. This is illustrated when an undergraduate is given special attention by her professor. He later makes sexual advances toward her. In a later section of this paper I will discuss why women of color may be vulnerable to sexual bribery and sexual coercion.

Sexual Imposition. Behaviors involved in sexual imposition include gross sexual imposition, assault, and rape (Fitzgerald, Shullman, Bailey, Richards, Swecker, Gold, Ormerod, and Weitzman, 1988). Others have described coercive power as the power base which underlies rape (*e.g.*, Anderson-Barboza, 1983). As Anderson-Barboza stated, "*Coercion*, a power type fundamental to understanding rape, reflects the means by which a rape victim is forced to succumb to her violator's sexual demands. . . . It deprives the victim of virtually all freedom of choice" (8). A full professor sexually assaults his undergraduate research assistant. The professor does not view this attack as rape because he believes that Hispanic women always desire sex. This is an example of sexual imposition with racist overtones.

RACISM AND SEXISM REVISITED

The failure to examine incidence rates of sexual harassment among women of color is alarming when one realizes that she may be particularly vulnerable to this form of victimization. As suggested by Harrigan in Betz and Fitzgerald (1987):

> The victim is a woman who is financially vulnerable and the perpetrator . . . is necessarily a male supervisor or employer who wield power over her. (231)

From the examples presented earlier in this paper, there are at least two types of factors which may serve to make women of color more vulnerable to harassment. These two factors are economic factors and images and stereotypes which are held about women of color.

Economic Factors

As pointed out in the quote by Harrigan, women who fall prey to harassment are often financially vulnerable. Women of color frequently hold positions which result in their economic vulnerability. As undergraduates they are often dependent upon financial aid to fund their education. Their family's income can not provide economic support (National Board on Graduate Education, 1976). As graduate students, they have loans and fellowships more often than research assistantships (Blackwell, 1981). Furthermore, female faculty members are more often concentrated in "gypsy scholar" positions. These are typically one year contracts. In some cases the appointments are only one semester or one quarter. And, faculty members who are in tenure track jobs are often untenured. A large number of women of color in academic settings are outside of the classroom. They are secretaries, administrative staff, cooks, and housekeepers. These are all jobs where the women are supervised (very often by men).

The financial vulnerability of women of color is further illustrated when one examines the 1980 U:S. Census Bureau figures of annual salaries (National Committee on Pay Equity, 1988). The annual salaries are as follows: Asian women 12,432; white women 11,213; Black women 10,429; Native American women 10,052; and Hispanic women 9,725. These salaries are 60.0 percent, 55.1 percent, 51.3 percent, 49.4 percent, 47.8 percent respectively of the average salary for white males.

Images of Women of Color

The images and perceptions of women of color also increase their vulnerability to harassment. These images either portray the women as weak and thus unlikely to fight back if harassed, or they are perceived as very sexual and thus desiring sexual attention. Hispanic women have been described as hot-blooded, ill-tempered, religious, overweight, lazy, always pregnant, loudmouthed, and deferent to men. Native American women are perceived as poor, sad, uneducated, isolated, and devoted to male elders. Asian women have been described as small, docile, and submissive. However, they are also viewed by some as the exotic sexpot who will cater to the whims of any man (Kumagai, 1978/1988). Black women have been perceived as domineering, having low morals, highly sexed, heads of households, and "loose." As pointed out by Tong (1984):

> Sexual harassers tend to take advantage of those whom they perceive as most vulnerable, and whether we care to face it or not, black women enflesh the vulnerability of their people's slave past. (165)

IMPLICATIONS FOR RESEARCH AND PROGRAM PLANNING

When doing work on women of color we must be careful of the types of research models that we use. Sue (1983) outlined two research models which negatively conceptualize the experiences of people of color. We must be careful not to use: (a) inferiority models that imply women of color are socially and intellectually inferior to white women as the result of biology and heredity; or (b) deficit models, which also assume that women of color are inferior but attribute their inferiority to external factors such as prejudice, discrimination and social and economic conditions. Sue points to the need for research which is bicultural or multicultural when examining ethnic minority issues. Bicultural research is thought to have the following properties, implicit values, or irientation:

1) attempts to conceptualize the influences of different cultures that interact with and are influenced by one another;
2) tends to emphasize understanding of ethnic minority groups on their own terms;
3) is concerned about within-group variations and individual differences.

For example, results of recent research have indicated that Black women may use a sociocultural model to explain harassment rather than the natural/biological or organizational explanatory models (Hunter College Women's Career Development Research Collective, 1988). According to the sociocultural model of harassment, men harass in order to assert their personal power as men. Women who attribute sexual harassment to the sociocultural viewpoint report that victims of harassment should notify a therapist, women's studies coordinator and faculty, women's center, and support groups for women who have been victimized (Hunter College

Women's Career Development Research Collective, 1988). In regards to black women, one must view the use of this strategy in the context of the history of African-Americans in this country. These women have seen that the legal system has not always worked for them in the past. As a result of this, they may just want social support for dealing with the psychological pain involved in the victimization process (Hunter College Women's Career Development Research Collective, 1988). In addition, different explanatory models of harassment may hold depending on whether the harasser is white or Black. As indicated by Tong:

> In those cases where their harassers are white men, black women generally observe that their harassers use sex as an excuse not only to control their *individual* bodies but also to exercise power over all of them as a *class* of persons: as women (sexism) or blacks (racism) or as disadvantaged blacks (classism). . . . That black women's reports of sexual harassment by white male superordinates "reflect a sense of impunity that resounds of slavery and colonization" is, in this connection highly significant. (165)

This is not to say that harassment is to be condoned depending on the race/ethnicity of the harasser. This is also not to imply that black women feel less violated when the harasser is a black male. The implication is that when racism, sexism, and classism combine, a qualitively different type of sexual harassment is the result (Tong). College campuses must recognize this issue when handling complaints of harassment, when designing prevention and intervention strategies, and when creating sexual harassment panels.

Historically research on gender and sexual harassment has excluded women of color. In the current paper I have outlined how types of power intersect with the various levels of harassment, and why women of color may be particularly vulnerable to harassment, as well as suggested a research model which could be used to study harassment among women of color.

References

Anderson-Barboza, L. (1983). *Women's perception of power and their vulnerability to coerced sexual experiences.* Unpublished doctoral dissertation, Columbia University, New York.

Betz, N., and Fitzgerald, L.F. (1987). *The career psychology of women.* New York: Academic Press.

Blackwell, J.E. (1981). Mainstreamin outsiders: *The production of black professionals.* Bayside: General Hall.

Bond, M. (1988). Division 27 sexual harassment survey: Definition, impact, and environmental context. *The community Psychologist, 21,* 7-10.

DeFour, D.C. (1988, July) Interface of racism and sexism in the academy. In M.A. Paludi (Chair), *Ivory power: Victimization of women in the Academy,* Symposium conducted at the 4th World Congress of Victimology, Tuscany, Italy.

Demby, L. (1989). In her own voice: A woman student's experience with sexual harassment. In M.A. Paludi (Ed.) *Ivory power: Sexual harassment on campus.* Albany, NY: State University of New York Press.

Dziech, B., and Weiner, L. (1984). *The lecherous professor: Sexual harassment on campus.* Boston: Beacon Press.

Fitzgerald, L.F., Shullman, S., Bailey, N., Richards, M., Swecker, J. Gold, Y., Ormerod, M., and Weitzman, L. (1988). The incidence and dimensions of sexual harassment in academia and the workplace. *Journal of Vocational Behavior, 32,* 152-175.

Fitzgerald, L., Weitzman, L., Gold, Y., and Ormerod, M. (1988). Academic harassment: Sex and denial in scholarly garb. *Psychology of Woman Quarterly, 12,* 329-340.

French, J., and Raven, B. (1959). The basis of social power. In D. Cartwright (Ed.), *Studies in social power.* Ann Arbor: University of Michigan Press.

Gutek, B., and Morasch, B. (1982). Sex ratios, sex-role spillover and sexual harassment of women at work. *Journal of Social Issues, 38,* 55-74.

Hunter College Women's Career Development Research Collective (1988, March). Woman's attitudes and attributions about sexual harassment. Paper presented at the 13th Annual Meeting of the Association for Women in Psychology, Bethesda, MD.

Huston, T. (1983). Power. In H. Kelley *et al.* (Eds.), *Close relationships.* New York: W.H. Freeman.

Kumagai, G.L. (1978/1988). The Asian woman in America. In P.S. Rothenberg (Ed.), *Racism and sexism: An integrated study.* New York: St. Martin's Press. (Reprinted from *Explorations in Ethnic Studies* 1978, *1.*)

National Board on Graduate Education (1976). *Minority participation in graduate education.* Washington, D.C.: National Academy of Science.

National Committee on Pay Equity (1988). The wage gap: Myths and facts. In P.S. Rothenberg (Ed.), *Racism and sexism: An integrated study.* New York: St. Martin's Press.

Raven, B.H. (1965). Social influence in power. In I.D. Steiner and M. Fishbein (Eds.), *Current studies in social psychology.* New York: Holt.

Raven, B.H., Centers, R., and Rodrigues, A. (1975). The basis of conjugal power. In R.S. Cromwell and D.H. Olsen (Eds.), *Power in families.* New York: Wiley.

Sue, S. (1983). Ethnic minority issues in psychology. *American Psychologist, 38,* 583-592.

Tong, R. (1894). *Women, sex, and the law.* Totowa: Rowman and Allanheld.

3

The Perils and Promise of Studying Sexist Discrimination in Face-to-Face Situations*

Bernice Lott

The objective of the research program discussed in this paper is a systematic investigation of sexist discrimination in face-to-face situations. My focus is on interpersonal discrimination, as distinct from institutional discrimination, with the former operationalized as distancing behavior. The central question addressed is what men *do* in the presence of women, not what they say they feel or believe about women.

From a social psychological/behavior oriented model of sexism in which prejudice, stereotypes, and discrimination are conceptually and operationally distinguished, I have derived predictions about men's behavior in the presence of women. The results of two studies (Lott 1987b, 1989) support the general proposition that men tend to distance themselves from women, and data from a third study (Lott, Lott, and Fernald, 1988) illuminate individual differences in such distancing behavior. This program of research is intended (in the long run): (1) to identify some of the conditions under which the probability of distancing responses to women by men will be increased (or decreased); (2) to relate individual differences in men's distancing behavior to other measures of sexism and to background variables; and (3) to examine such behavior in a wide range of samples in a variety of situations.

I have proposed that a social psychological analysis of interpersonal sexism should include three theoretically related but independently measurable components: prejudice, stereotypes, and discrimination. Translating these concepts into the language of general behavior theory (in the liberalized S-R tradition, cf. Lott and Lott, 1985) these components of sexism are distinguishable as follows: (1) *negative attitudes* toward women—hostility, dislike, misogyny—or, in more familiar terms, *prejudice*; (2) a set of *beliefs* about women which reinforce, complement, or justify the prejudice and involve an assumption of inferiority; these are the *stereotypes*—well-learned, widely shared, socially validated generalizations about women's nature or attributes; and (3) *overt behaviors* that achieve separation from women through exclusion, avoidance or distancing—behaviors that define *discrimination* in face-to-face situations.

If we were to place overt acts of face-to-face discrimination against women on a continuum, we would likely begin with sexist jokes or put-downs, cat-calls, leers, unwanted sexual attention of any kind and end with sexual assault, battering, and murder. Such a continuum includes behaviors that typically define sexual harassment as well as acts of devaluation, exclusion, and violence. While some of these specific behaviors clearly entail moving toward women and not away from them, it can be argued that their end result is to put a woman "in her place," to objectify her, and to thereby distance the actor from her.

The ample documentation of sexism in our society suggests that negative attitudes, beliefs, and behaviors directed toward women are acquired (primarily by men) under a wide array of differing circumstances. We know, of course, that men also learn positive attitudes, beliefs, and approach behaviors to women as a consequence of our association with nurturance and sexual pleasure. Because of the widespread reinforcement of sexism in our society, however, it is expected that sexist responses to women will predominate in relatively neutral situations.

Most psychological investigations of sexism have been concerned with beliefs or attitudes, and a large literature supports the conclusion that stereotyped beliefs and prejudice against women are common among men in our society (cf. Lott, 1987a). Yet, with the exception of harassment and assault, the overt behaviors of men toward women in face-to-face situations have rarely been the focus of study. As noted by Geffner and Gross (1984) "there have been . . . very few experiments investigating discriminatory behavior in actual interactions between men and women" (974).

The research program described in this paper is directly concerned with the behaviors of men that are instrumental in avoiding or distancing themselves from women in relatively neutral face-to-face situations. This program is thus an attempt to validate empirically the personal experiences reported anecdotally by many women—that men tend to ignore and turn away from us in situations in which there is minimal expectation of sexual, nurturant or other specifically positive consequences. Thus, for example, in describing the experiences of women administrators in universities, Mary Rowe (1973) has noted the frequency with which a woman found her name "mysteriously missing" from lists.

Hers are the announcements and invitations which fail to come . . . ,
the pages which were not typed . . . It is her work which by mistake
was not properly acknowledged, not reviewed, not responded to, not
published, her opinion which is not asked for. (4)

Rowe referred to such behaviors as "the minutiae of sexism." I have never
talked to a woman anywhere who did not report similar experiences of
sexist "minutiae" in work or social situations.

In its focus on empirical tests of this significant realm of women's
experience, the research reported here can be regarded as part of a
feminist/behaviorist agenda in social psychology that extends areas of
research to consider new questions stimulated by the study of women's
lives (Lott, 1985). In addition, this research moves beyond the existing
psychological literature on sexism by focusing on overt behavior (not self-
reported feelings or beliefs). As noted recently by Skinner (1987)

There can scarcely be anything more familiar than human behavior . . . We are always in the presence of at least one behaving
person. Nor can there be anything more important. . . . Nevertheless
it . . . has seldom been thought of as a subject matter in its own right,
but rather has been viewed as the mere expression or symptom of
more important happenings inside the behaving person. (780)

DISTANCING BEHAVIOR

The use of interpersonal distancing as a dependent measure of
attitudes was common in an earlier literature (cf. Lott and Lott, 1976) and
dates back to the classic work of Bogardus (1925) who developed "The
Social Distance Scale" to assess prejudice toward ethnic/racial groups. In a
review of the literature, Evans and Howard (1973) concluded that "The
preponderance of data suggest that persons who are friendly with each
other or wish to communicate a positive affect will tend to interact at
smaller interpersonal distances than those who are not friendly" (336f). A
sizable literature supports this conclusion. For example, it has been
reported (Allgeier and Byrne, 1973) that college students in a laboratory
situation placed themselves farther away from a disliked than from a liked
confederate; that a sample of college men (but not women) approached
more likable persons at closer distances than less likable persons (Wittig
and Skolnick, 1978); and that a sample of nonhandicapped college students
avoided sitting next to a person in a wheelchair when there was an
acceptable pretext for doing so (Snyder, Kleck, Strenta and Mentzer,

1979). Studies in which distancing is treated as an independent variable, and its consequences for observers are assessed, have generally found that positive and negative attitudes toward persons are communicated by smaller and larger distances, respectively (*e.g.*, Mehrabian, 1968).

That distancing behavior indicates a negative interpersonal response seems to be well supported by the literature. But are such responses made by men to women more often than to other men and more often than by women to either women or men? Such a proposition is supported by a variety of investigations using measures that have ranged from direct physical distance to the contents of dreams. In one study, for example (Barfoot, Hoople and McClay, 1972), male students were observed drinking from water fountains when either a male or female confederate sat some distance away. Only when the confederate was a woman did a greater percentage of men drink farther away than closer to her. In a different kind of investigation, college students were randomly assigned to work in pairs on a drawing task with either a nine-year-old boy or girl. The investigators (Hoffman, Tsuneyoshi, Ebina, and Fite, 1984) found that while the women participants did not respond differentially to boys and girls on any of the dependent measures, the college men spoke significantly less to girls than to boys. Suggestive data have also been reported by Hall (1984) on the contents of dreams studied across the world. Men, he found, in 29 of 35 samples, dream less frequently about women than about men while women dream equally of both. "The sex difference occurs in groups on every continent; in a diversity of cultures . . . ; in all age groups; in dreams collected in the laboratory, in the classroom, and in the field by many different investigators over a period of 30 years" (1115).

From another group of studies has come evidence that in certain situations men tend to approach women at closer distances than they approach men, particularly situations in which such approach behavior indicates the "invasion of the personal space" of another person. Nancy Henley (1977) has argued that persons in high status positions are more likely to encroach on the personal space of persons in subordinate positions than vice versa, and a review of research by Brenda Major (1981) led her to conclude that "men are overwhelmingly more likely to touch women than women are to touch men" (21). More recent reviewers, however, have questioned the earlier conclusions. For example, Hall (1987) concluded from her study of the literature on gender differences in nonverbal communication that the "evidence relating status to distance does not give much support to the assumption that low-status individuals are accorded smaller interpersonal distances" (190). And Stier and Hall (1984), who reviewed over 40 observational studies, reported no overall tendency for men to touch women more than vice versa.

There is certainly good reason to expect that under appropriate conditions men will respond to women with a variety of approach behaviors. Such conditions are likely to be defined by contextual factors that signal the probability of obtaining nurturant, sexual, or other goals, including status enhancement. But under circumstances where no specific gain from approach is likely, men are more apt to avoid, withdraw and separate themselves from women than from men, or than women from same- or other-gender persons.

The research described in this paper focuses on behavior that is instrumental in achieving separation, withdrawal, or distance from others. Most of us, I believe, would agree that we make judgments about persons' feelings toward one another by observing their behavior and, in particular, whether it is of an approach or avoidance nature. How accurately such behaviors reflect attitudes and beliefs is an important question, but *the overt behavior itself has primary social significance*. Regardless of what it may tell us about feelings and beliefs, interpersonal distancing tells us something about face-to-face discrimination, *per se*. When one person avoids, withdraws, or distances from another, this behavior directly and clearly denotes separation or exclusion. Separation may also function as a necessary antecedent to aggression. Rachel Hare-Mustin and Jeanne Marecek (1987) have recently suggested, for example, that "distancing permits hostility and abuse toward women, as seen in pornographic images and sexual and physical abuse."

A LABORATORY DEMONSTRATION AND PRIME TIME TV

Two completed studies have tested and found support for the general hypothesis that men tend to separate or distance themselves more from women than from men while women do not behave differently on this dimension toward same- and other-gender persons. In the first study (Lott, 1987b), men's and women's behavior toward same-gender and other-gender partners with whom they had no prior acquaintance was compared in dyads brought to a laboratory to participate in a domino contest (to be judged on originality and complexity). Each pair was instructed to work together for ten minutes to build a structure with dominos (as they used to do "when you were children"). In this task-focused situation, self-report paper-and-pencil measures did not reveal bias against other-gender partners in feelings or beliefs on the part of either women or men. However, the observations of trained observers who watched the pairs behind a one-way vision window indicated that men more frequently made negative statements and turned away from their partners when these were women than when these were men, and less frequently followed the advice of women partners than men partners. For the women, on the other hand, their partner's gender made no difference with respect to any of the measured behaviors. An additional finding was that the domino structures built by mixed-gender pairs were significantly more often closer to the man than to the woman, providing a concrete, physical illustration of the tendency of men to distance themselves from women.

In this study, no differences would have been found between men's responses to women and to other men had the data been restricted to self-reports of feelings and beliefs. Self-report measures did not reveal prejudice or stereotypes. Only observation of behavior revealed significant interactions between gender of actor and gender of partner, specifically, reliable differences in the way men responded to women partners and men partners, but no such differences in the behavior of women. These findings underscore the theoretical and practical necessity of separating the overt behavioral component of sexism (discrimination) from both the affective (negative attitudes) and the cognitive (stereotyped beliefs).

In the second study (Lott, 1989), the behavior of men and women toward same- and other-gender persons was observed on the television screen, as performed by characters in episodes of weekly dramatic or comedy shows. If sexism is a dominant feature of our present society, an assumption supported by a wide array of data, one would expect to find it reflected in the mass media which communicate to us so much about our culture's ideology. With respect to television, in particular, it has been amply demonstrated that this medium, both in programming and advertising, reinforces and perpetuates gender stereotypes (*e.g.*, Singer, Singer, and Zuckerman, 1981); *Window Dressing on the Set*, 1977). According to Liebert, Sprafkin, and Davidson (1982), for example:

> Content analyses invariably show that [men] enjoy highly prestigious
> positions [while] most TV women are assigned marital, romantic, and
> family roles. . . . In terms of how they behave, TV males are
> portrayed as more powerful, dominant, aggressive, stable, persistent,
> rational, and intelligent than females. Females are portrayed as more
> attractive, altruistic, sociable, warm, sympathetic, happy, rule abid-
> ing, peaceful, and youthful than males. . . . (163)

There is clear documentation for the conclusion that the television shows we watch carry a relatively consistent message that conforms to our society's stereotypes about gender. But do the characters behave in ways that also illustrate the discrimination component of sexism? Do men, in other words, tend to be shown distancing themselves from women?

To answer this question, ten primetime TV programs found to be most popular with a sample of eighth graders were observed by a group of trained college students. Men and women TV characters were observed interacting with same- and other-gender persons and the frequency of distancing behaviors (as well as positive approach and aggressive approach behaviors) was recorded. Observers were preassigned on a random basis to watch four programs and, for each, the gender of the character to be observed was also preassigned. During the first segment of a TV program, each observer chose a character of the preassigned gender who was then monitored in interaction with other persons during the second 10-12 minute segment. As predicted, men TV characters were observed more frequently to distance themselves from women than from men. Distancing responses by women TV characters, on the other hand, were not related to the gender of the person they were with. It was also found that women characters appeared less often in the TV programs than men, and that when they did appear they were significantly more likely to be shown interacting with men than with other women.

In this study, TV characters were observed across a wide variety of situations, and the finding of greater distancing by men from women was a general one, cutting across programs, specific circumstances, contexts, relationships, age and ethnic groups, geographic and environmental locations. The data obtained not only span diverse situations and conditions, but also come from a large number of independent observers who watched different characters on different shows. When the observations of women and men were analyzed separately, each sample of observers yielded the same findings in support of the hypothesis. The use of many participants observing a wide array of situations follows a model of research proposed by Egon Brunswik (1956). According to this model, the sampling of both observed stimuli and observers enables research to be done in natural situations where standard controls are not possible or desirable.

SOME NEGATIVE REACTIONS TO THIS RESEARCH

I thought the findings obtained from these studies were exciting and was, of course, interested in publishing them. As a well-seasoned contributor to professional journals I anticipated that I would get my share of suggestions, criticisms, questions, and both frustrating and helpful feedback from reviewers and editors. But I didn't expect a response to this work that was different in kind from reactions to previously submitted work. I will not identify the journal[s] from which this feedback came, but would like to share some of the comments that do not deal with issues of method, analysis, organization, or detail. These I appreciated and found generally constructive; it is with comments of a different sort that I had difficulty since they seemed to reflect an anxiety about both my conceptual analysis and the empirical findings.

To begin with, I found that my original title for these studies

"Women as Aversive Stimuli for Men" made some reviewers uncomfortable. When one reader called the title "provocative" (in the negative sense), I decided to change it. Several reviewers quarreled not with my designs or analyses but with my concepts, one saying that it is "ambiguous to call sexism . . . a psychological phenomenon," another arguing that women's lower pay, for example, is less a matter of discrimination than of men's "economic self interest."

Some reviewers simply refused to accept my definition of discrimination in face-to-face situations as distancing behavior, illustrated by the behavior observed by men toward women in the domino and TV studies. One reviewer suggested that men may actually feel more at ease with women since they can dominate them; and another suggested that TV "writers [may] believe that female characters are less interesting to viewers," and that this might be a better explanation of the observed paucity of interactions among women characters.

One editor, in commenting on the TV study, argued that some of the observers might "for some unconscious reason [have] preferred to watch male subjects behaving in a stereotypic fashion toward female targets [and] might well have selected a subset of characters who in fact confirmed the avoidant pattern, overlooking male characters who behaved differently." I wrote to this editor and told him that I considered this comment a "classic" and that I was looking forward to sharing it. This same editor did not believe that the findings of the TV study went beyond those obtained in the domino task study. "Certainly," he wrote, "the two studies together would have been an impressive package. In that the other paper is already forthcoming in the literature, the novelty of this contribution is somewhat attenuated." You can imagine the laugh I got out of that when I recalled the first paper of this "impressive package" having been turned town by the very same journal.

The comments I found most disturbing were those that accused me of going too far. One critic objected to my saying that the finding that women TV characters were shown significantly less often in the company of other women than in the company of men illustrates the general proposition that in our society women's value derives primarily from association with men. Another said that it was an overgeneralization to assert, as I had, that the dominant response of men to women in our society reflects prejudice and stereotypes. And one reader wrote the following:

> I do not subscribe to the view that psychology can be or should be value-neutral, but I find the conceptual framework offered . . . to be so heavily value-loaded that I wonder whether any data could disconfirm it.

The conceptual framework referred to by this reviewer is the same one I presented at the start of this paper.

Fortunately, some reactions were positive. Reports of both studies have been published in the *Psychology of Women Quarterly*, and the domino task paper received a distinguished publication award in 1987 from the Association for Women in Psychology.

PROPOSED NEXT STEPS

What are my next steps in this program of research? First, since most of the literature on sexist discrimination is concerned with its institutional forms—in the educational, political, legal and workforce systems, a thorough and careful review of the psychological literature dealing with face-to-face interaction between women and men is needed. Methodological and conceptual problems need to be identified and conclusions drawn from the empirical findings.

The general hypothesis that men (but not women) are more likely to distance themselves from other-gender than same-gender persons must be tested under varied and relatively natural conditions. These conditions should satisfy the criteria of not presenting cues that are likely to evoke expectations of possible sexual pleasure, nurturance, or other specific positive outcomes, nor expectations that distancing (discrimination) will be disapproved. Both demand characteristics and cues likely to evoke competing behavior (such as "helping") must be minimized.

Some studies will vary the conditions under which distancing behavior will be observed. For example, it is hypothesized that distancing responses by men to women will be less probably in situations in which the behavior will be observed by persons known to favor gender equality in opportunities, and more probable in situations in which the behavior will be observed by persons known to strongly support the *status quo*. It is also hypothesized that distancing responses by men to women will be less probably in situations in which face-to-face interaction is between persons of equal social or work status and more probable in face-to-face situations in which the man is of higher status. (Women's distancing behavior to men under these conditions will also be observed.)

It is likely that the extent to which men distance themselves from women will be related to their expectation of positive or aversive consequences for doing so. The most probably antecedent conditions for these expectations are one's own past experiences and the observation of the behavior of others and the consequences received by others. In a series of proposed studies, therefore, samples of adults and children will be exposed to conditions such as the following: they will observe a high status adult man interact with persons of both genders and consistently (or inconsistently) ignore/turn away from (or positively approach) women more than men (or men more than women); they will observe a highly liked peer of the same or different gender who has been the source of prior reward, interact with individuals of both genders and consistently distance (or not distance, or positively approach) girls/women (or boys/men). In each case the effects of the experimental conditions will be tested under new conditions. These studies will require the use of confederates (in live and/or videotaped scenes) and will necessitate careful debriefing of participants, a process through which information can be shared about the nature of sexism and the acquisition and maintenance of discriminatory behavior.

In an effort to identify other variables related to individual differences in men's distancing responses to women, measures of such behavior will be correlated with demographic/background variables and with other (affective and cognitive) measures of sexism, *e.g.*, attitudes toward women, tolerance for sexual harassment, belief that gender relations are adversarial, etc. For each of these variables, reliable and valid measures are available, thus enabling connections to be made among a wide range of phenomena.

My colleagues and I have developed a simulated measure of distancing behavior in the form of a Picture Choice Task that requires a participant to choose from pairs of photographs of middle-aged adults the one who is preferred for a particular interaction. Participants respond to a series of 24 cards, each of which contains the photographs of two adults previously judged by a sample of raters as being of moderate and relatively equal attractiveness. Each card presents a question beginning with "Who would you choose" and the participant is asked to choose from the two photographs the person who is preferred. Eight different sets of three cards present eight different service interactions (*e.g.*, "Who would you choose as your real estate agent?"). For each different service interaction (relatively non-stereotyped by gender) there are three different cards, one showing the photographs of two women, one showing two men, and one card showing a woman and a man. Thus, on eight of the 24 cards, a choice is requested between persons of different gender. There are 22 sets of 24 cards containing the photographs of 48 different persons in completely randomized orders.

In a study of a heterogeneous sample of 262 adult respondents (Lott, Lott, and Fernald, 1988), the number of men chosen over women has been related to gender and age of the chooser, and to scores on two widely used measures of beliefs developed by Burt (1980)—Adversarial Sex Beliefs, and Sex Role Stereotyping. As predicted, men, whether over 30 or younger than 30, chose women significantly below chance level, while women over

30 made other-gender and same-gender choices that did not differ from chance. Women under 30, however, chose women over men reliably more than chance. An examination of mean differences in belief scores among groups of persons whose scores on the Picture Choice Task were low, medium, and high revealed that men who were more likely to turn away from women in hypothetical situations were also more likely to adhere to stereotyped beliefs about sex roles and to view relationships between women and men as adversarial; this same pattern of individual differences was found among women.

Other studies are planned that will test relationships among behavioral measures of distancing, a simulated measure like the Picture Choice Task, demographic variables, and other self-reported affective and cognitive responses such as attitudes toward women (Spence and Helmreich, 1972) and tolderance for sexual harassment (Lott, Reilly, and Howard, 1982).

IMPLICATIONS FOR THE REAL WORLD AND SOCIAL POLICY

If the data from this research program continue to support the conclusion that sexist behavior (discrimination) in face-to-face situations is independent of what men say they feel or believe about women, then programs directed toward the reduction of sexism must provide for the separate assessment of actions, feelings, and cognitions and include strategies appropriate for each domain. Variables found to relate significantly to the increased (and decreased) probability of distancing responses to women will help us to understand how such behavior is learned and maintained, and will assist us in teaching what we know to others.

Porter and Geis (1981) have reported a similar lack of congruence among expressed beliefs and sexist behavior. They had participants in one study look at slides of five-person groups and make judgements about the group leader. The person sitting at the head of the table was seen as the group leader in same-gender groups, and in mixed-gender groups when the person at the head of the table was a man. But when a woman was seated at the head of the table in a mixed-gender group, participants tended not to name her as the group leader. In other words, as concluded by the investigators, "The only condition in which seeing was not believing was the one showing a woman in the leadership position in a mixed sex group" (58). What is most relevant to the present discussion is that this kind of sexist discrimination was not revealed by self-reports of belief in aspects of feminist ideology.

Taking a step-by-step approach to a major social problem (sexism), like the one described in this paper, permits us to concentrate on "small wins" and may temper the tendency to feel overwhelmed by the problem's enormity and complexity. As Karl Weick (1984) has argued, contributing to the difficulty of solving social problems is the fact that "people define these problems in ways that overwhelm their ability to do anything about them. Changing the scale of a problem can change the quality of resources directed at it" (48). If we redefine a social problem as a series of small tasks that can be accomplished, then a social problem becomes amenable to change by less than superhuman effort.

It is toward this social objective that the research program I have described is directed. Separating overt behavior from attitudes and beliefs is theoretically sound and empirically necessary, and it also increases the probability that we will understand more clearly and simply the conditions that influence the occurence of sexist discrimination in face-to-face situations. This, in turn, should help us to make thoughtful and realistic suggestions about ways to improve social life.

Notes

* This chapter is a revised version of a paper read at the national conference of the Association for Women in Psychology, March, 1988, Bethesda, MD.

References

Allgeier, A.R., and Byrne, D. (1973). Attraction toward the opposite sex as a determinant of physical proximity. *Journal of Social Psychology, 90,* 213-219.

Barefoot, J.C., Hoople, H., and McClay, D. (1972). Avoidance of an act which would violate personal space. *Psychonomic Science, 28,* 205-206.

Bogardus, E. (1925). Measuring social distance. *Journal of Applied Sociology,* 9, 299-308.

Brunswik, E. (1956). *Perception and the representative design of psychological experiments* (2nd ed.). Berkeley: University of California Press.

Burt, M.R. (1980). Cultural myths and supports for rape. *Journal of Personality and Social Psychology, 38,* 217-230.

Evans, G.W., and Howard, R.B. (1973). Personal space. *Psychological Bulletin, 80,* 334-344.

Geffner, R., and Gross, M.M. (1984). Sex-role behavior and obedience to authority: A field study. *Sex Roles, 10,* 973-985.

Hall, C.S. (1984). "A ubiquitous sex difference in dreams" revisited. *Journal of Personality and Social Psychology, 46,* 1109-1117.

Hall, J.A. (1987). On explaining gender differences: The case of nonverbal communication. In P. Shaver and C. Hendrick (Eds.), *Sex and gender* (177-200). New York: Sage.

Hare-Mustin, R.T., and Marecek, J. (1987, August). *Gender and the meaning of difference.* Paper read at the meeting of the American Psychological Association, New York.

Henley, N.M. (1977). *Body politics: Power, sex, and non-verbal communication.* Englewood Cliffs, NJ: Prentice-Hall.

Hoffman, C.D., Tsuneyoshi, S.E., Ebina, M., and Fite, H. (1984). A comparison of adult males' and females' interactions with girls and boys. *Sex Roles, 11,* 799-811.

Liebert, R.M., Sprafkin, J.N., and Davidson, E.S. (1982). *The early window: Effects of television on children and youth* (2nd ed.). New York: Pergamon.

Lott, A.J., and Lott, B. (1976). The role of reward in the formation of positive interpersonal attitudes. In T.L. Huston (Ed.), *Foundations of interpersonal attraction.* New York: Academic Press.

Lott, B. (1985). The potential enrichment of social/personality psychology through feminist research, and vice versa. *American Psychologist, 40,* 155-164.

———. (1987a). *Women's lives: Themes and variations in gender learning.* Pacific Grove, CA: Brooks/Cole.

———. (1987b). Sexist discrimination as distancing behavior: I. A laboratory demonstration. *Psychology of Women Quarterly.*

———. (1989). Sexist discrimination as distancing behavior: II. Prime time television. *Psychology of Women Quarterly,* in press.

Lott, B., Lott, A.J., and Fernald, J. (1988). *Individual differences in distancing responses to women on a photo choice task.* Unpublished paper, Dept. of Psychology, University of Rhode Island, Kingston, RI, 02881.

Lott, B., Reilly, M.E., and Howard, D.R. (1982). Sexual assault and harassment: A campus community case study. *Signs, 8,* 296-319.

Lott, B., and Lott, A.J. (1985). Learning theory in contemporary social psychology. In G. Lindzey and E. Aronson (Eds.) *The handbook of social psychology, Vol. II* (3rd ed.), 109-136, New York: Random House.

Mehrabian, A. (1968). Inference of attitudes from the posture, orientation, and distance of a communicator. *Journal of Consulting and Clinical Psychology, 32,* 296-308.

Porter, N., and Geis, F. (1981). Women and nonverbal leadership cues: When seeing is not believing. In C. Mayo and N.M. Henley (Eds.) *Gender and nonverbal behavior,* 39-61, New York: Springer-Verlag.

Rowe, M.P. (1973). *The progress of women in educational institutions: The Saturn's rings phenomenon.* Unpublished paper. Cambridge, MA: Office of the President and Chancellor of MIT.

Singer, D.G., Singer, J.L., and Zuckerman, D.M. (1981). *Teaching television: How to use TV to your child's advantage.* New York: Dial.

Skinner, B.F. (1987). Whatever happened to psychology as the science of behavior? *American Psychologist, 42,* 780-786.

Snyder, M.L., Kleck, R.G., Strenta, A., and Mentzer, S.J. (1979). Avoidance of the handicapped: An attributional ambiguity analysis. *Journal of Personality and Social Psychology, 37,* 2297-2306.

Spence, J.T., and Helmreich, R.L. (1972). The Attitudes toward Women Scale. *JSAJ Catalog Sel. Doc. Psychology, 2,* 66.

Stier, D.S., and Hall, J.A. (1984). Gender differences in touch: An empirical and theoretical review. *Journal of Personality and Social Psychology, 47,* 440-459.

Weick, K.E. (1984). Small wins: Redefining the scale of social problems. *American Psychologist, 39,* 40-49.

Wittig, M.A., and Skolnick, P. (1978). Status versus warmth as determinants of sex differences in personal space. *Sex Roles, 4,* 493-503.

II

Sexual Harassment

Impact on Cognitive, Physical, and
Emotional Well-Being

Editor's Notes

In the preceeding section, Drs. Fitzgerald, DeFour, and Lott alerted us to the consequences of sexual harassment for women's career development. Other researchers also confirm that women who have been harassed typically change their major or educational program as a consequence of being harassed.

In this section, the consequences of sexual harassment to women's emotional and physical health are discussed by three psychologists who conduct research in women's victimization. Each of the authors, Mary Koss, Kat Quina, and Vita Rabinowitz, acknowledge the paucity of research in emotional and physical health impacts of sexual harassment. Consequently they rely on the literature on child sexual abuse and sexual assault to describe the effects of sexual harassment on women's health. In addition, each of the authors discuss sexual harassment (as they do other forms of sexual victimization) in a social context in which women have not attained equal status and power. They illustrate the ways women victims experience physical hardship, loss of income, administrative neglect, and isolation. And, they describe the ways in which these experiences contribute to emotional and physical stress reactions.

Dr. Koss, in "Changed lives: The psychological impact of sexual harassment," cites statistics that indicate that depending on the severity of the harassment, between 21-82 percent of women reported that their emotional and/or physical condition deteriorated as a result of the harassment. Among the emotional reactions reported by the women were fear, depression, anxiety, irritability, feelings of low self-esteem and alienation, vulnerability, and helplessness. Physical symptoms frequently reported by women victims include gastrointestinal disturbances, sleep disorders, nausea, weight loss, crying spells, teeth grinding, and tiredness. Dr. Koss, relying on the literature on sexual assault, including her own national study on date rape, discusses the immediate postvictimization generalized distress response experienced by women victims of sexual harassment.

Dr. Quina, in "The victimizations of women," argues, as does Dr. Koss, that women victims of sexual harassment suffer long-term emotional aftereffects. Dr. Quina analyzes these responses according to common features of the victimization experience: (1) sexual assault is a severe trauma; (2) sexual assault is a violation; and (3) sexual assault causes secondary losses. Dr. Quina offers specific counseling approaches and guidance for women victims of sexual harassment, including finding individuals with similar experiences and sharing these experiences, allowing a grieving process to occur, and joining a feminist network and support group. These recommendations parallel those offered by Dr. Koss. Dr. Koss places the psychotherapeutic techniques in a developmental sequence, corresponding to women victims' cognitive appraisal of their victimization.

Dr. Rabinowitz, in "Coping with sexual harassment," argues that the ambiguity in women's defining sexual harassment is greater when the harassment occurs on college/university campuses, given the interaction of power relations, age differential, and sex stratification characteristic of the academic community. The stress reactions experienced by women students occurs gradually since, according to Dr. Rabinowitz, faculty can manipulate their authority over women students in subtle ways. Women may thus not label these experiences as sexual harassment (see Fitzgerald, in this volume). She also cites empirical evidence that suggests that the most severe emotional and physical consequences of sexual harassment are suffered by women students who have had a long-standing professional relationship with a male faculty member before the harassment began. Women begin to question their previous achievements, and become suspicious of male faculty in general. Her description of the college/university setting echoes Rollo May's (1972):

> If we take the university as the setting, we need only ask any graduate student whether his [sic] professors have power over him, and he will laugh at our naivete. The perpetual anxiety of some graduate students as to whether they will be passed or not is proof enough. The professor's power is even more effective because it is clothed in scholarly garb. It is the power of prestige, status, and the subtle coercions of others that follow from these. (102)

In a 1984 statement to all faculty at Harvard University, the Dean of Arts and Sciences, Henry Rosovsky reported on the Faculty Council's view of such inequalities in relation to all sexual contacts between students and teachers, the supposedly "consensual" as well as the obviously harassing:

Amorous relationships that might be appropriate in other circumstances are always wrong when they occur between any teacher or officer of the University and any student for whom he or she has a professional responsibility. Further, such relationships may have the effect of undermining the atmosphere of trust on which the educational process depends. Implicit in the idea of professionalism is the recognition by those in positions of authority that in their relationships with students there is always an element of power. It is incumbent upon those with authority not to abuse, nor to seem to abuse, the power with which they are entrusted.

Drs. Koss, Quina, and Rabinowitz offer suggestions for advocates, counselors, and educators who work with women victims of sexual harassment for (1) empowering these women, (2) facilitating their appropriate labeling of the victimization, and (3) helping women to view sexual harassment as resulting from the opportunities presented by power and authority relations which derive from the hierarchical structure of the college/university system. Each of the authors point out that cognitive reappraisals of beliefs shattered by sexual harassment will contribute to women's ability to become self-reliant, adapt, grow, and become confident in their abilities once again.

Drs. Koss, Quina, and Rabinowitz alert us to the continuum of issues in the area of sexual harassment that are not addressed by policy statements and laws. They agree that faculty responsibility is the way to ensure a campus setting free of sexual harassment. And, they express the sentiment of this entire volume: that we need to change the relative power of women in college/university settings that underlies sexual harassment. Women and women's experiences must be placed in the center of the academic environment.

Reference

May, R. (1972). *Power and innocence.* New York: Dell.

4

Changed Lives:
The Psychological Impact of Sexual Harassment

Mary P. Koss

> None of us can help the things that Life has done to us. . . . They're done
> before you realize it, and once they're done they make you do other things
> until at last everything comes between you and what you would like to be, and
> you've lost your true self forever.
>
> Eugene O'Neill, *A Long Day's Journey into Night*

Experiencing sexual harassment transforms women into victims and changes their lives. It is inevitable that once victimized, at minimum, one can never again feel quite as invulnerable. Much has been written about the experience of victimization including its impact on deeply held beliefs and values, immediate and long-term effects on mental health, and fallout in social and work arenas. The goal of this paper is to review the literature that documents these psychological impacts of sexual harassment and to present a cognitive model of victimization that attempts to explain the origin of these effects.

Although sexual harassment is currently considered sex discrimination and a violation of civil rights, this view only became public policy in 1980. As a result of the long historical period during which gender-based abuse in the workplace was condoned, strong forces toward secrecy exist which oppose disclosure of such incidents into the public record. Because sexual harassment is so infrequently discussed openly or formally grieved, one often hears skepticism about surveys which suggest that it has been experienced by 42 percent of women employees of the U.S. government (U.S. Merit Systems Protection Board, 1981). Yet, there are many reasons why victims of sexual harassment cannot or will not reveal their experiences.

Among these reasons is the traditional view of a victim as a loser

(Taylor, Wood, and Lichtman, 1983). Even in contemporary culture, a victim is often viewed as a precipitant or an actual participant in crimes with sexual components unless strong nonconsent and resistance can be demonstrated by the presence of serious injury (Bularzik, 1978; Burt and Katz, 1985). When people acknowledge their status as victims, some degree of devaluation and social stigma is inevitably incurred (Goffman, 1963). Thus, there is considerable motivation to reject the role of "victim" both to oneself and to others.

Other social forces have restrained research on the effects of sexual harassment including "the erroneous belief that gender-based abuse in the workplace is an insignificant life event" (Hamilton, Alagna, King, and Lloyd, in press, 5). Stigma may also infect researchers who study sexual harassment judging from tenure and promotion experiences where such work has been dismissed as lacking in importance and out of the mainstream, or discredited as political retoric and not objective science. In light of these compelling social forces and the short history of sexual harassment as a legitimate form of victimization, it is not surprising that the empirical database is too small to provide the basis for this chapter. Therefore, relevant work also has been sought to the literature on other forms of victimization including that caused by intimate violence (*e.g.*, child sexual abuse and sexual assault), crime, and disasters.

Yet, it must be acknowledged that various forms of victimization differ in important ways (*e.g.*, human induced versus natural causation; age and developmental stage of the victim; context, predictability, and duration of the abuse). As well, there are also important commonalities between sexual harassment and other forms of victimization of women. All these forms of abuse involve direct harm by another human being often with the specific intent to injure or control, and all occur in a social context in which women have yet to attain equal status and power (Burt and Katz, 1985). Like incest, sexual harassment is an abuse of power and a betrayal of trust; it is humiliating, which encourages women to keep it a secret; and it requires the victim to maintain interaction with the perpetrator (Hamilton *et al.*, in press). Like sexual assault victims who go to court, sexual harassment victims may experience a second injury when the investigator, judge, and jury support and protect the criminal (Hamilton *et al.*, in press). And, like crime victims, sexual harassment victims may lead to physical hardship, loss of income, frequent delays, administrative neglect and lack of information (Salisbury, Ginorio, Remick, and Stringer, 1986).

THE VICTIMIZATION PROCESS

Many women who sustain harm do not perceive themselves as victims. For example, Koss (1985) reported that only 57 percent of a group of college women, all of whom had had experiences that met legal definitions of rape, regarded themselves as rape victims. Among national sample, 30 percent of the women raped by strangers and 62 percent of the women raped by acquaintances did *not* view their experience as *any* type of crime (Koss, Dinero, Seibel, and Cox, 1988). The terms *acknowledged* and *unacknowledged* have been used to denote a raped woman's stance toward her victimization (Koss, 1985). Burt and Estep (1981) have suggested that there are three stages to becoming a victim. In stage 1, persons sustain injury. In stage 2, individuals perceive the injury as unfair and perceive themselves as victims. In stage 3, individuals seek redress from social control agents.

Among the reasons that victimization is aversive is that it involves losses (*e.g.*, control, value, self-esteem) and it forces people to label themselves in negative ways or to categorize themselves with other stigmatized individuals (Taylor *et al.*, 1983). To avoid these sources of aversion, victims may take steps to "de-victimize" themselves including trying to pass as nonvictimized and to engage in selective evaluations that allow them to limit the extent to which they see themselves as victims. For example, trivializing an experience that legally qualifies as sexual harassment may serve to protect the victim's sense of integrity and invulnerability. Research has shown that the desire to avoid identification as a victim is very high. For example, Curtis (1976) completed a reverse records study and found that only 54 percent of known acquaintance rape victims (*i.e.*, victims who had reported their assault to police) would admit to an interviewer that they had been raped. Such selective evaluation may be adaptive to the extent that it allows people to function in the face of catastrophe. However, it may be maladaptive if it prevents women from coming to terms adequately with their situation and uniting with others "to solve ligitimate common problems collectively" (Taylor *et al.*, 1983, 37).

Research designs that depend for participation on a subject's self-identification as a victim tap only that segment of those women who perceive themselves as victims while missing the many women who have sustained harm but may not see the injury as unfair. A question to be resolved by future empirical work is the severity and types of symptoms associated with various conceptual stages in the victimization process.

Realizing that One Is a Victim

Among persons in a large random sample who had experienced an act of sexual harassment, several different responses were reported: 46 percent of the victims objected directly to the perpetrator; 12 percent ignored the behavior; 11 percent reported it to a higher authority; and 2.5 percent used formal complaint channels (U.S. Merit Systems Protection Board, 1981). Factors that inhibited women from filing formal complaints included fear of retaliation and the belief that the behavior was not serious or would not be taken seriously (U.S. Merit Systems Protection Board, 1981). Many victims may have believed that men had the right—or even the duty—to pursue sexual encounters with women aggressively. This belief would have been reinforced by cultural norms that hold women responsible for stimulating men's sexual behavior (Burarzik, 1978; Burt, 1980).

Women who outwardly claim victim status are often disappointed by the response they receive from others. First, people frequently are not as helpful to victims as might be expected given our Judeo-Christian ethics and general tendency to help the powerless (Janoff-Bulman, and Frieze, 1986). People who have *not* been victimized by events such as illnesses, accidents, or crimes often maintain a belief that they are invulnerable or less vulnerable to victimization compared to other people (Perloff, 1983; Scheppele and Bart, 1983). The responses of nonvictimized persons often include one or more of the following: the victimization is either denied or trivialized (Frieze and McHugh, 1986); victims are seen as responsible for their fate (Lerner, 1970; Ryan, 1971); ignored (Reiff, 1979); seen as losers (Bard and Sangrey, 1979); feared (Frederick, 1980); or avoided because they are depressed (Coates, Wortman, and Abbey, 1979). Some of these responses serve the purpose of maintaining the nonvictimized person's sense of invulnerability at the expense of validating the victim's experience.

Clinical work with women who had experienced sexual harassment has revealed that considerable time often elapsed before many realized the wrongness of the perpetrator's behavior and acknowledged their status as legitimate victims:

> Because sexual harassment and other forms of employment discrimination are so prevalent, these experiences are likely to fade into the background of our lives as women at work. Since we as women have also been taught to devalue our talents . . . and to lower our expectations, the realization that we have experienced even profound discrimination is often slow in coming. Instead of conceptualizing our experiences as "discrimination," most women initially report confusion and bewilderment. Isolation and lack of validation and reality-based feedback also undermine trust in one's own perceptions. . . . A specific incident such as an unexpected termination or nonrenewal, or a lack of promotion may finally spark a woman's anger . . . a woman often decides to fight when she realizes that there is nothing else to lose. . . . Once the realization of profound discrimination sinks in, there is generally the gradual recognition of a large number of inequities that occurred previously but were deflected . . . (Hamilton *et al.*, 12-13)

Blowing the Whistle

The decision to seek redress changes a woman's status from simply a victim/loser to a victim/"whistleblower" (Glazer, 1983). Often, the woman who speaks out is a person with a strong sense of integrity who can no longer ignore injustice. Institutional responses to formal complaints of sexual harassment are typically defensive: "It didn't happen, if it did happen, it wasn't intentional, even if it did happen, the woman brought it on herself due to her peculiar personality; even if it did happen, the good work done by the discriminator or the institution outweighs the bad" (Hamilton et al., in press, 19). About two-thirds of a group of victims who requested help from Working Women's Institute reported apparent retaliation including being criticized unduly or held up for ridicule before subordinates or clients, refused promotions, kept out of training programs, and denied letters of reference (Crull, 1982). The experience of another group who filed complaints included: prolonged harassment; retaliation by the harasser or the organization in the form of psychological abuse; lowered evaluations, denied promotions or firing; shunning by co-workers; withdrawal of any social support previously derived from work-group interaction; and financial despair (Salisbury et al., 1986, 320).

The refusal of co-workers to contribute corroborating information was an extreme disappointment to many victims and felt like collusion or betrayal. Hamilton and colleagues have concluded, "To the extent that women have a decision about discrimination, it is fundamentally a choice between miserable alternatives: to speak out, and become a pariah; or to suffer in silence" (in press, 16). Thus, it is not surprising that women who file formal complaints or seek legal help experience "dramatically" higher rates of physical and psychological symptoms compared to those who do not file charges (Livingston, 1982).

THE IMPACT OF SEXUAL HARASSMENT ON WOMEN

The impact of sexual harassment is considered in the following sections including behavioral, mental health, and cognitive changes.

The Behavioral Impact

Among the women in one large random sample who spoke up when confronted with sexual harassment, close to half (43 percent) stated that their most assertive response "made no difference" (U.S. Merit Systems Protection Board, 1981). Subsequent to sexual harassment, 16 percent of victimized federal employees reported adverse employment effects in the form of poor working conditions or diminished opportunities for advancement and nine percent reported changing jobs as a direct result of the harassment (U.S. Merit Systems Protection Board, 1981). Behavioral changes in work behavior attributed to sexual harassment included decreased morale, absenteeism, and loss of concentration which were estimated to cost the federal employment system 90 million dollars per year (U.S. Merit Systems Protection Board, 1981).

Behavioral effects appeared to be even greater among women whose employment lacked the diversity and protections of the federal system. For example, among 88 cases of sexual harassment filed with the California Fair Employment and Housing Department between 1979 and 1983, almost half of the complainants were fired and an additional quarter quit in fear or frustration (Coles, 1986). Among a non-random group of 262 women who contacted the Working Women's Institute for help, more than a quarter were fired or laid off and an addition 25-42 percent (depending on whether they were in the questionnaire or interview sample) resigned (Crull, 1982). The costs of leaving jobs under duress included loss of confidence, income, seniority, a disrupted work history, problems with references, and often a failure to qualify for unemployment (Hamilton *et al.*, in press).

Among college students, behavioral impacts take different forms. According to Dziech and Weiner (1984) harassment often "forces a student to forfeit work, research, educational comfort, or even career. Professors withhold legitimate opportunities from those who resist, or students withdraw rather than pay certain prices" (10). In a 1983 study conducted at Harvard University, 15 percent of the graduate and 12 percent of the undergraduate students who experienced harassment changed their academic major or educational program as a result (cited in Fitzgerald and Shullman, 1987).

Mental and Physical Health Impacts

Depending on the severity of the abuse, between 21-82 percent of women reported that their emotional or physical condition worsened as a result of harassment (Crull, 1982; Loy and Stewart, 1984; U.S. Merit Systems Protection Board, 1981). Among the emotional reactions reported by victims of sexual harassment were anger, fear, depression, anxiety, irritability, loss of self-esteem, feelings of humiliation and alienation, and a sense of helplessness and vulnerability (Gutek, 1981; Safran, 1976; Working Women's United Institute, 1978). For example, among one sample of victims, 78 percent reported feeling angry, 48 percent felt upset; 23 percent were scared; 27 percent felt alone, helpless, guilty, and alienated (Silverman, 1976-77). Among victims who had reached the point of filing formal charges, the magnitude of anger often exceeded the likely organizational remedies (*e.g.*, transfer to an equivalent job, sexual harassment prevention training for management, discipline of the harasser, or implementation of an adequate complaint procedure) (Salisbury *et al.*, 1986). The physical symptoms frequently reported by these victims included: gastrointestinal disturbances, jaw tightness and teeth grinding, anxiety attacks, binge-eating, headaches, inability to sleep, tiredness, nausea, loss of appetite, weight loss, and crying spells (Crull, 1982; Salisbury *et al.*, 1986).

As can be seen from the studies cited above, the research on the psychological impact of sexual harassment is still in the description mode. Studies are yet now available in which victims were followed prospectively in time from the point of victimization and administered standardized diagnostic interviews and psychological tests. Therefore, related work will be considered including studies of the range and severity of the initial and long-term psychological impacts of several forms of victimization. Reviews of this material are available including the aftereffects of child maltreatment (Lamphear, 1985), child sexual abuse (Augoustinos, 1987; Browne and Finkelhor, 1986); adult sexual assault (Holmes and St. Lawrence, 1983; Ellis, 1983; Resick, 1987), criminal victimization (Kilpatrick *et al.*, 1987); and marital rape (Frieze, 1983).

These studies reveal that most victims experience an immediate postvictimization generalized distress response characterized as a state of psychological shock (*i.e.*, emotional numbing, constriction of affect, repeated re-experiencing of the trauma by intrusive waking images or dreams, anxiety, and depression). For many victims the immediate distress fails to resolve but instead develops into a chronic, thoroughly heterogeneous symptom picture that may persist for a considerable length of time. The core features of the long-term symptommatic responses to a variety of victimizing experiences include fear/avoidance responses, affective constriction, disturbances of self-esteem/self-efficacy, and sexual dysfunction (Koss, 1987). These physical, cognitive, and behavioral responses which are induced by violent victimization are consistent with the DSM-111-R criteria for post-traumatic stress disorder (American Psychiatric Association, 1987). In fact, rape victims constitute the largest single group of PTSD sufferers (Foa, Olasov, and Steketee, 1987).

Several random sample community surveys have found that adult women who were victims of child sexual abuse, sexual assault, and criminal victimization had identifiable degrees of impairment when compared with nonvictims. For example, 17 percent of adult women abused as children were clinically depressed as measured by the Center for Epidemiologic Studies-Depression Scale [CES-D] and 18 percent were considered severely psychoneurotic (Bagley and Ramsay, 1985). Adult victims of completed rape and aggravated assault, compared to nonvictims, were significantly more likely to have increased levels of Hostility, Depression,

Paranoid Ideation, Psychoticism, Anxiety, and Obsessive-compulsive symptoms as measured by the Symptom Checklist [SCL-90] (Kilpatrick, Best, Veronen, Amick, Villeponteaux, and Ruff, (1985). In their lifetimes, rape victims compared to nonvictims were more likely to have had problems with depression, alcohol and drug use, somatization, schizophrenia, post-traumatic stress, generalized anxiety, panic, and obsessive-compulsive symptoms (George and Winfield-Laird, 1986). Even when evaluated many years after the sexual assault, victims were significantly more likely than nonvictims to qualify currently for psychiatric diagnoses including major depression, alcohol abuse/dependence, drug abuse/dependence, generalized anxiety, obsessive-compulsive disorder, and post-traumatic stress disorder and equally likely to be diagnosed as somatization or schizophrenia/schizophreniform (George and Winlfield-Laird, 1986). Furthermore, a strong correlation between history of violent victimization and suicidal ideation or deliberate attempts at self-harm has been found consistently (*e.g.*, Bagley and Ramsay, 1985; George and Winfield-Laird, 1986; Kilpatrick *et al.*, 1985; Kilpatrick, *et al.*, 1987). To the extent that sexual harassment resembles the trauma of rape and incest, these studies suggest that it could be a stressor which poses significant obstacles to women's achievement of mental health and well-being. A state-of-the-art, prospective study of the impact of sexual harassment should be a priority item on the research agenda.

The Cognitive Impact

Rich clinical observations of sexual harassment victims (82 percent of whom had filed formal complaints) are available in the literature (Hamilton *et al.*, in press; Salisbury *et al.*, 1986). The sequence of reactions to harassment that were observed by Salisbury and colleagues (1986) are described below. In addition to the affective responses that can be seen, here are a sequence of changes in the victim's central beliefs about herself, her co-workers, and the workworld:

(1) *Confusion/Self-Blame.* The sexual harassment was a series of events. After each incident, the victim believed that the harassment was going to level off or eventually stop. When the harasser's behavior escalated, which it did in virtually all of the cases studied, the victim felt out-of-control and helpless.

(2) *Fear/Anxiety.* Subsequent to the harasser's continuing behavior, the victim felt trapped and became "paranoid." She feared potential retaliation at work, the future of her career, and potential financial ruin. Outside of work, she feared being called on the phone in the early morning, having her home watched, or being followed in a car. Concentration,

motivation, work performance, and attendance were adversely affected and self-esteem declined.

(3) *Depression/Anger.* Once the woman recognized that she was a legitimate victim who was not to blame for her harassment, anxiety often shifted to anger. Often this shift occurred when she decided to leave her job or was fired. This anger about being treated unfairly was a prime motive to file charges. While filing charges may have represented a positive step by the victim to take control of her destiny, it often led to a decided deterioration in the work situation. Hamilton and colleagues (in press) describe the psychological burden of sexual harassment at this point in the sequence of events:

> In order to survive once the realization of harm occurs, the woman must rely on protective mechanisms that include renewed efforts at denial and suppression of affect. At this point—because of the despair and efforts at denial—the woman's controls are likely to be erratic. It is common for a woman to express extreme ambivalence. She may both curse the unfair way she's treated, and alternately descredit her own abilities. . . . There are few, if any, role models for successfully responding to severe discrimination. . . . A central issue becomes the woman's sense of control. If we believe that we are being harmed irrationally, then we may feel even more helpless and out of control. One alternative is to believe that the abuse is justified—then at least it appears "rational" and perhaps we could learn to change it. One way to achieve a sense of control is through identification with the aggressor. The stress of being devalued internally and externally, by powerful authorities, can push intelligent, rational, and otherwise well-functioning women to an extreme crisis of self-doubt. (13-15)

(4) *Disillusionment.* The organizational response to sexual harassment was often hurtful and disappointing. By speaking up, the woman encountered a whole new set of institutional abuses. For women in science, in particular, the discovery of the extent to which scientists can be prejudiced and can both lie and falsify the data, shook beliefs about trust and scientific objectivity (Gornick, 1983). Often, the woman eventually realized that she had been naive about getting help in the system—courts, federal and state agencies, or internal organizational procedures. She questioned her expectations about fairness, loyalty, and justice. These ingenuous beliefs gradually became replaced by the insight that justice doesn't always prevail.

VICTIMIZATION INDUCED AFTEREFFECTS:
THEORETICAL EXPLANATIONS

Currently, most research on victimization induced traumatic responses uses a behavioral/conditioning framework to account for the development of symptoms. Sexual and fear related symptoms are explained on the basis of classical conditioning (*e.g.*, Kilpatrick, Veronen, and Resick, 1979; Becker and Skinner, 1983). Higher order conditioning effects are suggested to account for the observed diffuseness, persistence, potency, and individual variations in victimization induced aftereffects. However, sexual harassment presents challenges to a conditioning model. Compared to criminal victimization, sexual harassment is much more likely to be a cumulative series of escalating episodes rather than a single, blitz attack. Many incidents of sexual harassment do not involve paralyzing levels of fear regarding imminent death or mutilation. In fact, the level of emotional arousal conducive to conditioning may not occur at all in the early stages of sexual harassment when the victim may believe that she has misinterpreted the behavior or that the offender was just joking. Coupled with possibly lower levels of aroused fear, a series victimization like sexual harassment may involve a number of different approaches and settings which would mitigate against the development of focalized fear reactions.

The key to understanding the psychological impact of sexual harassment may have more to do with the kinds and consequences of the victim's perceptions and cognitive appraisals of her experience rather than with simple or complex conditioning effects. Clinical work with victims reveals the "overwhelming assault victimization is to the child's and adult survivor's world of meaning" (Conte, 1987, 24).

Stress and Cognitive Appraisal

Cognitive appraisal (Lazarus and Folkman, 1984) is a key concept of considerable value in accounting for the variations in sensitivity and vulnerability to stressors as well as the differences in adaptation. Cognitive appraisal refers to the process by which an individual evaluates a particular stressor (*e.g.*, Lazarus and Folkman, 1984; Folkman, 1984). The amount of psychological distress experienced by an individual is not determined by the stressor alone but by the relationship between the person and environment. Appraisals are influenced by both *situation* factors (*e.g.*, predictability, duration, and ambiguity of the stressor) and person factors (*i.e.*, "*commitments*—what is important to the person; . . . *beliefs*—personally formed or culturally shared . . . preexisting notions about reality which serve as perceptual lens; and existential beliefs—faith in God, fate, or some natural order . . . that enable people to create meaning out of life even out of damaging experiences, and to maintain hope" (Lazarus and Folkman, 1984, 58-77).

Victimization by sexual harassment is likely to be appraised as harmful and threatening because it (1) interferes with a woman's ability to meet important financial commitments to family; (2) by its nature, occurs in situations that are unpredictable, ambiguous, and long-lasting; and (3) poses serious challenges to important, central beliefs such as personal invulnerability, the perception of the world as meaningful, and the positive view of ourselves (Janoff-Bulman, 1985; Taylor, 1983). To victims who were cautious and good people (e.g., who dressed for success and took their job seriously), the world does not appear meaningful (Scheppele and Bart, 1983; Silver and Wortman, 1980). Victims are no longer able to say, "It can't happen to me," and must confront a challenge to their beliefs that bad things happen only to bad people. It is possible that sexual harassment and subsequent workplace retaliation are even more likely to create such obstacles than some other forms of victimization. Whereas stranger attacks and civilian disasters shatter the sense of invulnerability, they can be attributed to fate which may preserve some sense of life purpose and self-esteem. Because of its intimate linkages with work performance, a central adult life role, sexual harassment directly activates identity issues raises questions about life purpose.

The process of victimization activates negative self-images. Victims see themselves as weak, needy, frightened, and out of control (Horowitz, Wilner, Marmar, and Krupnick, 1980; Krupnick, 1980). The common thread among all forms of victimization is the psychological loss of one's cherished beliefs following the experience (Janoff-Bulman, 1985). Being a victim forces individuals "to realize that their 'cognitive baggage'—the assumptions and expectations that have held about themselves and their world—have been severely challenged and may no longer be viable" (Janoff-Bulman and Fireze, 1983, 3). Victims experience a "loss of equilibrium. The world is suddenly out of wack. Things no longer work the way they used to" (Bard and Sangrey, 1979, 14).

The cognitive processing of trauma is theorized to involve a "completion tendency," which is a predisposition to "integrate reality and schemata" (Horowitz, 1976, 249). Experiences that contradict deeply held beliefs have no emotional location where they can be assimilated. For example, the perception "I have been victimized" is inconsistent with a schemata of invulnerability. The perception that "I am criticized and shunned" is inconsistent with a schemata of being a good person. The perception that people are lying and covering up is inconsistent with a schemata that work, or science, is a meaningful and exhalted life endeavor.

Victimization "will eventually change inner models. . . . The mind continues to process important new information until the situation or the models change, and reality and models of reality reach accord (Horowitz, 1982, 727). While in active memory, traumatic experiences often intrude on mental life through dreams, memories, and uncontrollable, distressing images. Alternating with intrusiveness, numbing may also occur which represents the individual's attempts to slow down cognitive processing and reduce the anxiety associated with intrusive representations (Horowitz, 1980, 1982). This process accounts for periods of high anxiety and intrusiveness which alternate with periods of avoidance and depression.

Eventually, however, beliefs must be altered to assimilate the trauma so that resolution can occur. These victimization-induced cognitive alterations have important and long-lasting implications for victims, because cognitive schema function as anticipatory mechanisms that determine what people attend to in their future encoding of reality (Greenberg and Safran, 1981). Thus, the woman who eventually comes to believe that life isn't always fair may have enhanced work-related coping skills in the future. In contrast, the woman who comes to believe that she is defective and damaged may evidence impaired work and interpersonal effectiveness.

Cognitive Assimilation and Resolution versus Accommodation

For a victimization to be resolved, shattered beliefs must be reformulated to assimilate the traumatic experience. This process has been called cognitive re-adjustment (Taylor, 1983). Taylor suggested that the cognitive readjustment process involves three important themes: (1) the search for meaning (Why me?); (2) attempts to gain mastery and control (How can I prevent a re-occurrence?); and (3) attempts to promote self-enhancement (Now that I am victimized, who am I?). Successful cognitive re-appraisals of beliefs shattered by victimization emphasize attributes including the discovered ability to cope, adapt, learn, grow, and become self-reliant; and produce a greater sense of strength, depth, maturity, sensitivity, honesty, and self-confidence (Finkel, 1975).

Kilpatrick and Veronen (1983) provided three ways in which rape, for example, was assimilated positively: as a consciousness raising experience ("Now I see how women are treated in our society—I'm glad I don't have a blindfold on anymore."), as a life appreciation lesson ("Since I got out of this alive, I promised myself to live each day to the fullest."), and as a challenge to overcome ("I'm a survivor and I won't let this get in my way."). These new beliefs allowed assimilation of the traumatic experience and functioned to restore previous meaning, mastery, and self-esteem. Empirically developed "growth scales" have produced evidence of positive change in the attitudes and beliefs of victims undergoing treatment at rape crisis centers (Burt and Katz, in press). Among untreated victims of rape and incest, however, evidence exists which suggests that even 20 years after their victimization, many do not feel that they have resolved their trauma, found meaning in it, or returned to the way they were before it happened (Burgess and Holmstrom, 1979; Silver, Boon, and Stones, 1983).

Given the widespread acceptance of myths that support female responsibility for sexuality (e.g., Burt, 1980) and the general treatment accorded the victimized in our society (e.g., Taylor et al., 1983), positive outcomes are not highly likely to occur spontaneously among victims. Several sources of evidence suggest that without clinical intervention successful cognitive re-adjustment subsequent to sexual harassment is especially unlikely. First, the reality is that most women work out of economic necessity and have lower-status jobs with less seniority and training than male co-workers. "It is likely that the woman's harasser will have some form of authority or advantage over her in the work hierarchy and, thus, be able to win out in any confrontation that results from the sexual harassment" (Crull, 1982, 542). Second, compared to assaults by strangers, sexual harassment (as well as acquaintance rape and incest) more strongly evoke cultural stereotypes about the victim's responsibility for enticing the offender's behavior and require the victim to continue interaction with the offender who may hold power over her. Third, as opposed to victimizations which can be ascribed to fate—although they indirectly challenge important beliefs—sexual harassment is a direct assault on identity, self-worth, and the meaning of work, a central role of adult life.

As long as traumatic memories remain unassimilated, symptoms of avoidance and intrusion will persist. An alternative to successful assimilation is accommodation in which shattered beliefs are modified maladaptively by the victimization. "Victims who become psychologically impaired do so in environments in which they accommodate or adjust to the judgements that others made about the abuse" (Rieker and Carmen, 1986, 363). These accommodations can be seen as "survival strategies" to deal with ongoing abuse, yet ultimately they form the basis of the "damaged self" (Carmen, Reiker, and Mills, 1984; Reiker and Carmen, 1986). Sexual harassment is one of the important ways in which inequality impacts directly on women's mental health (Carmen, Russo, and Miller, 1981).

IMPLICATIONS FOR CLINICIANS

There are no published guidelines for therapeutic treatment of sexual harassment victims but reports of two group treatment approaches are available (Hamilton et al., in press; Salisbury et al., 1986). Clients may initially appear extremely unstable, histrionic, paranoid, or depressed.

Extreme behavior should be interpreted in terms of victimization as a normal response to a social problem until proven otherwise (Crull, 1982; Hamilton *et al.*, in press). It may be helpful for the clinician to adopt the following assumptions when approaching such a client (Hamilton *et al.*):

1. The woman actually has experienced discrimination.
2. She probably has an adequate or better work history.
3. She probably has reacted in some way to the discrimination and this already has been brought to her attention by this time.
4. If she has complained, there has been retaliation.

In this work, it is very important that the counselor keep roles straight. As the assumptions listed above illustrate, the clinician is not a judge and doesn't have to be concerned with whether sexual harassment as legally defined has occurred. Likewise, the clinician is not an attorney. Clinicians should only help clients with their options, not advise them on their civil rights (Salisbury *et al.*, 1986). Also, clinicians must make clients aware that making a claim of psychological damages will require them to waive their right to confidentiality in the sessions and the treating therapist may be called to trial to present an assessment of the client (Salisbury *et al.*).

Dealing with sexual harassment taxes psychological resources, often over a long period of time as delay is a time honored defense tactic. Whether in individual or group therapy format, clinicians may serve victims best by providing emotional support, a safe forum for expressing feelings, monitoring physical symptoms and coping behavior, and engaging in specific problem solving. Experience to date suggests that progress on significant therapeutic issues is not realistic while a woman is actively confronting a chronic, highly abnormal environment—akin to a concentration camp experience—to which exaggerated self-protective behaviors are necessary for day-to-day psychological survival.

The psychotherapeutic techniques that have proved valuable in applications to date are entirely consistent with a view of sexual harassment as an assault on significant beliefs and the woman's world of meaning. Recommended interventions include:

(1) *Validation of feelings: I didn't make it up.* Emotional support and statements that legitimate victim status may help the client resist self-devaluation.

(2) *Search for meaning: Why me?* Discussion of gender inequity may help the client realize that sexual harassment is inevitable given current workplace culture and power distribution.

(3) Expression of Anger. Provision of a safe forum for the expression of anger may help the client to contain her feelings in the workplace and preserve effective job performance as much as possible. Also, psychotherapeutic expression of anger may drain away feelings that could otherwise occur at home.

(4) Monitor Damage. The strain of coping with sexual harassment will impact on the client's supportive relationships. The therapist should monitor the use of maladaptive strategies for managing stress by the victim and her family (Hamilton *et al.*, in press). While the clinician should share techniques for stress management and effective problem solving, the client may also be advised to seek documentation of health problems and difficulties as a form of legal protection (Crull, 1982).

(5) Provision for mourning losses. Inevitably, sexual harassment changes victims' lives. Whether in small or large ways, their beliefs are shattered, their life is changed, they're not the people they were. These loses have to be mourned as a first step to re-building new beliefs, new lives, and new support systems.

(6) Offer hope. Virtually all whistleblowers were able to rebuild their careers and their belief in their own competence and integrity (Glazer, 1983). Filing a complaint ultimately had beneficial effects on resolution of traumatic experiences (Schoener *et al.*, 1983). Becoming different doesn't mean becoming worse!

In the coming years, a generation of young women will enter the job market who have been raised with expectations that they can be what they want to be and can have it all. If the prevalence of sexual harassment continues at current rate, an enormous number of these young women face the realization that their expectations were naive. Clinicians are available to offer the support and hope. Hopefully, many of these victims will have a sufficient sense of injustice to file charges and will face a system that offers them reasonable avenues for redress.

References

American Psychiatric Association. (1987). *Diagnostic and statistical manual of mental disorders* (4th ed). Washington, D.C.: American Psychiatric Association.

Augoustinos, M. (1987). Developmental effects of child abuse: Recent findings. *Child Abuse and Neglect*, 11, 15-27.

Bagley, C., and Ramsay, R. (1986). Sexual abuse in childhood: Psychosocial outcomes and implications for social work practice. *Journal of Social Work and Human Sexuality, 4,* 33-47.

Bard, M., and Sangrey, D. (1979). *The crime victim's book.* NY: Basic Books.

Becker, J.Y., and Skinner, L.J. (1983). Assessment and treatment of rape-related sexual dysfunctions. *The Clinical Psychologist, 36,* 102-105.

Browne, A., and Finkelhor, D. (1986). Impact of child sexual abuse: A review of the research. *Psychological Bulletin, 99,* 66-77.

Bularzik, M. (1978). Sexual harassment at the workplace: Historical notes. *Radical America, 12,* 25-43.

Burgess, A.W., and Holmstrom, L.L. (1979). Rape: Sexual disruption and recovery. *American Journal of Orthopsychiatry, 49,* 648-657.

Burt, M.R. (1980). Cultural myths and supports for rape. *Journal of Personality and Social Psychology, 38,* 217-230.

Burt, M.R., and Estep, R.W. (1981). Who is a victim? Definitional problems in sexual victimization. *Victimology: An International Journal, 6,* 15-28. (1983).

Burt, M.R., and Katz, B.L. (1985). Rape, robbery, and burglary: Responses to actual and feared criminal victimization with special focus on women and the elderly. *Victimology: An International Journal, 10,* 325-358.

———. (in press). Dimensions of recovery from rape: Focus on growth outcomes. *Journal of Interpersonal Violence.*

Carmen, E.H., Rieker, P.P., and Mills, T. (1984). Victims of violence and psychiatric illness. *American Journal of Psychiatry, 141,* 378-383.

Carmen, E.H., Russo, N.F., Miller, J.B. (1981). Inequality and women's mental health: an overview. *American Journal of Psychiatry, 138,* 1319-1330.

Coates, D., Wortman, C.B., and Abbey, A. (1979). Reactions to victims. In I.H. Frieze, B. Bar-Tal., and J.S. Carroll (Eds.) *New approaches to social problems: Applications of attribution theory.* San Francisco, CA: Jossey-Bass.

Coles, F.S. (1986). Forced to quit: Sexual harassment complaints and agency response. *Sex Roles, 14,* 81-95.

Conte, J.R., (in press). The effects of sexual abuse on children: Results of a research project. In R. Prentky and Y. Quinsey (Eds.). *Human sexual aggression*. NY: New York Academy of Sciences.

Crull, P. (1982). Stress effects of sexual harassment on the job: Implications for counseling. *American Journal of Orthopsychiatry, 52*, 539-544.

Curtis, L.A. (1976). Present and future measures of victimization in forcible rape. In M.J. Walker, and S.L. Brodsky (Eds.) *Sexual assault* (61-68). Lexington, MA: D.C. Heath.

Dziech, B.W., and Weiner, L. (1984). *The lecherous professor: Sexual harassment on campus*. Boston, MA: Beacon Press.

Ellis, E.M. (1983). A review of empirical rape research: Victim reactions and response to treatment. *Clinical Psychology Review, 3*, 473-490.

Finkel, J.J. (1975). Stress, traumas, and trauma resolution. *American Journal of Community Psychology, 3*, 173-178.

Fitzgerald, L.F., and Shullman, S.L. (1987, March). The development and validation of an objectively scored measure of sexual harassment in higher education: Some extensions and applications to theory. Paper presented to the convention of the Association for Women in Psychology, Denver, CO.

Foa, E.B., Olasov, B., and Steketee, G.S. (1987, September). Treatment of rape victims. Paper presented at the conference, "State of the Art in Sexual Assault." Charleston, S.C.

Folkman, S. (1984). Personal control and stress and coping processes: A theoretical analysis. *Journal of Personality and Social Psychology, 46*, 839-852.

Frederick (1980). Effects of natural versus human-induced violence. *Evaluation and Change*, 1980, 71-75.

Frieze, I.H. (1983). Investigating the causes and consequences of marital rape. *Signs, 8*, 532-553.

Frieze, I.H., and McHugh, M.C. (1986). When disaster strikes. In C. Tavris (Ed.) *Everywoman's emotional well-being* (349-370). NY: Nelson Doubleday.

George, L.K., and Winfield-Laird, I. (1986). Sexual assault: prevalence and mental health consequences. Final report submitted to the National Institute of Mental Health.

Glazer, M. (1983). Ten whistleblowers and how they fared. *The Hastings Center Report, 13*, 33-41.

Goffman, E. Stigma: Notes on the management of spoiled identity. Englewood Cliffs, NJ: Prentice-Hall, 1963.

Gornick, Y. (1983). *Women in science.* NY: Simon and Schuster.

Greenberg, L.S., and Safran, J.D. (1981). Encoding and cognitive therapy: Changing what clients attend to. *Psychotherapy: Theory, Research, and Practice, 18,* 163-169.

Gutek, B.A. (1981, August). Experiences of sexual harassment: Results from a representative survey. Paper presented at the annual meeting of the American Psychological Association, Los Angeles, CA.

Hamilton, J.A., Alagna, S.W., King, L.S., and Lloyd, C. (in press). The emotional consequences of gender-based abuse in the workplace: New counseling programs for sex discrimination. *Women and Therapy.*

Holmes, M.R., and St. Lawrence, J.S. (1983). Treatment of rape induced trauma: Proposed behavioral conceptualization and review of the literature. *Clinical Psychology Review, 3,* 417-433.

Horowitz, M.J. (1979). *States of mind.* NY: Plenum Medical.

———. (1980). *Stress response syndromes.* NY: Jason Aronson.

———. (1982). Stress response syndromes and their treatment. In L. Goldberger and S. Breznitz (Eds.), *Handbook of Stress.* NY: Free Press.

Horowitz, M.J., Wilner, N., Marmar, C., and Krupnick, J. (1980). Pathological grief and the activation of latent self-images. *American Journal of Psychiatry, 137,* 1137-1162.

Janoff-Bulman, R. (1985). Criminal versus non-criminal victimization: Victim's reactions. *Victimology: An International Journal, 10,* 498-511.

Janoff-Bulman, R., and Frieze, I.H. (1983). A theoretical perspective for understanding reactions to victimization. *Journal of Social Issues, 39,* 1-17.

Kilpatrick, D.G., and Veronen, L.J. (1983). Treatment for rape related problems: Crisis intervention is not enough. In L.H. Cohen, W. Claiborn, and G. Specter (Eds.), *Crisis intervention* (165-185). NY: Human Sciences Press.

Kilpatrick, D.G., Veronen, L.J., and Resick, P.A. (1979). Assessment of the aftermath of rape: Changing patterns of fear. *Journal of Behavioral Assessment, 1,* 133-148.

Kilpatrick, D.G., Best, C.L., Veronen, L.J., Amick, A.E., Villeponteaux,

L.A., and Ruff, G.A. (1985). Mental health correlates of criminal victimization: A random community survey. *Journal of Consulting and Clinical Psychology, 53,* 866-873.

Kilpatrick, D.G., Veronen, L.J., Saunders, B.E., Best, C.L., Amick-McMullan, A., and Paduhovich, J. (1987). The psychological impact of crime: A study of randomly surveyed crime victims. Final report on grant No. 84-IJ-CX-0039 submitted to the National Institute of Justice.

Koss, M.P. (1985). The hidden rape victim: Personality, attitudinal, and situational characteristics. *Psychology of Women Quarterly, 9,* 193-212.

———. (1987, October). The women's mental health agenda: Violence against women. Paper presented at a conference of the National Institute of Mental Health and the National Coalition for Women Mental Health entitled, "The Women's Mental Health Agenda." Washington, D.C.

Koss, M.P., Dinero, T.C., Seibel, C., and Cox, S. (in press). Stranger and acquaintance rape: Are there differences in the victim's experience? *Psychology of Women Quarterly.*

Krupnick, J. (1980). Brief psychotherapy with victims of violent crime. *Victimology: An International Journal, 5,* 347-354.

Lamphear, V.S. (1985). The impact of maltreatment on children's psychosocial adjustment: A review of the research. *Child Abuse and Neglect, 9,* 251-163.

Lazarus, R.S., and Folkman, S. (1984). *Stress, appraisal, and coping.* NY: Springer Publishing Company.

Lerner, M.J. (1980). *The belief in a just world.* NY: Plenum Press.

Livingston, J.A. (1982). Responses to sexual harassment on the job: Legal, organizational, and individual actions. *Journal of Social Issues, 38,* 5-22.

Loy, P.H., and Stewart, L.P. (1984). The extent and effects of the sexual harassment of working women. *Sociological Focus, 17,* 31-43.

Perloff, L.S. (1983). Perceptions of vulnerability to victimization. *Journal of Social Issues, 39,* 41-61.

Reiff, R. (1979). *The invisible victim: The criminal justice system's forgotten responsibility.* NY: Basic Books.

Resick, P.A. (1987, September). *The impact of rape on psychological functioning. Paper presented at the conference, "State of the art in sexual assault."* Charleston, SC.

Reiker, P.P., and Carmen, E.H. (1986). The victim-to-patient process: The disconfirmation and transformation of abuse. American Journal of Orthopsychiatry, 56, 360-370.

Ryan, W. (1971). Blaming the victim. NY: Basic Books.

Safran, C. (1976). What men do to women on the job: A shocking look at sexual harassment. Redbook, 149, 217-224.

Scheppele, K.L., and Bart, P.B. (1983). Through women's eyes: Defining danger in the wake of sexual assault. Journal of Social Issues, 39, 63-80.

Schoener, G., Milgrom, J., Gonsiorek, J. (1983, mimeo). Responding therapeutically to clients who have been sexually involved with their psychotherapists. Walk-In Counseling Center, Minneapolis, MN.

Silver, R.L., and Wortman, C.B. (1980). Coping with undesirable life events, In J. Graber and M.E.P. Seligman (Eds.) Human helplessness. NY: Academic Press.

Silver, R.L., Boon, C., and Stones, M.H. (1983). Searching for meaning in misfortune: Making sense of incest. Journal of Social Issues, 39, 81-102.

Silverman, D. (1976-77). Sexual harassment: Working women's dilemma. Quest: A Feminist Quarterly, 3, 15-24.

Summitt, R. (1983). The child sexual abuse accommodation syndrome. Child Abuse and Neglect, 7, 177-193.

Taylor, S.E. (1983). Adjustment to threatening events: A theory of cognitive adaptation. American Psychologist, 38, 1161-1173.

Taylor, S.E., Wood, J.V., and Lichtman, R.R. (1983). It could be worse: Selective evaluation as a response to victimization. Journal of Social Issues, 39, 19-40.

U.S. Merit systems Protection Board (1981). Sexual harassment in the federal workplace: Is it a problem? Washington, D.C.: U.S. Government Printing Office.

Working Women's Institute (1979). The impact of sexual harassment on the job: A profile of the experiences of 92 women. New York: Working women's Institute Research Series, Report No. 2.

5

The Victimizations of Women

Kathryn Quina

In the comic strip *Beetle Bailey*, common forms of sexual harassment are carried out by harmless characters whom we are supposed to love, or at least feel a kind of charitable forgiveness toward. General Halftrack is the archetypic older gentleman whose dowdy wife starves him for affection. His secretary Miss Buxley—who can't type—drives him wild with her sexy figure and short skirts. "Killer" (short for "lady-killer," a curiously violent name) is always whistling at "chicks" (who love it), accompanied by Beetle, who is equally aggressive but not as successful. Zero just stares at women's bodies.

Played out in the real world, these scenarios are not funny. The similarity of a university department to a comic strip seems especially incongruous, yet many of us have had to cope with Generals, Killers, Beetles, and Zeros in our professional as well as personal lives. In my first five years as an academic, I had an older professor literally chase me around a desk, similar-aged colleagues determined to bed me, and a dean who simply could not stop staring at my chest (and I'm not Miss Buxley!). Sadly, I am not the only one to relate these experiences. In most of the instances described above, I learned about other victims of the same offenders; in my research on sexual harassment and rape, I have met many more victims of other offenders.

The striking thing about sexual harassment is that it is almost never harmless. In this paper, I will argue that sexual harassment is a sexual assault which shares important commonalities with rape, an offense few of us today believe is harmless. While harassment is less physically intrusive and usually less violent or life-threatening, it is not substantially different structurally or socially from rape. In this view, the burgeoning literature on the issues of rape victimization allows important insight and understanding of the sexual harassment situation and survivor reactions.

The conceptual framework for this position is that rape and harassments are both sexual assaults which lie on a continuum of sexual exploitation, varying primarily in degree of physical intrusion and potential physical injury to the victim.[1] On the least physically violent pole, this continuum begins with verbal assaults, including sexually offensive jokes or degrading comments. At the most violent pole are rape-murder and femicide. On this scale, sexual harassment and rape are relatively close together. In fact, many assaults now called harassment—those involving sexual contact—are legally the equivalent of rape.

Six major commonalities underlying this continuum are discussed here, illuminated with stories from students and colleagues and from my own life to provide a glimpse of the reality of these sexual assaults.[2] These areas of commonality are: (1) power dynamics; (2) gender roles and relationships; (3) offender characteristics; (4) cultural stereotyping; (5) emotional reactions of survivors; and (6) paths to resolution.

Power Dynamics

Researchers have now clearly established that rape is not sexually motivated, but is a violent way to achieve a sense of power (Groth, 1979). Case studies support a similar psychological mechanism among sexual harassers. The rapist is likely to use his physical strength advantage over his victim, or to wield a gun or knife. The sexual harasser uses his age or social position, or wields economic power and authority as his weapons (Alliance Against Sexual Coercion, 1981; Fitzgerald, Gold, Ormerod, and Weitzman, 1987; Hall and Sandler, 1982). Both clearly rely on the fear and vulnerability of their victims.

Ann was a new assistant professor, the only woman in a large department. Only one colleague, Ed, had welcomed her arrival. Late one night, Ed called her to "discuss a problem." He began talking about her future tenure decision and her need to be more "friendly." He also suggested they have dinner to discuss their relationship, since he knew it would "help her get ahead." At the same time, he warned her not to associate with students (the only other women) or any of the women's groups on campus, because such associations would "look bad" in the eyes of her colleagues. Already isolated, she now avoided him as well as the women.

Gender Roles and Relationships

By far, the sexual offender is most likely to be a male: an estimated 99 percent of rapists (Groth, 1979) and 75-90 percent of sexual harassers (Reilly, Lott, and Gallogly, 1986) are men. The victim is most likely to be female and young (Finkelhor, 1979, Reilly et al., 1986). Cultural gender roles are also important to rape and harassment. By their own admission, rapists believe in, and attempt to act out, extreme versions of the cultural stereotype of masculinity as dominance over women (Beneke, 1982). There is evidence that sexual harassers hold the same stereotypes and desire the same macho image (Dziech and Warner, 1984). Furthermore, both kinds of offender hold extreme stereotypes of women, including the mythical images described later in this paper of women as masochistic and secretly desiring their "attentions." Finally, cultural demands on women to be "feminine"—that is, to be passive, submissive, helping, and nurturant— probably increase the likelihood of being victims of rape or harassment (Bart, 1986).

For several months, Beth remained silent about her major professor's sexual comments and the way he touched her whenever they were alone. She tried to be nice, partly to avoid his wrath and partly because she didn't know what else to do. Meanwhile, other graduate students were beginning to tease her about him. One day, as she described it, she "freaked out." She yelled at him to get out of her office and quit bothering her. Not only did his abuse stop, but the other students, who overheard the interaction, began to treat her with greater respect. Until she spoke up, they had assumed she was "using her femininity."

Characteristics of the Abuser

Sexual abusers, from harassers to rapists, from child molesters to murderers, are "habitual" offenders, many assaulting hundreds of women, children, and men (Rosenfeld, 1985; Freeman-Longo and Wall, 1986). Furthermore, these offenders carry out their repeated assaults in a highly stereotypical fashion, or modus operandi. Even those who claim to be in love with their victims are likely to have a characteristic pattern of behaviors leading up to, during, and following the assault (Holroyd and Brodsky, 1977).

Cindy, a student tutor, was assaulted by a client, who accused her of "exuding sexuality all over the place." She remained silent, embarrassed by the experience and frightened by the powerful message she felt she must be projecting. A month later, a coworker filed a complaint of sexual assault against the same man, and Cindy spoke up. In the ensuing legal proceedings, another student victim came forward, and records revealed that several previously reliable tutors had resigned after working with this client.

This has important implications for any victim: someone else probably has a similar story to tell. Unfortunately, we have a tendency to view each assault as an isolated incident, attributing the cause to the victim's character or behavior (Cann, Calhoun, Selby, and King, 1981), and fail to look for a pattern. The legal implications are also important: it may be possible to identify others who have shared the experience and to pursue a group grievance.

Cultural Images and Mythologies

Brownmiller (1975) provided an excellent review of the cultural mythologies surrounding rape, and the images of rape victims, extending back to Biblical writings. Thanks to extensive educational efforts and willingness of survivors to speak up, these attitudes have become less prevalent with respect to rape (Kanarian and Quina-Holland, 1981). However, stereotypes and misinformation continue to be applied to sexual harassment. These mythologies consistently blame the victim for sexual abuse, and on a larger scale, act to keep women "in their place" (MacKinnon, 1979). The most common attributions about sexual harassment fall into three categories:

(1) *Sexual assault is a form of seduction.* In history (*e.g.*, Homer's sirens) and in our contemporary culture (*e.g.*, Cindy's case), sex is imbued with images of women as temptresses and men as helpless slaves to powerful sexual drives. MacDonald (1971) wrote a handbook for police officers describing 27 ways in which women "precipitated" rape. While his data were seriously flawed (Hursch, 1977), similar warnings are now being given with respect to sexual harassment. Meyer (1981) suggested that women in the workplace must be careful about the way they dress and talk, because it could cause their coworkers to harass them. Fitzgerald *et al.* (1987) found that professors who dated students were more likely (than non-dating professors of the same students) to perceive that women students had approached them. These ideas are summed up by the classic first response to all victims of sexual assault: What were YOU doing, and what were YOU wearing?

(2) *Women secretly need/want to be forced into sex.* Not long ago, masochism was considered an essential element of women's personality (Deutsch, 1944). Young men learn from an early age that women like to be forced into sex (Malamuth and Briere, 1986), and that they "say no but mean yes."[3] It is not surprising, then, that harassment usually continues or escalates when the victim has given no positive response, or a negative response (Alliance Against Sexual Coercion, 1981). Harassers offer such excuses as "I know her better than she knows herself," while onlookers— like Beth's fellow graduate students—may suspect the victim really enjoys the attention.

(3) *Women do not tell the truth.* The historical distrust of women's

words influenced legal statutes and practices concerning sexual assault until the 1970s, and still affects attitudes towards survivors. For example, charges of rape had to be corroborated by a witness in some states, and the judge's instructions to the jury included a warning that rape is easy to accuse, and hard to prove (Brownmiller, 1975). Such suspicion clouds survivors of sexual harassment as well. The first concern is often whether she or he had any reason to harm the alleged offender. At a conference I attended last year, a university counsel (a woman!) recommended that *any* time a sexual harassment case ended in acquittal, the university should consider bringing charges of perjury (for false accusation) against the alleged victim.

Survivor Reactions

Individual responses to rape and sexual harassment, of course, vary widely as a function of the severity of the assault, the victim's personal style, and the availability of social support afterward. However, survivors of all the sexual assaults on our continuum have described long-term emotional aftereffects: grief, anger, fear, lowered self-esteem, helplessness, guilt and shame, body image distortion, sexual dysfunction, and problems in other relationships. Underlying these survivor reactions are three common features of the victimization experience.

(1) *Sexual assault is a severe trauma.* Even when harassment is not physically violent, survivors report strong fear reactions (Alliance Against Sexual Coercion, 1981), loss of control, and disruption of their lives— experiences shared with survivors of more physically dangerous assaults such as rape, accidents, or natural disasters.

"Looking back, I don't know what I was afraid of," mused Deborah some years after her experience as a student worker fondled by a professor, "but I was terrified each time this man came toward me." At the end of the semester, Deborah wrote a short note about the professor's advances, gave it to her dorm advisor, and left school. She gave up her ambitions to become a scientist, and didn't return to college for many years.

(2) *Sexual assault is a violation.* Physical contact is not necessary to create a feeling of being violated, as noted in the reactions of intense disgust by women who receive obscene phone calls or street harassment. Since in sexual harassment the victim frequently knows the offender, a violation of trust is almost always experienced. Most survivors also report feeling degraded by the experience, stripped of their dignity by the abuser.

When a nationally known scholar asked her to participate in his research project, Ellen was thrilled. Flattered by his attentiveness and excited by promises of a letter of recommendation to top graduate schools, she worked long hours, collecting data and writing up a paper herself. Shortly before it was to be sent for publication, Dr. X delivered his ultimatum: no sex, no authorship. Ellen submitted, although disgusted by him physically, because she was so invested in the project. After they had sex, he laughed at her tears. The next day, he told her he did not consider her contributions very thoughtful or important, certainly not sufficient to deserve authorship; and that he had only allowed her to work on these projects because he knew how much she wanted to be near him. Ellen lost a year of work and a publication. More importantly, she lost her confidence. Dr. X's comments were emotionally devastating, and ultimately more degrading than the sexual act.

(3) *Sexual assault causes secondary social losses.* Too often, survivors find no social comfort and support after rape or harassment. Those who remain silent, like Ann, often become increasingly isolated and begin to view themselves as deviant. To those who tell, family and friends often offer rejection, blame, or disbelief, rather than the support and comforting they need. Employees who file charges of sexual harassment face a range of harmful social responses, including being demoted or fired (Farley, 1978). These secondary betrayals increase the severity of long-term emotional reactions, and interfere with healthy resolution.

At first, Faye didn't tell her mother about the abuse she was experiencing at work, or about the charges she had filed against the department chair. Unfortunately, a local newspaper picked up the story, and her mother learned about the case when a friend who lived near the university called her. Faye's mother, embarrassed by the publicity, accused Faye of "bringing shame upon the family," and said "a lady would never have gotten herself into a mess like this!" Soon after, Faye dropped the case, too emotionally exhausted to continue.

Paths to Resolution

Individual resolution needs are as varied as the emotional responses to sexual assault. Many emotional responses, such as stress behaviors and fear, reduce with time and distance from the trauma. Others, notably guilt, depression, helplessness, and relationship problems, may continue or grow worse with time, and may need more direct intervention. However, some paths to resolution have been found to help survivors of any sexual assault. For those wishing further information, specific counseling approaches and guidance are offered in a forthcoming book by Quina and Carlson.

(1) *Cast the experience as a sexual assault, and recognize its effects.* Survivors frequently use terminology that does not include the word "rape" (Russell, 1984), and until recently we didn't even have a term for

"harassment." Thus many have difficulty recognizing their experience as victimization. It is helpful to use the words that fit the experience, validating the depth of the survivor's feelings, and allowing her to feel her experience was serious. In some cases, the terminology of sexual assault can help a person recognize the relationship among victimizations, as in Ellen's case.

After her professor's sudden change of behavior, Ellen found herself mistrusting everyone. Her relationships with men, including other professors, became more sexual, although she didn't want to have sex with anyone. Finally, through counseling, she was able to describe for the first time a sexual assault by a favorite uncle during her childhood. As she told of growing up with her uncle's praise and the devastating reversal of feelings she experienced after he assaulted her, she began to see both incidents clearly as sexual assaults rather than seductions. She recognized that she had begun to respond to all men with a sense of resigned dread, anticipating a sexual assault. In fact, she interpreted any compliment from a man as a signal he wanted to have sex with her, since that was where kindness had led in the past.

(2) *Find others with similar experiences and share stories.* It is essential to know that we are not alone. In therapy groups or just in self-disclosing conversations, or even in reading the stories of others, the sexual assault survivor can discover she is rational, her reactions are normal, and that others have overcome this trauma. Furthermore, as stories are compared, the cultural and social pattern emerges, and victim blame becomes more difficult to maintain.

Eventually, Ann went to a campus professional women's function, sitting quietly in the back of the room. A woman faculty member from another department came over to talk, and befriended her. In their discussion, Ann's new friend disclosed that one of Ann's colleagues—the same man who had approached Ann—had acted very strangely toward her. She described a conversation much like Ann's. Suddenly, Ann felt relieved of all her self-doubts about her situation. She also realized that sexual harassment was a serious problem on campus. She became active in the organization, and helped organize a campus "speak-out" on harassment.

(3) *Recognize the personal losses of sexual assault, and allow a grieving process.* In addition to betrayals and life changes such as being fired or rejected by friends, the experience of sexual assault constitutes a major personal loss. Recovery from sexual assault often follows the analytic grief process, described by Rando (1984). The mourning process takes time, perhaps a year or more, and involves stages of acute stress, denial, depression, and anger prior to achieving peace with the reality of the loss. Survivors need to appreciate the depth of their feelings of loss, and to allow

themselves to mourn, in order to achieve that peace.

Faye spent months being "tough" about her lawsuit—she described it as having to block out all emotions in order to survive (denial). When her mother called and accused her of shaming the family, her well-crafted armor came crashing down. She found herself unable to get up and get dressed in the morning, and had to seek therapy. Her therapist wisely recognized the signs of mourning and the reasons for Faye's grief, and eased her fears about her normalcy. When Faye did not feel strong enough to pursue the lawsuit, her therapist helped her mourn that loss as well, appreciating that she had done all she could, and helping her feel like a survivor rather than a victim.

(4) *Join or form a feminist network and support group, to prevent future traumas for others as well as oneself.* In addition to rich friendships and the feelings of mutual caring in such a group, self-esteem can be raised by helping others, and a good strong feminist support group can provide real empowerment. Some campuses have formed casual support groups for women in general, where sexual harassment might be discussed (*e.g.*, first year graduate student women, women in science); some counseling and women's centers provide facilitators for sexual assault survivors' groups. Any format is possible.

I finally left my first job, where I was the only woman, and moved to a department with three faculty women. We started meeting for lunch regularly, just to touch base about ongoing events and to do problem solving when necessary. At least once a semester we went to dinner with the women secretaries, and had an evening of fun, support, empathy, and genuine mutual admiration. Now the number of women faculty in our department has grown to six, our dinners have expanded to include women from related departments, and our empowerment—as well as our deep friendships—are extraordinary. Recently a male colleague told us he envied our relationship, because it allowed us to disclose and discuss our *problems* as well as our successes. We helped him form his own support group of gentle men!

Notes

1. This framework is laid out in the student/staff handbook on sexual harassment and assault distributed at the University of Rhode Island, coauthored by Quina, Carlson, and Temple (1982/84), and fully described in the forthcoming guide for counseling sexual assault survivors by Quina and Carlson (forthcoming by Praeger). Other support for this

view is found in Chapman and Gates (1978) and in Stanko (1985).

2. All stories in this paper are based on true situations. The names are fictitious, and details of the stories have been altered slightly, to protect the identities of the victims and perpetrators. I am grateful to these women for sharing their deep personal pain with me. I have chosen to use the term "victim" to refer to the dynamic, and survivor to refer to the individual after the assault.

3. Several male friends have described the early inculcation of these images of women—and of what "real men" do to women—especially through peer pressure during adolescence. I appreciate their honesty, and their efforts to overcome their own sexism.

References

Alliance Against Sexual Coercion. (1981). *Fighting sexual harassment: An advocacy handbook.* Boston, MA: Alyson.

Bart, P. (1985). *Stopping rape: Successful survival strategies.* Elmsford, NY: Pergamon.

Beneke, T. (1982). *Men on rape.* NY: St. Martin's Press.

Brownmiller, S. (1975). *Against our will: Men, women, and rape.* NY: Simon and Schuster.

Cann, A., Calhoun, L.G., Selby, J.W., and King, H.E. (Eds.) (1981). Rape [Whole Issue]. *Journal of Social Issues, 37* (4).

Chapman, J.R., and Gates, M. (Eds.) (1978). *The victimization of women.* Beverly Hills, CA: Sage.

Deutsch, H. (1944). *The psychology of women, Volume I.* NY: Grune and Stratton.

Dziech, B.W., and Weiner, L. (1984). *The lecherous professor: Sexual harassment on campus.* Boston: Beacon Press.

Farley, L. (1978). *Sexual shakedown: The sexual harassment of women on the job.* New York: McGraw-Hill.

Finkelhor, D. (1979). *Sexually victimized children.* NY: The Free Press.

Fitzgerald, L., Gold, Y., Ormerod, M., and Weitzman, L.M. (1987, May). *The lecherous professor: A study in power relations.* Paper presented at the Midwestern Society for Feminist Studies, Akron, OH.

Freeman-Longo, R.E., and Wall, R.V. (1986, March). Changing a lifetime of sexual crime. *Psychology Today*, 58-64.

Groth, A.N. (1979). *Men who rape: The psychology of the offender.* NY: Plenum.

Hall, R.M., and Sandler, B.R. (1982). *The classroom climate: A chilly one for women?* Washington, D.C.: Project on the Status and Education of Women.

Holroyd, J.C., and Brodsky, A.M. (1977). Psychologists' attitudes and practices regarding erotic and nonerotic contact with patients. *American Psychologist, 32*, 843-849.

Hursch, C.J. (1977). *The trouble with rape.* Chicago, IL: Nelson-Hall.

Kanarian, M., and Quina-Holland, K. (1981, April). *Attributions about rape.* Paper presented at Eastern Psychological Association, New York City, NY.

MacDonald, J.M. (1971). *Rape: Offenders and their victims.* Springfield, IL: C.C. Thomas.

Mackinnon, C.A. (1979). *Sexual harassment of working women.* New Haven, CT: Yale University Press.

Malamuth, N.M., and Briere, J. (1986). Sexual violence in the media: Indirect effects on aggression against women. *Journal of Social Issues, 42* (3), 75-92.

Meyer, M.C. (1981). *Sexual harassment at work.* Princeton, NJ: Petrocelli.

Quina, K., Carlson, N., and Temple, H. (1982/84). *Sexual harassment and assault: Myths and reality.* Kingston, RI: University of Rhode Island [Contact Women's Studies Program, URI, Kingston, RI 02881].

Rando, T. (1984). *Loss and grief.* Lexington, MA: Lexington Books.

Reilly, M.E., Lott, B., and Gallogly, S.M. (1986). Sexual harassment of university students. *Sex Roles, 15*, 333-358.

Rosenfeld, A.H. (1985, April). Discovering and dealing with deviant sex [Report on work of Abel, Becker, and Mittleman]. *Psychology Today*, 8-10.

Russell, D.E. (1984). *Sexual exploitation.* Beverly Hills, CA: Sage.

Stanko, E.A. (1985). *Intimate intrusions: Women's experience of male violence.* Boston: Routledge and Kegan Paul.

6

Coping with Sexual Harassment

Vita C. Rabinowitz

Wherever it occurs, from the street to the workplace, the experience of sexual harassment defines and limits women in sexual and gender-specific terms. When sexual harassment occurs in the academy, the repository of our best traditions and highest intellectual and moral aspirations, it is experienced by women as a particularly devastating betrayal of trust. Sexual harassment gives the lie to the belief that women compete on the same terms as men for the training and credentials required for professional careers.

This chapter addresses the questions of how female student victims of sexual harassment by male professors in the academy come to label, accept, and cope with their experiences. It begins by considering how students cognitively appraise harassment by faculty and why there is such deep-seated resistance to acknowledging the fact of their victimization. Next, it reviews the literature on the aftereffects of experiencing sexual harassment by a faculty member. Many women display a constellation of cognitive, behavioral, emotional, and physical symptoms following harassment that may persist long after the harassment ends and even change the course of their lives. Finally, it explores the implications of this analysis for future research in sexual harassment and for those advocates, counselors and educators who seek to help victims of harassment become survivors.

COGNITIVE APPRAISAL OF HARASSMENT

Most surveys of sexual harassment on college campuses define harassment in ways that include the following behaviors (See Fitzgerald in this volume):

— gender harassment
— seductive behavior—inappropriate and offensive but sanction-free sexual advances,
— sexual bribery—solicitation of sexual activity or other sex-linked behavior by promise of rewards,
— sexual coercion—coercion of sexual activity by threat of punishment, and
— sexual assault—gross sexual imposition or assault.

It is a reliable finding in the literature on sexual harassment on college campuses that about 30 percent of undergraduate women experience harassment by at least one of their professors during their four years in college (Dziech and Weiner, 1984; Adams, Kottke, and Padgitt, 1983). Yet, only about 5 percent report the harassment or file a grievance (See Fitzgerald in this volume), and on average only between 2 and 7 percent of the undergraduates report having directly confronted their harassers (UCLA Survey, 1985; Koss, in this volume). Many have speculated about why so few women seem to fight their harassment. To understand this, we need to understand the victimization process generally, and how it operates within the particular context of the university.

The Power of the Professorate

Research demonstrates that there is a high level of ambiguity among victims and observers about what causes and constitutes sexual harassment (Fitzgerald, 1986; Jensen and Gutek, 1982; Somers, 1982). Perhaps nowhere is this ambiguity greater than in the academy, and it places female students at a distinct disadvantage.

Unlike employers in the workplace, professors usually do not have the power to hire and fire students, determine the size of their paychecks, or control their prospects for promotion. Their power as classroom instructors, research directors, and academic and career advisors is relatively indirect, and is often more subtly exercised than the power of employers. For this reason, it is easy for students and professors alike to underestimate the power a professor possesses in his interactions with his students. In fact, professors wield a great deal of power over students who depend on them for grades, letters of recommendation, academic and career counseling, and research and clinical opportunities. This is especially true of particular subgroups of students whose power and control in their relationships with their professors are constrained. These subgroups might include the following:

— graduate students, whose future careers are often determined by their association with a particular faculty member,

— students in small colleges or small departments, where the number of faculty available to students is quite small

— women of color, especially those with "solo" or "token" status (DeFour, in this volume)

— students in nontraditional fields for women, like engineering, where women are vastly outnumbered by men (Dziech and Weiner, 1984)

— students who are economically disadvantaged, and work at school for pay.

Further contributing to the power difference between male professors and female students is the issue of the students' age. For the most part, female college students are younger and less experienced than their professors. They are at that developmental stage in which it is common to question values and standards of behavior and open themselves to new viewpoints and experiences. Professors are among the most available, attractive and salient role models for undergraduates. Students often look up to their professors with great admiration, and attribute to them such appealing characteristics as brilliance, sophistication, wisdom, and maturity.

It is precisely this interaction of power relations, age difference, and gender stratification that makes the intruism of sexual interest by male faculty members so problematic in the academy. Dziech and Weiner (1984) have written extensively about the vulnerability in the student status that makes sexual harassment by faculty a most intimate betrayal of trust. They state that sexual harassment by faculty injects a note of "incestuous sexuality" into the faculty-student relationship that shocks the average student. Indeed, research suggests that most students initially react with disbelief and doubt about even the most blatant sexual advances by faculty. And students often continue to believe that they have misinterpreted their instructor's behavior long after the facts warrant an appraisal of harassment (See Zalk in this volume).

Contributing to this ambiguity is the type of harassment that is so common to university settings. To be sure, physical assault, sexual coercion, and sexual bribery exist in the academy. In the UCLA Survey (1985), twenty nine percent of those students who reported being harassed described the harassment as including unwanted touching, sexually-related attempted assault or physical assault. Ordinarily, however, professors exert more subtle pressure on students than many other authority figures apply to those over whom they have the power, commensurate with their more diffuse power and higher level of sophistication. For instance, their inducements are more gradual and less overtly linked to concrete rewards or immediate sexual obligation than employers'. For example, instructors may accumulate credit over time for potential sexual favors by extraordinary friendliness, extra help with assignments, lenient grading, and extended deadlines. Benson and Thomson (1982, 243) describe an interview with a male faculty member who characterized some of his colleagues as being "fundamentally dishonest" in their dealings with female students. He noted that they praised female students to render them more vulnerable to future sexual advances, and may have laid the groundwork for such overtures through patterns of selective attention and reward. Thus, through the considerable latitude inherent in the faculty role, a professor can avoid the potential danger of a blunt proposition while manipulating his authority over female students.

Despite the ambiguity inherent in most types of sexual harassment on campus, and the initial tendency of most students to give their professors the benefit of the doubt in labelling their behavior as harassment, students who are the targets of unwanted sexual interest will eventually come to acknowledge and manage this sexual pressure (UCLA Survey, 1985; Bensonson and Thomson, 1982). The preponderance of research on harassment is clear in indicating that most harassers are persistent, harassment rarely ends spontaneously, and often escalates in the absence of direct action. But even after students correctly perceive their professors' sexual intent, they rarely come to view themselves as being harassed or victimized (Dziech and Weiner, 1984).

Self-Blame Among Victims

There is ample evidence that women experience an enormous amount of guilt and self-blame surrounding harassment, just as they do over rape and incest (Dziech and Weiner, 1984; Koss, in this volume; The Alliance Against Sexual Coercion, 1981). In a society where women are held and hold themselves responsible for arousing men's sexual interest, it is easy to understand how female students can become conflicted about their own motives and behaviors. Students who have been harassed by professors frequently report worrying about what it was that they did to lead their professors on, or wondering what they might have done earlier to discourage him. Like other victims, students also report asking, "Why me?" or "What did I do to deserve this?" Theorists have come to understand these questions as reflecting the victims' search for meaning and control in their victimization, and as having some adaptive value (cf. Janoff-Bulman and Frieze, 1983; Wortman, 1983). But these questions also have the effect of putting the focus on the victims' behavior and "character-blaming" the victims instead of the perpetrator. Even if the victim could avoid second-guessing her behavior and motives, she knows that others would judge her harshly if the situation became known (Jensen and Gutek, 1982; Kenig and Ryan, 1986). In cases with sexual overtones, male and female observers typically wonder, "Did she encourage him?" or "Did she enjoy it?" (Dziech and Weiner, 1984).

Commenting on the notions that men are at the mercy of their sexual appetites, which women need to curb, Dziech (1985) observed:

> I think it's really damning that a handful of people have allowed us to believe that such behavior is normal of men. It's not a woman's job— it's certainly not an 18-year-old student's job—to control her 40-year-old professor's sexual outbursts. . . . (7)

There are other aspects of harassment by college professors that facilitate self-blame by students. Some students exonerate their professors and blame themselves because they have been flattered by their professors' interest in them. As noted previously, harassers in the academy frequently lay the groundwork for sexual advances by treating potential targets in a special way and convincing them that they occupy a unique place in the professors' thoughts and affections. All of us want to be attractive to others, and enjoy being well-treated. Women of college age may be especially vunerable to flattery by professors because they exhibit a lesser sense of self-control over their own fates and less self-confidence in their academic abilities than do men of similar age (Kenig and Ryan, 1986). It can be an exhilarating experience for a young woman to be the object of attention from someone who holds the prestigious position of professor, someone who might choose any one of a hundred students to favor, but has chosen *her*. It is easy for her to fall into the trap of blaming herself for her normal desire to be noticed and appreciated. Another self-blaming scenario among students, albeit a self-serving one, centers on the belief that the professor's passion is fueled by relatively noble sentiments, like spiritual kinship and romantic love, that she alone inspires. Not surprisingly, research suggests that self-blame is especially prevalent among women who have complied with their harassers in any way (The Alliance Against Sexual Coercion, 1981).

Rejection of Victim Status

As uncomfortable and distorted as it may seem to blame oneself for unwanted sexual attention, there is much evidence from the literature on victimization that blaming oneself and refusing to acknowledge that one is being harassed or victimized is preferable to claiming the status of the victim (cf. Janoff-Bulman and Frieze, 1983). Many women who sustain harm do not perceive themselves as victims. Koss (1985) reported that only 57 percent of college women, all of whom had experiences that met legal definitions of rape, regarded themselves as rape victims. Similarly, she also noted that in a national sample, 30 percent of the women who were raped by strangers and 62 percent of the women who were raped by acquaintances did not view their experiences as any type of crime. So common is this refusal to accept victim status among people who have suffered that Estep (reported in Koss, in press) proposes that people do not become victims simply by virtue of sustaining injury or loss. According to Estep, there are three steps to becoming a victim: a) sustaining damage; and b) perceiving the injury as unfair and oneself as victimized; and c) seeking redress. There is great resistance from moving from step a to step b because almost no one covets the lable of victim. The traditional view of victim, particularly in our society, is that of a loser.

To acknowledge victimization is to acknowledge the following losses:

— control over one's future,
— the belief in a "just world," where good things happen to good people,
— the belief in personal invulnerability,
— a belief in the world as safe and predictable,
— a positive image of the self

More than anything else, these shattered assumptions may be the vehicle through which negative life events like harassment wreak their damage.

STUDENT COPING STRATEGIES

Denial, Avoidance, and Deceit

Given this cognitive appraisal by student victims, we can now consider the coping behaviors commonly exhibited by students who are compelled to deal with unwanted sexual attention by faculty.

Initially, many victims attempt to deny that unwanted sexual advances took place. Surveys of harassment repeatedly cite such self-statements by students to the effect that the professor could not have been just kidding, or lonely, or interested in their social lives, or in being friends, or in trying to be nice, etc. (cf. Benson and Thomson, 1982; Dziech and Weiner, 1984; the Alliance Against Sexual Coercion, 1981). Those students who acknowledge the sexual intent early on typically deny the power relations that underly the situation and thus fail to regard those intentions as harassing. Researchers have found that student responses to recognizing this sexual pressure range from the belief that the professor is in love with them, to the notion that "That's how men are; you can't blame a guy for trying," (Dziech and Weiner, 1984; the Alliance Against Sexual Coercion, 1981). Underlying the first belief is the assumption that the relationship is one between equals, and the student is truly free to behave as she pleases. The second belief is predicated on the notions that sexually harassing behaviors by men are inevitable and normal, if not harmless.

When the coercive nature of the sexual advances cannot be denied, the relationship becomes a distinct source of distress for students. Students attempt to ignore or trivialize unwanted sexual advances for as long as possible (Benson and Thomson, 1982; Reilly, Lott, and Gallogly, 1986).

It is a very common coping mechanism for women to believe that the harassment will stop if they are unresponsive or unavailable, despite evidence to the contrary. Women receive a good deal of social support from men and other women for denying, ignoring, and trivializing harassment (The Alliance Against Sexual Coercion, 1981; Reilly, Lott, and Gallogly, 1986). Reilly, Lott, and Gallogly cite the report of one victim of sexual harassment in the academy that highlights this problem:

> Her boyfriend told her that "you should expect it, and you shouldn't run in shorts when other people aren't." Others told her: "You should just ignore it, don't respond, don't yell, don't throw things. (147)

Reporting that one has been harassed by a professor may be met with skepticism or ridicule, and attracts scrutiny of one's behavior or motives.

For the vast majority of undergraduate victims, coping with the problem of harassment means using indirect tactics to forestall escalation. Benson and Thomson (1982) report that most women invent other appointments or enlist friends to accompany them to instructors' offices to avoid being alone with their harassers. Many students in their survey cut class and even hid to prevent encounters. Two respondents in the Benson and Thomson study wrote: "I never went to his office hours," and "I no longer went to his section because of the uncomfortable situation" (245). Dressing down, and trying to appear less attractive, is another strategy frequently employed to avoid notice (Dziech and Weiner, 1984).

Even when undergraduate women are directly confronted with the bluntest propositions, their management tactics remain indirect. A majority of the students who responded to the Reilly, Lott, and Gallogly and Benson and Thomson surveys who experienced the most persistent, coercive harassment reported counteracting propositions by talking about their boyfriends or husbands, expressing reluctance to becoming sexually involved with faculty or married men, or claiming no time for social activities. Students seemingly resort to these tactics to try to keep their professors at bay at the same time that they avoid the dreaded direct confrontation. Yet the mention of a boyfriend or other social concerns as an excuse for a rebuff legitimizes the intrusion of sexual interest in the faculty-student relationship, reaffirms that women continue to be defined in relation to men, and undermines the perception of women as independent scholars and professionals.

Study after study confirms that students rarely express their true feelings in these situations (Kenig and Ryan, 1986; Dziech and Weiner, 1984; Benson and Thomson, 1982; Reilly, Lott, and Gallogly, 1986; Jenson and Gutek, 1982). The widespread incidence of denial, avoidance, and deceit leads to the inescapable conclusion that, on some level, most students are highly sensitive to the power imbalance between faculty and students. Students do not in fact feel free to refuse unwanted advances. There is evidence to suggest that fear of retaliation by the scorned professor is the paramount reason that students attempt to cope with harassment by indirect means (Dziech and Weiner, 1984; Benson and Thomson, 1982). More than one third of the harassment victims in Jenson and Gutek's study reported that they did not file a grievance against their professors because they "thought it would be held against [them] or that [they] would be blamed" (128).

Some victims do not report the harassment because they feel some sympathy for their harassers. Students frequently express great concern over whether the harasser might lose his job or his family if a complaint is filed against him (The Alliance Against Sexual Coercion, 1981; Dziech and Weiner, 1984). It is not uncommon for harassers to count upon—and play upon—this concern (Dzeich and Weiner, 1984).

Finally, there is some evidence that students fail to report cases of harassment because they are unaware that the university makes provisions for such complaints and feel powerless to act effectively (Reilly, Lott, and Gallogly, 1986).

What do the student victims eventually do? Research suggests that students who have had little prior involvement with a harasser most often try to withdraw from future interactions whenever possible (cf. Dziech and Weiner, 1984; Benson and Thomson, 1982). Missed educational opportunities are the most obvious price paid for this coping strategy. Students quit research teams, drop courses, switch majors, and drop out of college altogether in numbers that we will never know because of what many people perceive as harmless flirtations. Dziech and Weiner (1984) suggest that the extraordinary drop-out rates among women in non-traditional fields like engineering are largely due to the high rates of sexual and gender harassment encountered there.

Sexual Advances in Well-Established Relationships.

Some of the most severe consequences of harassment appear to be suffered by students who enjoy long-standing professional contact with a faculty member before his sexual interest in them becomes evident (Glaser and Thorpe, 1986; Benson and Thomson, 1982). Studies suggest that students in these situations come to question the reasons for their previous academic success. They become skeptical about the value of their professor's praise and encouragement. And they tend to become suspicious of male faculty in general, as these students report to Benson and Thomson:

> I became disillusioned with academia. [The experience] lessened by confidence on whether it was worth going through with it all.

> [With male faculty, I am] more cautious about being open and friendly. (246)

Sexual Intimacies Between Professors and Students

The consequences of harassment are apt to be particularly severe when students enter into sexual relationships with faculty members (The Alliance Against Sexual Coercion, 1981; Glaser and Thorpe, 1986; Reilly, Lott, and Gallogly, 1986). Becoming sexually involved with a professor increases the likelihood that the student will report feelings of being in love, being used or betrayed, and of being responsible for her professor's behavior (See Zalk in this volume).

Recent research by Glaser and Thorpe (1986) surveyed 464 female clinical psychologists about their graduate school experience of sexual intimacy with and sexual advances from psychology educators. Consistent with earlier research (cf. Pope, Levenson, and Schover, 1979), the results indicated that the sexual contact is quite prevalent overall, with 17 percent of respondents reporting sexual contact, and 22 percent of recent doctoral recipients reporting sexual intimacy. As Pope et al. found, the rate of sexual intimacy with professors was especially high (34 percent) among doctoral candidates who were divorcing or separating during training.

At the time of the sexual contact, 72 percent of the respondents reported receiving unwanted sexual advances from educators that did not lead to sexual contact. The majority of these women declined the advances directly (30 percent) or indirectly (60 percent), suggesting that graduate women may be more likely to reject advances directly than their undergraduate counterparts. But they paid a price for this directness: 45 percent of respondents who declined advances reported not only significant subsequent harm to the working relationship but also punitive damage from educators. These include lowered grades, withdrawal of support and opportunities, and sharply sarcastic criticism of work once praised. Many respondents volunteered that they had seriously considered leaving graduate studies in the face of these pressures.

These findings, along with the results of previous studies on the sexual harassment of students, led Glaser and Thorpe to issue this stern warning to psychologists:

> The profession needs to acknowledge and address the reality of a population of women of unknown numbers who after gaining keenly competitive admission to doctoral studies in psychology, take leave of that effort, not through lack of ability or diligence, but through disgust, dissuasion, and misuse. The numbers need not to be large for that to be an appalling and shameful situation. (50)

Sexual Harassment Syndrome

Missed educational opportunities, lost time and effort, and feelings of disillusionment and disappointment are high prices indeed to pay for one's victimization by harassment. But they are not the only costs. Tong (1984) has identified a "sexual harassment syndrome" that describes the emotional and physical symptoms suffered by victims of sexual harassment generally. Based on her analysis and the survey data on reactions of student victims in the academy (cf. UCLA Survey, 1985; Reilly, Lott, and Gallogly, 1986; Benson and Thomson, 1982; Dziech and Weiner, 1984; Jenson and Gutek, 1982), the following consequences of harassment may be experienced by student victims:

— general depression, as manifested by changes in eating and sleeping patterns, and vague complaints of aches and pains that prevent the student from attending class or completing work;
— undefined dissatisfaction with college, major, or particular course;
— sense of powerlessness, helplessness, and vulnerability;
— loss of academic self-confidence and decline in academic performance;
— feelings of isolation from other students;
— changes in attitudes or behaviors regarding sexual relationships;
— irritability with family and friends;
— fear and anxiety;

— inability to concentrate;
— alcohol and drug dependency.

Previous research has not yet systematically investigated the conditions under which victims will experience any of these consequences. There is some evidence to suggest that to the extent that the sexual harassment resembles the trauma of rape or incest, the student may exhibit the characteristics of the Post-Traumatic Stress Disorder as described in DSM-3R (cf. Koss, in this volume; Gagliano, 1987). These characteristics include intense terror, reexperiencing the event, hypervigilance, helplessness, increased arousal, eating disorders, avoidance of stimuli associated with the event and numbing of general responsiveness.

DIRECTIONS FOR FUTURE RESEARCH

Clearly, future research needs to address the questions of what factors increase the likelihood that sexual harassment will occur, will persist, and will cause emotional, academic, physical or other harm to students. We need information about the structural, the institutional, and departmental factors that encourage or sustain harassment. We also need further information about the faculty, student, and relationship characteristics that increase the chances that harassment will take place or will be especially harmful to victims. Based on this review of the sexual harassment literature, we can isolate certain characteristics that merit further investigation for their possible contribution to the experience of harassment:

Faculty Characteristics:

— Faculty member is tenured (cf. UCLA Survey, 1985; Dziech and Weiner, 1984).
— Faculty member has senior status in the department (Dziech and Weiner, 1984).

Student Characteristics:

— Woman is a graduate student (Glaser and Thorpe, 1986).
— Student, if undergraduate, is a graduate school aspirant (Benson and Thomson, 1982; Dziech and Weiner, 1984).
— Student has returned to school after a hiatus (Dzeich and Weiner, 1984).
— Student is divorced or separated (Glaser and Thorpe, 1986; Pope, Levenson, and Schover, 1979).
— Student is a member of a racial or ethnic minority (DeFour, in this volume).

— Student holds traditional, as opposed to progressive, sex role beliefs (Jenson and Gutek, 1982).
— Student is economically disadvantaged (Dziech and Weiner, 1984; The Alliance Against Sexual Coercion, 1981).
— Student is a "loner"—has no visible ties to other students, or faculty or family (Dziech and Weiner, 1984).
— Student is physically attractive (Dziech and Weiner, 1984).

Characteristics of the Faculty/Student Relationships:

— Faculty member and student are in the same field (Dziech and Weiner, 1984).
— Faculty member has more than the usual amount of power over student's evaluations, outcomes, or prospects (*i.e.*, is a mentor, dissertation advisor, honors sponsor, employer) (Glaser and Thorpe, 1986; The Alliance Against Sexual Coercion, 1981).
— Faculty member and student have had a long, well-established relationship prior to the onset of harassment (Benson and Thomson, 1982).
— Faculty member and student have had a sexual relationship (Glaser and Thorpe, 1986; The Alliance Against Sexual Coercion, 1981).

MOVING FROM VICTIM TO SURVIVOR: IMPLICATIONS FOR ADVOCATES AND COUNSELORS

The present chapter conceptualizes sexual harassment in the academy as coercive because it is supported by and can be enforced through the power of the professorate and is reinforced through its confounding with age and gender. The implications of this analysis for the therapeutic treatment of harassment are that victims have suffered from the abuse of power, feel powerless, and need to be empowered.

Specifically, victims need validation of their perception and feelings about their experiences. They need to know how common the experience of harassment is, and how common are the tendencies to deny, ignore, and trivialize those experiences. They need to understand harassment in terms of power relations instead of sexual relations, and to debunk the myths about how such behavior is normal among men. Depending upon the particulars of their situation, victims may need referals to psychologists, physicians, college officials, or lawyers. More commonly, however, they may need information about interventions that are inherently supportive and empowering for harassment victims. These include skill-training, participation in support groups, and the sharing of information about confronting harassers or filing formal complaints against them.

Several therapists and researchers have begun the process of elucidating the specific steps that counselors might take in treating victims of harassment (cf. Hamilton, in press; Koss, in this volume; Gagliano, 1987). The following prescriptions borrow from their work and the present analysis of sexual harassment.

Specific Advice for Counselors, Advocates, and Educators:

— Acknowledge her courage by citing how difficult it is to label, report, and discuss harassment.

— Encourage the ventilation of her feelings and perceptions and validate them. It is not the role of a counselor to determine whether harassment as legally defined has occurred. Female students have little to gain from making false charges of harassment against professors and rarely make them (cf. Fitzgerald, 1987).

— Provide information to students about the incidence of harassment to assure her that she is not alone. Communicate the research findings about the consequences of harassment—emotional, behavioral, and physical—to assure her that the harassment is not harmless to victims and that she is not overreacting.

— Counteract her tendencies to blame herself for the harassment by explaining its origins in power relations. Assure her that she is in no way responsible for her professor's sexual interest in her, regardless of her behavior or dress. Tendencies to self-blame are likely to be strongest in women who have delayed reporting the harassment or who have complied with the harassers in any way. Self-blame is also likely to be high in those who have "voluntarily" entered into sexual relationships that they now wish to end, but cannot because of pressure to continue. These women need to know that their past behavior may well have been constrained, and in any case that past activities do not control future choices.

— Aid the student in her search for meaning in the victimization. She will need to rebuild shattered assumptions. As Koss (in this volume) notes, the experience of sexual harassment can change people's lives. Cherished, life-long beliefs about authority figures, men, academia, and the professorate may be lost forever. The student's positive self-image and professional prospects may be blighted. She will need to acknowledge, assess, and "mourn" these losses before she can establish the new beliefs and support systems that will guide her future academic and professional career.

— Monitor the physical, emotional, academic, and interpersonal toll of harassment. The strain of coping with harassment will have some predictable effects on a woman's physical and emotional health. The student may need help in seeing seemingly unrelated problems in her life as the consequences of harassment. The counselor should monitor the use of maladaptive coping strategies like denial and avoidance. The counselor should be cognizant of the incident of illness and emotional distress so that he or she can help the client make the correct attributions about the sources of the problem so that the proper referrals will be made.

— Offer a safe forum for the expression of anger and resentment. Victims sometimes become very angry when they become fully aware of how their lives have been changed by this experience. Many resent how their behavior has been manipulated and constrained by the harasser. Some have experienced reprisals in the form of lowered grades, unfair criticism, and lost opportunities. Anger is an entirely normal and appropriate response to being harassed. Because it is so dangerous to express their anger to the harasser and so unrewarding to seek sympathy from friends and fellow students, it is critical that women have a safe place to ventilate their anger. Without such a place, women sometimes allow their anger to damage their other relationships (cf. The Alliance Against Sexual Coercion, 1981).

— Offer skills-training. Depending upon the particular problems presented by the harassment and the personality of the victim, the student may need training in one of the following areas: assertiveness, problem solving, decision making, self-efficacy, or stress management.

— Teach the student to validate herself. The socialization process turns women into skillful self-discounters. Gagliano (1987) has proposed a way to counteract this pattern through positive "self-talk"—silently repeating to oneself validating, supportive, positive messages. Another of her suggestions is the use of "stoppers." Stoppers are easy and effective behavioral techniques designed to cut off self-blaming, powerless, and other negative cognitions. Clients may receive significant validation and support from participating in self-help groups for victims of harassment or speaking to member of a sexual harassment panel.

The goal of the intervention should be to enlighten the client about her options and support her to make informed choices about her life, even if the counselor disagrees with those choices. This is the crux of empowerment.

References

Adams, J.W., J.L. Kottke, J.L. and Padgitt, J.S. (1983) Sexual harassment of university students. *Journal of College Student Personnel*, *24*, 484-490.

The Alliance Against Sexual Coercion (1981). *Fighting Sexual Harassment: An advocacy handbook*. Boston: Alyson Publications, Inc., and The Alliance Against Sexual Coercion.

Benson, D.J. and Thomson, G.E. (1982) Sexual harassment on a university campus: The confluence of authority relations, sexual interest, and the gender stratifications. *Social Problems*, *29*, 236-251.

DeFour, D.C. (this volume) Interface of racism and sexism. In M. Paludi (ed.) *Ivory Power: Victimization of Women in the Academy*. Albany: SUNY Press.

Dziech, B.W. (1985). Indiana University Women's Affairs Office develops sex education package. *Behavior Today Newsletter*. July 15, 1985, 5-7.

Dziech, B.W. and Weiner, L.L. (1984). *The Lecherous Professor: Sexual Harassment on Campus*. Boston: Beacon Press.

Fitzgerald, L.F. (1986). The lecherous professor: A study in power relations. Paper presented at a meeting of the American Psychological Association, New York. August, 1986.

———. (1987). Sexual harassment: A new look at an old issue. Symposium presented at a meeting of the American Psychological Association, New York. August, 1987.

Gagliano, C. (1987). Surviving sexual harassment: Strategies for victims and advocates. Paper presented at the Women in Higher Education Conference, Orlando, Florida. January 27, 1987.

Glaser, R.D. and Thorpe, J. (1986). Unethical intimacy: A survey of sexual contact and advances between Psychology educators and female graduate students. *American Psychologist*, *41*, 43-51.

Hamilton, J.A., Alagna, S.W., King, L.S., and Lloyd, C. (Forthcoming). The emotional consequences of gender-based abuse in the workplace: New counseling programs for sex discrimination. *Women and Therapy*.

Janoff-Bulman, R. and Frieze, I.H. (1983). A theoretical perspective for understanding victimization. *Journal of Social Issues*, *39*, 1-17.

Jensen, I.W. and Gutek, B.A. (1982). Attributions and assignment of responsibility in sexual harassment. *Journal of Social Issues*, *38*, 121-136.

Kenig, S. and Ryan, J. (1986). Sex differences in levels of tolerance and attribution of blame for sexual harassment on a university campus. *Sex Roles*, 15, 535-549.

Koss, M.P. (1985). The hidden rape victim: Personality, attitudinal, and situational characteristics. *Psychology of Women Quarterly*, 9, 193-212.

———— . (this volume) Changed lives: The psychological impact of sexual harassment. In M. Paludi (ed.), *Ivory Power:* Victimization of Women in the Academy. Albany: SUNY Press.

Pope, K.S., Levenson, H., and Schover, L. (1979). Sexual intimacy in psychological training: Results and implications of a national survey. *American Psychologist*, 34, 682-689.

The Sexual Harassment Survey Committee (1985). A survey of sexual harassment at UCLA. *Administrative Report:* February, 1985.

Somers, A. (1982). Sexual harassment in Academy: Legal issues and definitions. *Journal of Social Issues*, 38, 23-37.

Tong, R. (1984). *Women, Sex, and the Law.* Totowa, N.J.: Rowman and Allanheld.

Weber-Burdin, E. and Rossi, P.H. (1982). Defining sexual harassment on campus: A replication and extension. *Journal of Social Issues*, 38, 121-136.

Wortman, C.B. (1983). Coping with victimization: Conclusions and implications for future research. *Journal of Social Issues*, 39, 195-221.

III

Sexual Harassment

A Look at Harassers

Editor's Notes

In a classroom setting it is entirely appropriate that personal and professional lives be separated. However, undergraduates doing honor's research and graduate students become junior colleagues; a close personal relationship is to be encouraged.

Just because I personally haven't engaged in close personal or sexual relationships doesn't mean that I disapprove. Whatever the adults feel that they must do, as responsibly as they can, is just fine.

It has been my observation that students, and some faculty, have little understanding of the extreme pressure a male professor can feel as the object of sexual interest of attractive women.

(Responses From Male Faculty; Fitzgerald, Weitzman, Gold, and Ormerod, 1988)

In the last section, Drs. Koss, Quina, and Rabinowitz emphasized the role of the faculty in creating a campus atmosphere free of sexual harassment so as to empower women, not intimidate them. In this section, Louise Fitzgerald and Lauren Weitzman, in "Men who harass: Speculation and data," report that male faculty members typically do not label their behavior as sexual harassment despite the fact they report they frequently engage in initiating personal relationships with women students. Male faculty denied the inherent power differential between faculty and students, as well as the psychological power conferred by this differential (that is as salient as the power derived from evaluation).

These results support those obtained by Pryor (1987), who reported that the man who is likely to initiate severe sexually harassing behavior appears to be one who emphasizes male social and sexual dominance, and who demonstrates insensitivity to other people's perspectives. And, as Fuehrer and Schilling (1988) point out, because there is a lack of understanding between men and women about what a common set of behaviors mean and a difference in perspectives on the role of relationships in the academic environments, conflict is likely to result.

Kenig and Ryan (1986) also indicated that faculty men were less likely than faculty women to define sexual harassment to include jokes, teasing remarks of a sexual nature and unwanted suggestive looks or gestures. In addition, women faculty were more likely than men to disapprove of romantic relationships between faculty and students. Men were also significantly more likely than women to agree with the following statements: "An attractive woman has to expect sexual advances and learn how to handle them," "It is only natural for a man to make sexual advances to a woman he finds attractive," and "People who receive annoying sexual attention usually have provoked it." Finally, faculty men were more likely than women to believe individuals can handle unwanted sexual attention on their own without involving the college or university. Male faculty, thus, view sexual harassment as a personal, not an organizational issue.

These findings suggest that women are more likely than men to assign a central role to the college for preventing and dealing with all levels of sexual harassment. Since the research indicates that men attribute more responsibility to women victims of sexual harassment, men would also be likely to minimize the potential responsibility of college/university officials. Thus education is needed in men's perceptions of the misuse of power, their perceptions about women who have been harassed, and their attitudes toward sexual interactions.

Sue Rosenberg Zalk, in "The lecherous professor: Psychological profiles of professors who harass their women students," also argue that there is no such thing as women students' informed consent in a sexual relationship with male faculty members:

> The bottom line in the relationship between faculty member and student is POWER. The faculty member has it and the student does not. As intertwined as the faculty-student roles may be, and as much as one must exist for the other to exist, they are not equal collaborators. The student does not negotiate—indeed, has nothing to negotiate with.

Rosenberg Zalk also highlighted the need for educating male faculty about power in the classroom. Sandler (1988) has offered suggestions for meeting this goal, including (1) establishing a policy statement that makes it clear that differential treatment of professional women on campus will not be tolerated; (2) establishing a permanent committee to explore and report on professional climate issues; and (3) publishing an annual report on progress in regard to women on campus.

Cyril and Egelman (1988) provided additional suggestions for addressing sexual harassment on campus, including: (1) conducting information sessions for faculty, staff, and students on the policy toward sexual harassment on campus; (2) holding noontime brown bag seminars on the issue; (3) using peer educators among students; and (4) including materials on sexual harassment in courses on human sexuality.

K.C. Wagner has offered suggestions for interventions that can be implemented in order to challenge attitudes that perpetuate harassment. These techniques are presented in the Appendix, along with materials developed by Richard Barickman and Michele Paludi for training faculty in issues relating to sexual harassment. Issues these workshop materials address include (1) learning how informal and formal power or authority in the college/university setting is perceived by students and faculty; (2) learning the politics involved in such nonverbal gestures as touch, body position, personal space; and (3) learning the social meanings attributed to behaviors that legally constitute sexual harassment.

References

Cyril, J., and Egelman, C. (1988, April). *Educational strategies.* Workshop presented at the Cornell Conference on Sexual Harassment on Campus, New York, NY.

Fitzgerald, L.F., Weitzman, L., Gold, Y., and Ormerod, M. (1988). Academic harassment: Sex and denial in scholarly garb. *Psychology of Women Quarterly, 12,* 329-340.

Fuehrer, A., and Schilling, K. (1988). Sexual harassment of women graduate students: The impact of institutional factors. *The Community Psychologist, 21,* 13-14.

Kenig, S., and Ryan, J. (1986). Sex differences in levels of tolerance and attribution of blame for sexual harassment on a university campus. *Sex Roles, 15,* 535-549.

Pryor, J. (1987). Sexual harassment proclivities in men. *Sex Roles, 17,* 269-290.

Sandler, B. (1988, April). Sexual harassment: A new issue for institutions, or these are the times that try men's souls. Paper presented at the Cornell Conference on Sexual Harassment on Campus, New York, NY.

7

Men Who Harass: Speculation and Data

Louise F. Fitzgerald and *Lauren M. Weitzman*

Although the great majority of published studies of academic sexual harassment have concerned themselves with documenting the existence, extent and dimensions of the phenomenon, a few have attempted to address other questions: "Who is the harasser?" "Are some groups or types of professors more likely to harass than others?" "Are there any variables or characteristics that are reliable predictors of harassing behavior?" A related issue, and one that may have received more attention than it deserves based on data so far examined, is the extent to which women faculty harass male students. This chapter will review the available evidence bearing on these issues. We begin by examining what little is formally known about the "lecherous professor" and then move to a discussion of the workplace harasser.[1] Following this, we review recent efforts to develop measures that may indicate a propensity to harass, and conclude with a discussion of the data and issues concerning whether or not women can and do harass men, either in academia or the workplace.

Academic Harassers

In a provocatively titled chapter, "The Lecherous Professor: A Portrait of the Artist," Dziech and Weiner (1984) suggest that academic harassers can be classified into two very different types: the public and the private. The public harasser is described as engaging in flagrant sexist or seductive behavior towards students. Dziech and Weiner (1984) describe a man who is articulate, funny, glib and sarcastic; one who tells amusing but sexist or off-color jokes, and who engages in seductive, sometimes intrusive but rarely explicitly coercive behavior. The public harasser is informal, often young, and unusually available to students. According to these authors, "He spends enormous amounts of time with students—in his office, in the halls during breaks, in the student union or at the nearby bar when the day or week ends. His informality is a welcome contrast to the authoritarian style of most of his colleagues" (120). The picture that emerges here is that of the "radical young faculty" member, jeans-clad and student-oriented, using his position to enhance his ego. Despite his posturing and doubtless often offensive behaviors, the public harasser is thought less likely to be directly coercive than his more private counterpart.

The private harasser, on the other hand, is in many ways the direct opposite. Dziech and Weiner (1984) suggest that he conforms to the academic stereotype, often dressing formally and conservatively, a bearing that is reinforced through a generally restrained, even intimidating, demeanor. Rather than a seductive openness, it is his formal authority that gives him access to the student, an access that he can initiate by the simple directive, possibly scrawled on a term paper, "Please see me." Once in the privacy of his office, the student is unprepared for the change in his demeanor, a change that may eventually culminate in the classic confrontation, in which she is faced with outright sexual coercion with respect to her grade or some other academic outcome.

In addition to these two "types," Dziech and Weiner (1984) also suggest other roles that may be assumed by the harasser, such as the counselor/helper; the confidante; the intellectual seducer (who encourages or requires self-disclosure as part of class activities, which he then uses to gain personal information about the student); and the opportunist, who takes advantage of the physical setting or unusual or occasional circumstances to gain intimacy with his students. Finally, they speculate about demographic, characterological and life events that may stimulate or support harassing behavior by faculty members.

The picture drawn by these authors is a fascinating one, heuristic in nature and seemingly intuitively true to women's experiences. Rich with the contextual detail that is the strength of qualitative methodology, it is also subject to the disadvantages of such a "broad brush" approach, and leaves many questions unanswered. For example, how prevalent is the "lecherous professor?" Where can the distinction be drawn between showing positive interest in students and the more exploitive behaviors outlined by Dziech and Weiner (1984)?

Little is known concerning the prevalence of academic harassers, as opposed to academic harassment. Investigations of incidence rates, utilizing students as subjects, are increasingly common and usually report widespread incidence of harassment, the exact rates varying with the definition used in the study. Such, while extremely valuable, are unable to determine whether such behaviors are typical of few or many. For example, 500 women at a university may report having experienced off-color jokes, sexist comments, suggestive or pornographic teaching materials, and crudely sexual remarks—and all may be referring to the same professor, who teaches perhaps an introductory course meeting general requirements. At the other extreme, a far smaller number of women may note that they have been stared at or ogled, pressed for dates, or even coerced into sex—and each may be referring to a different man. Common sense tells us that gender harassment (Fitzgerald *et al.*, 1988; Franklin *et al.*, 1981) can involve few professors yet affect many women, while the more sexually oriented forms are more "labor intensive," as it were, implying as they do more one-on-one interaction; however, such reasoning gives no clue to the actual numbers of professors who engage in any such behaviors. And, although speculation and anecdote abound, little is formally known about faculty members who actually initiate romantic or sexual relationships with students.

It was to address these issues that our research group attempted an initial effort at such scrutiny (Fitzgerald, Weitzman, Gold, and Ormerod, 1988). Although far from definitive, our data does provide a preliminary profile of social and sexual interaction between faculty and students from the faculty member's perspective, as well as some data on the faculty members themselves. Our subjects were 235 male academics employed at a prestigious research-oriented university, who responded to a questionnaire sent via campus mail. All faculty ranks were represented, as well as a wide range of ages and academic disciplines. These professors responded to a 22-item questionnaire designed to tap four of the five types of sexually harassing behaviors identified by Till (1980) through content analysis of his national survey of college women (seductive behavior, sexual bribery, sexual coercion, and sexual assault). In an attempt to "defuse" the questionnaire, items measuring such behaviors were paired with others that asked about comparable student behavior. For example, the item "Has a student ever made an unsolicited attempt to stroke, caress, or touch you?" was followed by one that read "Has the reverse ever been true (*i.e.*, have you ever attempted to stroke, caress, or touch a student)?" These sensitive items were then embedded in a group of distractor questions that focused on friendship or mentoring behaviors. The final two items asked whether the faculty member believed he had ever sexually harassed a student, and whether he felt that he himself had been sexually harassed by a student. Table 1 presents the frequency and percentage of the sample that reported engaging in each behavior, in order of frequency of response. As would be expected, mentoring and friendship behaviors were the most frequently endorsed items; however, more than 37 percent indicated that they had attempted to initiate personal relationships with students (defined as dating, getting together for drinks, etc.). Nearly half of these (40.2 percent) noted that this behavior was directed exclusively at female students. Over 25 percent of the sample indicated that they had dated students (who had been defined as anyone enrolled at the university, whether or not they were enrolled in one of the respondent's classes), while a slightly larger percentage noted that they had engaged in sexual encounters or relationships with students. Eleven percent reported that they had attempted to stroke, caress or touch female students. However, only one subject reported that he believed he had ever sexually harassed a student. A small group of faculty reported that some students had themselves initiated sexual interactions by touching or caressing, or by implying sexual favors in return for some reward. Approximately 6 percent believed they had been sexually harassed by their women students.

TABLE 1

Frequencies and Percentages of Item Endorsement on the FEQ
in Order of Item Endorsement[1]

Item # *	Item	N	%	Male	Female	Both
2.	Have you ever made your personal professional library available to students for their personal use?	208	88.51	5.45	1.00	93.56
6.	Have you ever established what you considered to be a friendship with a student?	189	80.42	8.70	3.26	88.04
3.	Have you ever tried to identify particularly talented undergraduates and encourage them to apply to graduate study in your field?	185	78.72	6.56	1.09	92.35
1.	Would you say that you have ever been a "mentor" to a student (i.e., provided support, encouragement, and tutelage beyond the normal faculty/student interaction)?	185	78.72	10.93	3.83	85.25
4.	Has a student ever called on you for advice or support concerning their personal life (e.g., family, financial, or sexual matters)?	179	76.11	13.22	9.20	77.59
7.	Have you ever had a student to your home for dinner with your family?	169	71.92	13.42	1.83	84.76
9.	Has a student ever attempted to initiate a personal relationship with you?	128	54.47	6.45	41.94	51.61

Item #	Item	N	%	Male	Female	Both
8.	Have you ever attempted to initiate a personal relationship with a student (*e.g.*, asking for a date, suggesting you get together for a drink, etc.)?	88	37.44	6.90	40.23	52.87
11.	Have you ever had a sexual encounter or relationship with a student?	62	26.38	—	96.50	3.50
10.	Have you ever dated a student?	60	25.53	—	95.0	5.0
13.	Have you ever loaned money to a student?	50	21.27	68.09	10.64	21.28
18.	Has a student ever made an unsolicited attempt to stroke, caress, or touch you?	41	17.45	2.44	78.05	19.51
12.	Has a student ever asked you for a loan?	36	15.32	65.71	20.00	14.29
14.	Has a student ever implied or offered you sexual favors or cooperation in return for some reward (*e.g.*, a grade, assistantship, etc.)?	33	14.04	2.94	91.18	2.94
5.	Have you ever attempted to draw a student into a discussion of personal or sexual matters (*e.g.*, attempted to discuss or comment on their sex life)?	29	12.34	10.71	14.29	75.0
19.	Have you ever attempted to stroke, caress, or touch a student?	26	11.06	3.85	57.70	38.46
16.	Has a student ever hinted, implied, threatened or actually carried out some retaliation against you for personal reasons?	26	11.06	54.17	33.3	12.5
22.	Do you believe you have ever been sexually harassed by a student?	14	5.96	7.69	84.62	7.69

* Three items, each having to do with explicit attempts to sexually harass students, received item endorsement of < 1%.

[1]Total N = 235. Figures reported in columns labeled Male, Female and Both indicate percentage of faculty responding affirmatively to the item who noted that this behavior involved male students, female students or both.

In addition to these computations, we also examined the data for possible differences related to age, rank, and scholarly discipline. Only a few scattered differences were found, however, and these seemed most appropriately attributed to chance. We were particularly interested in that small subset of our sample who reported believing that they themselves had been harassed by their students. When their questionnaires were examined closely, however, it became apparent that they differed from their colleagues in only one respect: they were significantly more likely to report dating or becoming sexually involved with a student or students. Interestingly enough, it was those professors who reported engaging in these behaviors "more than once" who were most likely to indicate that they had been sexually harassed by their students.

Our data led us to two preliminary conclusions. First, 25 percent, or one in four, can be tentatively considered a lower bound estimate on the number of faculty members who become sexually involved with students. We suggest this because the actual number may be considerably higher; our data are based on the subset of faculty (30 percent) who were willing to report on their own sexual behavior. While possibly a minority of faculty, such professors in no way represent isolated instances of inappropriate behavior. Rather, they constitute a relatively large subset of academic faculty, at least at the university where our data were collected.

Secondly, such faculty are not distinguishable from their colleagues with respect to age, marital status, rank or academic discipline. Full professors in their 50s and 60s were just as likely to report dating their students as assistant professors in their 20s and 30s, and were just as likely to be social or biological scientists as engineers or scholars of the visual or performing arts. It should be noted, however, that the conclusions concerning age and rank may be flawed, as subjects were not required to state *when* the romantic or sexual encounters took place; it is possible that the older, more senior subjects were referring to incidents that occurred some time ago. Future research should be more specific in this respect.

Workplace Harassers

Unlike their counterparts in academia, men in the non-university workplace have yet to be examined directly with respect to their participation in sexually harassing behaviors. However, two large-scale and important studies have appeared that report data on such men from the perspective of their women victims. The first of these investigations, conducted by the National Merit Systems Protection Board (1981), constitutes the largest study of workplace harassment reported to date.

Questionnaires were sent to over 23,000 men and women civilian employees of the Executive Branch of the United States government, with a response rate of nearly 85 percent. Among other objectives, the authors note "We were interested in learning a number of things about the perpetrators of sexual harassment: whether they are found in disproportionate numbers within certain job classifications, racial categories, age brackets, educational levels and grade levels; whether harassers of men and women differ markedly; whether certain types of victims typically are bothered by certain types of harassers; and whether incidents tend to be one-time acts, or whether some harassers show a pattern of sexually bothering others" (57). These researchers found that women in the federal workforce typically are harassed by a male coworker who is married, older than the victim, and white, and who is likely to have harassed other women at work as well.

The women reported that most harassers acted alone (79 percent) but that a substantial minority of incidents involved two or more men acting in concert. As noted above, these men tended to be older than their victims. According to the respondents, 68 out of 100 women were younger than their harassers. Furthermore, at least two-thirds of the men were married at the time of the incident that the woman was describing; this point is important, as it underscores the fact that harassment is not likely to be based on authentic personal/romantic interest in the woman, but rather has a more pragmatic purpose. Contrary to classic views of harassment, in this sample the harasser usually had no supervisory authority over the victim (although 37 percent of the women did report that they were harassed by their immediate supervisor, or by a higher level supervisor). It should also be pointed out that in the most severe forms of harassment—actual or attempted rape, or sexual assault—supervisors were more likely to be the harasser than in less severe situations.

Finally, many of these women reported being harassed by someone who had also harassed others on the job. While a slight majority of victims indicated that they did not know whether the harasser had bothered others, 43 percent noted that this was indeed the case, and only 3 percent were sure that it was not. Again, there were differences with respect to the most severe forms of sexual harassment; in this case, victims of such severe and traumatic behavior were more likely to be bothered by repeat offenders than were victims of less severe harassment.

Although the majority of information was provided by female victims, the researchers did make an attempt to gather more direct data by asking their respondents whether they had been accused of "sexually bothering" someone within the last 24 months. Of the men who responded affirmatively, the vast majority (82 percent) felt that they had been unjustly accused, while only 8 percent thought the charge was fair, and 10 percent indicated that they were not sure whether or not the charge was justified. When these men were asked why they considered the accusation to be unfair, 48 percent said their motives had been misunderstood, 45 percent believed that the accuser wanted to cause trouble, and 29 percent reported that they had done nothing wrong. The authors note "since far fewer men report being accused of sexual harassment, whether fairly or not, than the number of women who report being harassed by men, it would appear that few women victims confront their harassers" (62).

The portrait of the harasser that emerges from these data is the somewhat unsavory one of an older, married man, possibly a supervisor, who makes a habit of harassing young women, and then maintaining that he meant no harm, did nothing wrong, and that his accuser was simply trying to cause trouble. Although this may be an accurate portrait, it should also be noted that these data are probably most representative of the more severe forms of harassment, as women respondents were told to respond in terms of the most recent incident or *the incident that had the greatest effect on them*. It is possible that "garden variety" harassers are much more diverse.

In addition to these data on the public sector, some information is also available concerning harassment in the private sector workplace, the most comprehensive of which is provided by Gutek (1985). Her study reports the results of a random sample of working men and women in Los Angeles County, interviewed by telephone in their homes. The final sample consisted of 827 women and 405 men, all of whom were 18 or older, employed outside the home, and who regularly came in contact with members of the opposite sex as coworkers, clients, customers, supervisors and so forth. Those who indicated that they had experienced any of several harassing behaviors were asked to respond to questions about the harasser, including how long they had known him, whether or not he was a supervisor, age, marital status and physical attractiveness, and whether or not he behaved in a similar fashion toward other women at work. Most of the victims reported that they had been acquainted with their harasser for some time (50 percent had known him for over six months). As in the public sector investigation described above, the majority of the harassers were coworkers (56 percent); however, a substantial minority were supervisors. These men were further described by their victims as older (approximately half were 40 or more), married (65 percent), and below average in physical attractiveness (58 percent).[2] The great majority of these men (71 percent) were reported to behave in a similarly harassing fashion toward other women in the workplace. It can easily be seen that the characteristics of harassers described in these two large samples are remarkably similar, allowing some confidence that the results are generalizable. However, it should also be pointed out that Gutek (1985) reports that the characteristics of harassers in her sample were similar to those of the average male worker (at least with respect to her sample). She notes "Of the men in the sample, 53 percent are thirty-six or over and 68 percent of them are married. By comparison, 49 percent of the (harassers) are forty or over and 65 percent are married" (63). This suggests it may be difficult to make predictions concerning which men are likely to harass and which are not, at least on the basis of easily available demographic variables.

Such findings present somewhat of a dilemma; on the one hand, there is the repeated finding that sexual harassers have somewhat of a "reputation" for harassment (i.e., most women report that their harasser has also approached other women, and professors who feel harassed by their students tend to be those men who make a practice of dating or sleeping with their students). Such findings suggest that individual differences may be important predictors of harassing behavior; however, Gutek's (1985) finding that descriptions of harassers resembled the typical male worker in her sample indicate that such individual differences may be somewhat difficult to identify.

An extremely interesting approach to this problem is that of Pryor (1987). Noting that sexual harassment (at least, in its more severe forms) bears a conceptual similarity to rape, this researcher developed a self-report measure based on Malamuth's (1981) likelihood of rape measure. Briefly, Malamuth asks his male subjects to indicate on a 5-point scale (ranging from *not at all likely* to *very likely*) the probability that they, personally, would rape if they were certain not to be caught and punished. Scores on this measure are related in theoretically expected ways to variables that have been shown to differentiate between rapists and nonrapists. Based on this work, Pryor (1987) developed 10 hypothetical scenarios of situations that provided opportunities for sexual harassment if the man so chose. Pryor writes "Each depicted a male who by virtue of his social role or the particular circumstances described had the power to control an important reward or punishment for a female target. . . . Instructions asked respondents to imagine themselves in the roles of the males and to consider what they would do in each situation. (They) were further instructed to imagine that, whatever their chosen course of action no negative consequences would result from their choices" (273). After reading each scenario, subjects were required to rate the probability of their engaging in the various courses of action described, one of which involved sexual exploitation of the female target. For example, one scenario read:

Imagine that you are the news director for a local television station. Due to some personnel changes you have to replace the anchorwoman for the evening news. Your policy has always been to promote reporters from within your organization when an anchorwoman vacancy occurs. There are several female reporters from which to choose. All are young, attractive and apparently qualified for the job. One reporter, Loretta W., is someone whom you personally find very sexy. You initially hired her, giving her a first break in the TV news business. How likely are you to do the following things in this situation? (273-274)

Among the alternatives was one that read "Assuming that you fear no reprisals in your job, would you offer Loretta the job in exchange for sexual favors?" In a sample of college men, scores on this measure (entitled likelihood of sexual harassment, or LSH) were positively related to adversarial sexual beliefs (*e.g.*, "In a dating relationship, a woman is largely out to take advantage of a man"), rape myth acceptance, and likelihood of rape, as measured by Malamuth's (1981) scale. Interestingly, this last was the single best predictor of LSH. LSH scores were also related to sex role stereotyping and negatively related to feminist attitudes and that component of empathy having to do with the ability to take the standpoint of the other. Thus, according to this research, the man who is likely to initiate severe sexually harassing behavior appears to be one who emphasizes male social and sexual dominance, and who demonstrates insensitivity to other people's perspectives. In a particularly creative validation study, Pryor (1987) demonstrated that college men with high LSH scores were more likely than their low LSH counterparts to engage in sexually exploitive behaviors in a laboratory situation.

Women Harassers?

In all informal discussions of harassment, and the majority of formal ones, one is likely to hear at some point the remark that this is not "just" a women's issue, and that "men can be harassed, too." Popular culture abounds with descriptions of the sexy undergraduate, clad in a clingy sweater and pleading soulfully that she is willing to do "anything" for a good grade. And, serious books and training tapes make a point of including scenarios in which lecherous female supervisors or teaching assistants issue seductive invitations to uncomfortable and befuddled male subordinates to "Drop over after dinner and we'll discuss your work." Even researchers with feminist orientations, while acknowledging that the problem is likely to be a minor one, scrupulously include both men and women in their samples in an attempt to be "fair." This section of the present chapter examines several large data sets that bear on this issue, as well as critically analyzes the *meaning* of data purportedly depicting women's harassing behavior in an attempt to address the question "Can women harass men?"

Academic Women. As part of the study of academics reported above (Fitzgerald *et al.*, 1988) our research team also examined data on 79 women faculty members. This number represented approximately one-third of the female faculty at the target institution and was representative of this population with respect to both academic rank and scholarly discipline. The profile of faculty-student interactions described by these women is one where mentoring and friendship behaviors predominate. The most frequently endorsed item was that of mentoring a student. Eighty-three percent of the sample responded affirmatively to this item, with the majority indicating mentoring both male and female students. Over one-quarter of the sample reported mentoring women students only, and only three percent reported mentoring men students exclusively. The item asking whether the faculty member had ever established a friendship with a student was answered affirmatively by 83 percent of the women. The great majority of these women reported friendships with both men and women, with the remainder reporting friendships exclusively with women. None of the women faculty reported establishing friendships solely with male students.

In contrast to these frequent reports of mentoring relationships and friendships, and also in contrast to their male colleagues, very few women (7 percent) reported dating a student, and even fewer engaged in sexual encounters. And, in fact, there was some suggestion in the data that these women were themselves the target of sexual approaches from their male students. For example, 9 percent of the sample indicated that male students had made unsolicited attempts to stroke or caress them and 15 percent noted attempts to establish a personal relationship through requests for dates, drinks, etc. Only three subjects, however, believed they had been sexually harassed by a student. This rate of endorsement is low relative to the reported behavior of the students, and is also lower than the male faculty's endorsement of this item. This parallels other findings (Fitzgerald, Shullman, *et al.*, 1988) in which women do not label such behavior as sexual harassment. In contrast, the male faculty were much more likely to label a wide variety of student behavior as sexual harassment, and were also much more likely to date and/or sleep with their students, which they did not see as harassment!

Many of the women academics in the sample took the opportunity to comment on sexual interactions between faculty and their students. Unlike their male colleagues, who went into much detail concerning the conditions and circumstances under which such interaction was appropriate, these women were more likely to share their feelings regarding the prevalence and injustice of sexual harassment. One woman professor wrote poignantly:

> . . . I resent horribly the exploitation of female students by male faculty. Too many male teachers are using (this campus) as a sexual supermarket, and I grieve for my female students who are (rightly) awed by these men whom they see as so wonderfully appreciative of their minds, only to find out that this man simply gets off on the adoration of nineteen-year-old women. It's still offensive to see aging male faculty members with nubile, pregnant wives who are former graduate students, many of whom will never finish. . . .

The three female faculty who had engaged in sexual relationships with male students all expressed a sense of discomfort and uncertainty about the relationship that increased with time. One subject wrote:

> . . . I became involved with a student after he was no longer my student. While he was my student, considerable flirtation occurred— but we became friends only. Nonetheless, I probably gave him excess help in pursuing his professional career. The relationship probably did not hurt him—but it *could* have. And it was most definitely damaging to me.

A dramatic example of the harm that can come to women faculty members was illustrated by the comments of one subject who reported being raped by a former student. Another felt that there should be some official channel for reporting students who behave inappropriately, but noted that the administration would probably not be sensitive to the issue, or take such reports seriously.

Working Women. The U.S. Merit System Protection Board study (USMSPB, 1981) also provides data bearing on the question of whether women harass men. Their subjects were asked to respond to a series of items describing their most recent experience of harassment or the one that had the greatest impact on them. The responses of the male subjects indicated that their experiences were quite different from those of their female colleagues. First, the actual incidence of such behavior was very small: 10 percent of the men reported being the target of unwanted sexual teasing, jokes, etc.; 8 percent received "suggestive looks"; 7 percent reported deliberate touching, leaning over, etc.; 3 percent experienced pressure for dates; 2 percent for sexual favors; and 0.3 percent reported rape or attempted rape. Secondly, some of this behavior (22 percent) was directed at these men by other men, although it is not possible to tell from the report which incidents can be attributed to which sex. Only 3 percent of the women victims in this study reported being harassed by other women.

The characteristics of the women labeled as "harassers" in the USMSPB study also differ from those of male harassers. Male harassers are likely to be older than their victims and married; women were likely to be younger than the men they approach, and single. They rarely held any supervisory authority over the men. This finding parallels that of Gutek (1985) who reports that female "initiators" tend to be younger, unmarried, and above average in physical attractiveness. According to Gutek ". . . men describe a female initiator who is not at all like the average female worker. The average woman who makes advances is young, attractive, not married and not a supervisor. It seems unlikely that such a female employee is in an organizational position to harass anyone" (64).

Do/Can Women Harass Men? The data reviewed so far suggest the following summary comments: first, women academics are highly unlikely to date or initiate sexual relationships with their male students. The great majority of their interaction with students involves mentoring or friendship behaviors, most of which involve women students. Secondly, a small number of men in the federal workforce report (mostly) low level and indirect sexual advances at work (Levels I and II, in the Fitzgerald *et al.*, 1988, terminology) initiated by young, attractive single women with little or no workplace authority. A somewhat larger percentage of men in the private sector (37 percent) believe they have been sexually harassed (Gutek, 1985) but describe their harassers in similar terms. Thus, it seems that, although it is a rare occurrence, some small number of women do indeed make approaches to male coworkers, approaches that are interpreted by these men as sexual. The question, of course, is whether or not such behavior constitutes sexual harassment.

Many writers have suggested that sexual behavior is interpreted differently by men and women. First, men are more likely than women to interpret a particular behavior as sexual. Data provided by Gutek and her colleagues (Gutek, Morasch, and Cohen, 1983) and by Abbey (1982) support this assertion. Gutek and her colleagues found that men were more likely to label any given behavior as sexual; thus, a business lunch becomes a "date," if it is with a woman. And, Abbey (1982) demonstrated that friendliness on the part of a woman is often interpreted by a man as a sexual gesture. This tendency to misattribute women's motives was sometimes apparent in our study of college faculty. One professor stated that he knew a student was interested in having sex with him because of "the way she sat" and the fact that she made an appointment to see him shortly before the end of the working day. One of Gutek's (1985) subjects noted "We were at the lunch desk. I was contacted under the table. She stepped on my foot. That told me she was interested in sexual relations" (79). This tendency to sexualize their experiences makes it difficult to interpret men's reports of seductive advances.

A second point has to do with differing reactions to sexual overtures when they do occur. Although there are some exceptions, the great majority of male subjects report that they are flattered by such advances, whereas women report feeling annoyed, insulted and threatened (Gutek, 1985, and others).

Finally, it is extremely rare for a woman to hold the organizational power that would allow her to reward a man for sexual cooperation, or punish him for withholding it, even if sex-role prescriptions did not ensure that she was extremely unlikely to demand sexual "favors" in the first place. Thus it was with our women professors. They held the same power as their male colleagues, but virtually never became sexually involved with their students. One in four of the men did.

We conclude that although it is theoretically *possible* for women to harass men, it is, in practice, an extremely rare event. This is due both to the women's relative lack of formal power, and the socialization that stigmatizes the sexually aggressive woman. Reports by male subjects of sexual overtures by women coworkers not only do not constitute harassment in any formal sense, but must also be evaluated in light of data suggesting that men are likely to interpret relatively innocuous behavior as invitations to sexual contact.

Finally, we are struck by Mills' (1959) distinction, of which Hoffman (1986) has reminded us, between *private troubles* and *public issues*. Hoffman writes "Private troubles occur when isolated events cause personal difficulties for individuals—they are the vicissitudes of individual biographies, related peripherally at best to the location of the individual in the social structure. Public issues, on the other hand, are structurally induced problems affecting large numbers of individuals in particular social locations. Since they are the consequences on individual lives of the institutional arrangements within which individuals live, they are not amenable to individual solutions. . . . The sexual harassment of men by women is a private trouble, that of women by men a public issue" (110).

Conclusion

This chapter has attempted to review what is known about those who engage in sexual harassment. We conclude that harassers, whether in the academy or the world of work, have no easily identifiable characteristics by which they may be distinguished. Although recent research has identified attitudinal correlates of the propensity to harass, such variables are not readily observable outside the laboratory. In short, the harasser is similar, perhaps disturbingly so, to the "average" man. Although further research will doubtless uncover additional psychological predictors of harassing behavior, it seems to us that it may be equally possible (and of more practical value) to identify the situational, structural and organizational variables that allow and support the practice of such behaviors, thus suggesting appropriate systemic interventions.

Notes

1. Because there is, as yet, very little formal research concerning professors who sexually exploit students, we have included the available data on non-academic harassers. Although we hope that this will prove to be heuristic, the actual similarities between the two groups of harassers still awaits formal examination.

2. Dziech and Weiner (1984) speculated that the academic harasser was likely to be physically unattractive to his victims. Gutek's data thus provide some empirical support for this assertion.

References

Abbey, A. (1982). Sex differences in attributions for friendly behavior: Do males misperceive females' friendliness?" *Journal of Personality and Social Psychology, 47,* 830-838.

Dziech, B.W., and Weiner, L. (1984). *The lecherous professor: Sexual harassment on campus.* Boston: Beacon Press.

Fitzgerald, L.F., Shullman, S.L., Bailey, N., Richards, M., Swecker, J., Gold, Y., Ormerod, A.J., and Weitzman, L. (1988). The incidence and dimensions of sexual harassment in academia and the workplace. *Journal of Vocational Behavior, 32,* 152-175.

Fitzgerald, L.F., Weitzman, L.M., Gold, Y., and Ormerod, A.H. (1988). Academic harassment: Sex and denial in scholarly garb. *Psychology of Women Quarterly, 12,* 329-340.

Franklin, P., Moglin, H., Zatling-Boring, P., and Angress, R. (1981). *Sexual and gender harassment in the academy.* New York: Modern Language Association.

Gutek, B.A. (1985). *Sex and the workplace.* San Francisco: Jossey-Bass.

Gutek, B.A., Morasch, B., and Cohen, A.G. (1983). Interpreting social-sexual behavior in a work setting. *Journal of Vocational Behavior, 22,* 30-48.

Hoffman, F.L. (1986). Sexual harassment in academia: Feminist theory and institutional practice. *Harvard Educational Review, 56,* 105-121.

Mills, C.W. (1959). *The sociological imagination.* New York: Grove Press.

Pryor, J.B. (1987). Sexual harassment proclivities in men. *Sex Roles, 17,* 269-289.

Till, F. (1980). *Sexual harassment: A report on the sexual harassment of students.* Washington, D.C.: National Advisory Council on Women's Educational Programs.

U.S. Merit Systems Protection Board. (1981). *Sexual harassment in the federal workplace: Is it a problem?* Washington, D.C.: U.S. Government Printing Office.

8

Men in the Academy:
A Psychological Profile of Harassment

Sue Rosenberg Zalk

What prompts a faculty member to sexualize his relationship with a student and cross over the parameters of his professional role by simultaneously engaging in an incompatible role?

This chapter explores some of the psychological dynamics of male faculty who relate sexually to female students and the structural context of the academy within which they operate.[1] "Relate sexually" is being used to refer to sexual overtures (*e.g.*, aggressive demands or subtle seductions), respectivity to students' sexual invitations, and behavior designed to achieve sexual intimacy with a student or to establish a special, exclusive bond built on flirtatious relating. Gender harassers whose behaviors are not directed toward sexual intimacy are excluded. Gender harassment is so pervasive that it would require a lengthy, almost endless analysis of the "hows, whys and wherefores" of misogyny.

There is remarkably little literature which specifically addresses the psychological dynamics of male teachers who sexually harass students. Dziech and Weiner (1984) dedicated a chapter of their book to a discussion of "The Lecherous Professor: A Portrait of the Artist" (115-146). Many of their observations and analyses are referred to later in the chapter. Using an anonymous questionnaire, Fitzgerald *et al.* (1988b) asked male professors their thoughts about sexual encounters with students. The rationales for condoning the behavior varied somewhat in angle, but they all had one common feature—*denial of power*.

Short of these pieces, however, the literature is sparse. The reasons for the blank pages are obvious. How does one collect data that sheds light on the psychological dynamics of these men? Professors who sexually harass women students are understandably reticent to volunteer as participants for such a study. They do not, as a rule, declare themselves publicly. There are no lists from which to solicit participants or clinics or self-help groups for harassers. In short, these men do not judge their behavior to be in any way symptomatic of a personal problem. They do not apply the label "sexual harasser" to themselves.

A number of researchers have collected demographic data on faculty sexual harassers from faculty as well as students who were subject to incidences of sexual harassment. Professors who sexually harass students cross all ages, professorial ranks, disciplines, and family situations (e.g., Fitzgerald et al., 1988b; Sandler, 1981). Similar findings have been reported in research on sexual harassment in the workplace, and Tangri et al. (1982) suggest that the behavior is so multi-determined that it may approximate a random event. If this is so, what, if anything, is to be learned by studying the sexual harasser?

It is clear that we cannot understand sexual harassment without placing it within the context of misogyny and sexist oppression. As such, although individuals commit the act of harassment, can it be understood as an individual dynamic? Can we understand why some male professors harass women students by studying these men? Is sexual harassment indicative of a maladjustment of the harasser or of society? While one can argue either position (assuming they accept the premise that it is evidence of a pathology), the two may not be so easy to separate. These men are products of, and mirror, a sexist culture. But one cannot stop here, for *that culture also reflects the psychology of men.*

Sexual harassment is a symptom—both of the individual and society. It is one among countless expressions of gender stratification. In most societies men have more power than women and they use that power differential to maintain it. Power provides many licenses, including the right to exploit the less powerful. Sexual harassment conforms to role expectations and operates within cultural guidelines.

Placing sexual harassment within the context of sexual oppression paves the way for an analysis of the academy and its role in promoting harassment. Nonetheless, not all male professors sexually harass female students. There is valuable psychological and social information embedded in the dynamics of sexual harassment.

An analogy to misogyny elucidates this point. The fact that misogyny is rampant in most societies and that these societies provide for and promote its expression does not explain why men hate women. Concluding that men hate women because they *can* is nonsensical. Just as hating women is not simply an expression of many individuals' idiosyncratic psychological histories existing in a societal vacuum, neither is sexual harassment the acting out of isolated individuals' emotional irritants.

Not all men sexually harass women, but it is pervasive enough in most societies to indicate that the social structure nurtures a male psychology that finds gratification in this behavior. It is instilled in the psychological development of these males and is sufficiently pervasive to reflect a pattern of shared experience. The study of men who sexually harass women will enlighten our understanding of male psychological development, gender dynamics, and the ways in which cultural definitions and roles shape the repetition of patterns through psychological needs.

Behaviors, even emotions, do not exist in a vacuum. As such, an understanding of the professor who engages in a sexual liaison with a student requires an understanding of the context with which these events occur.

The Academy: A Model Patriarchy

The academy is, in many ways, a microcosm of the larger society. The differences that do exist, however, seem striking for their exaggeration of roles—roles created and legitimized by an institutional design that fosters power and status inequities ripe for exploitation.

The formal academy was instituted to educate men for the betterment of society (which was to be achieved by providing educational resources to an elite few whose social status targeted them as the future leaders). Men teaching men. Women were intruders and their presence was strongly resisted. But that is history. Today, most academic institutions educate women as well as men. However, the Academy is still a male domain, dominated by men (e.g., there are more male professors, males hold higher professorial ranks and more top administrative positions). Women's very presence in the academy represents their movement out of traditional spheres and into male turf and is resisted.[2]

Academic institutions are structured hierarchically. Students are at the bottom of the hierarchy,[3] "officers" (e.g., presidents, provosts, deans) are at the top. In the middle sit the faculty—with their own hierarchical markers. There is little mobility between these categorical ranks and some within them. Students usually remain students until they leave the institution and few faculty are promoted to college president. The professor's recognition comes from peers, where "he" must be a "man among men," receive acknowledgement from "his" peers for the quality of "his" work, and, as a result, move into leadership positions and reap the rewards.

College professors are admired. Many people are in awe of us. They think we know more than we do and they think we are smarter than we are. But our professional contributions are generally acknowledged by a narrowly defined group of colleagues. Our incomes are limited and our power is elusive. Few of us become advisors to political leaders and our achievements and status grant us few social "perks."

But there are many benefits to being an academician. In many ways the role of professor in the academy is a unique work situation. Tenure, once achieved, means job security (barring some outrageous, illegal or indefensible unethical behavior) and the pressure to "prove" oneself is no longer tied to continued employment. The job is somewhat unstructured and flexible. Although fulfilling professorial obligations responsibly can be demanding and time consuming, the range of demonstrable commitment is wide and there is considerable freedom in organizing one's time. In the U.S. professors are given tremendous autonomy. The status of the role and a commitment to academic freedom makes administrators, deans, chairs and colleagues most reticent to judge a professor's competence or style in carrying out the role.

Not surprisingly, there are also few guidelines for faculty-student relations. Faculty can commit a minimum amount of time to students' individual needs or exceed professional expectations; they can meet students in their offices or outside of institutional grounds; they can cultivate friendships, share personal histories, feelings and non-academic activities or remain strictly business and focus only on the specific academic issues at hand.

This autonomy exaggerates the professor's sense of self-importance and contributes to arrogance (Dziech and Weiner, 1984). It readily lends itself to feeling "licensed." Exactly what the license legitimates is a reflection of the psychological dynamics of the professor operating in this particular context. It also contributes to an aura which shrouds the professor in the eyes of many.

Students, the raison d'etre of the academy and the complement to the professor, enter this setting and must adapt to it—it will not accommodate to them. Although students are at the bottom of the hierarchy (and sadly treated as such), they are not support staff or employees. Theoretically, the organization exists to serve them. The product of their work is theirs. Its assessment is a measure of personal achievement. And, students are definitionally non-permanent. They do, and are supposed to, move out and on.

Students attend college to advance themselves intellectually and, as a result, in the social order. The professor is the vehicle for doing this—even in the more progressive institutions. So the role of professor and student are intertwined—although it is not an equal partnership. However, the "contract" does not operationalize roles. The scripts are not clearly delineated and the professorial role, in relationship to the student, is vague and somewhat confusing. The "job description" outlines professional obligations but hints at roles which nurture the intellectual and emotional maturity of the individual—a task which encourages, perhaps requires, more personal relating. The student also struggles with her or his script in the complementary scenario.

Whatever form their relationship takes, students are another source of recognition for the professor. The professor "knows" what the student wants to "know," is looked upon by the student as an authority, as smart, as having "proved" him- or herself in a way students have yet to realize. The professor is often admired, and students frequently believe they will never be as clever, no matter how much they learn.

Who among us would not be flattered by such idealization? This admiration is not the same, however, as recognition by one's colleagues. One need not compete by the standards set by peers to attain it. The recognition lacks status, but it is most gratifying. It feeds one's sense of self-worth, importance, superiority—in short, one's ego. Students are a powerful, sometimes pervasive, source for the gratification of emotional needs—needs which can dominate and motivate behavior.

Power and Faculty-Student Roles

It is not just the distorted aggrandisement by the students or the greater store of knowledge attributed to the professor that "feels good" and is emotionally gratifying. These can be problematic, and they are fragile. They are not guaranteed (they have to be cultivated) and many students do not get hooked by them.

The bottom line in the relationship between faculty member and student is POWER. The faculty member has it and the student does not. As intertwined as the faculty-student roles may be, and as much as one must exist for the other to exist, they are not equal collaborators. The student does not negotiate—indeed, has nothing to negotiate with. There are no exceptions to this.

All the power lies with the faculty member—some of it is real, concrete, and some of it is imagined or elusive. Professors give grades, write recommendations for graduate schools, jobs and awards and the like, and can predispose colleagues' attitudes towards students. But it goes beyond this.

Knowledge and wisdom are power. While superior knowledge, and thus presumably greater wisdom, are often ascribed to faculty members by society at large, the students' adolescent idealism exaggerates its extent. The knowledge and experience ascribed to age add to this source of power. The extension of the power of knowledge is often made into the realm of values and students often accept, uncritically, as true or right what the professor espouses.

It is easy to see how this imbalance of power exacerbates the vulnerability of all students. One can also understand what a heady experience it is for the student who is singled out as "special" by a professor.

There is another dimension to the professor's power which is more elusive. The professor's purpose does not stop at feeding information and facts. Professors are expected to nurture a student's capacity to think analytically, to reason logically, to harness creativity, in short, to mature intellectually and esthetically. This implies that the professor's power extends over the minds of his students. Whether or not this is true, many professors believe it. The more humble refer to it as tapping and nurturing potential; the more grandiose think in terms of unformed minds to be "shaped." Dziech and Weiner (1984) refer to this dynamic as it operates in the context of sexual harassment as the Galatea/Pygmalion myth: The professor believes that female students are drawn to male faculty "as necessary and desirable guides to maturity" and the students are portrayed as needing their touch for intellectual and sexual vitality. So the faculty member's aura of power far exceeds his official assessment of students' performance.

Finally, the professor's greatest power lies in the capacity to enhance or diminish students' self-esteem. This power can motivate students to master material or convince them to give up. It is not simply a grade, but the feedback and the tone and content of the interaction. Is the student encouraged or put down? Does the faculty member us his/her knowledge to let students know how "stupid" they are or to challenge their thinking? This is *real* power.

What about the professor? Isn't all this power enough? How is it some use this power to sexually exploit female students? Faculty members are well aware of the imbalance of power, although they commonly deny the relevance of power in their sexual encounters with students (Fitzgerald *et al.*, 1988b). Nonetheless, they have chosen this relationship for the unequal balance of power. They feel safer, by far, holding all the high cards than in relationships of greater equality.

The above blueprint describes the setting in which the sexual harassment of students occurs. It is necessary background for a fuller understanding of the psychology of harassment. Not only is the environment conducive to sexual harassment, it can stimulate, as opposed to inhibit, intense, unresolved conflicts and provides the setting for acting them out. These conflicts are more likely to surface, the terrain nurtures them, and the props are available to perform the script.

Professorial Style: Assumed Roles and "Seduction" Scripts

Professors have styles of relating and interacting with students. They execute the role of professor in very different ways. These roles are generally quite apparent, and students recognize them from a distance. Dziech and Weiner (1984) cite five "classical" professorial roles assumed by male faculty who sexually harass female students. Their discussion of how these roles serve to facilitate sexual exploitation is valuable, particularly for community educational endeavors. Additionally, attention to the subtle dynamics of the faculty-student script each role elicits reveals the required, and potentially exploitable, power differential that form their common foundation.

A brief description of the five professorial roles described by Dziech and Weiner follow.

1. *The Counselor-Helper* takes the role of nurturer and caretaker. By encouraging students' confidences, he uncovers vulnerabilities and information which are useful in deciding on the seduction script. The student is flattered by his concern and active interest in her life.

2. *The Confidant* treats students as friends and equals. He readily shares personal information with them while inviting them to do the same. Feeling trusted and valued, the student finds herself unwittingly engaged in an emotional intimacy that she sees no way out of. He may also create feelings of obligation by doing favors for the student.

3. *The Intellectual Seducer* impresses students by flaunting his knowledge. He may use his class for eliciting personal information about students that enable him to select his target or determine his approach. Students are often coerced into revealing personal information about themselves under the guise of intellectual, content relevant, course experiences.

4. *The Opportunist* uses physical settings and circumstances or infrequently occurring opportunities to mask premeditated or intentional behavior. This may involve inappropriate touching while obstensibly providing instruction (*e.g.*, "guiding" a student through a movement exercize) or changing the environment in order to minimize the inhibitory effects of the institution (*e.g.*, field trips, conferences).

5. *The Power Broker* uses his professorial "right" to determine grades, write recommendations, and so forth, in order to obtain sexual "favors" from students. It may take the form of promises of rewards or threats of punishment. It may be overt, the "trade" directly communicated, or it may be hinted at and subtle.

Dziech and Weiner present these five roles as typical *modus operandi* of the faculty "seducer." They are plays, varying in degree of elaboration and camouflage, for achieving sexual intimacy with students. But most of us in the academy can recognize similarities between our own styles with students and some of these roles and can probably slot most of our colleagues into one or the other category. Introspection will reveal to use the emotional needs the role reflects and gratifies.

Professors motivated to establish sexual liaisons with students use these roles as a seduction ploy. Whether the role taken is consciously deceptive and premeditated or integral to the self-image, successfully assuming and/or identifying with it and the "strokes" it provides, is not sufficiently affirming, gratifying or meaningful to these men. It does not provide an adequate defense against underlying emotional conflicts and the professor lacks the emotional maturity to settle within the limits of the symbolic meaning the role holds. Like the child who cannot resist the forbidden when no one is watching, they act-out because the environment does not provide controls and they have not sufficiently internalized control. While the more mature individual diverts needs rooted in early disappointments into appropriate adult endeavors (*e.g.*, professional achievements), the sexual harasser lacks adequate defenses and coping strategies and must "play out" the conflict.

Power Dynamics and Professorial Style. Dziech and Weiner's "seduction" role classification is particularly useful in the ways it highlights the common theme of power and control. The faculty member controls the circumstances and orchestrates the opening scenario. The imbalance of power is easily apparent in four of the five scripts. The Counselor-Helper, Intellectual Seducer, Opportunist, and Power Broker roles require, by definition, a power differential. The power element is more elusive in the Confident role—but it is there. Because the power dynamic of this style is so easily missed, it is useful to look more closely at how the Confident operates.

The professor's confidences are a "gift" he bestows. Its very value rests on the power and prestige of his position. His confidences and pretense of friendship between equals is manipulative. It is the power of his position that is used to "set her up," that exaggerates the appeal of her assigned role and that eventually renders her its victim.

Although students initially feel flattered and privileged by the attention the Confidant offers, they also feel uneasy. Their histories in relationships, with family, peers, bosses and teachers, provide neither guidelines for participating in this new friendship nor hints about the rules of the game. The desire to measure up, the uncertainty about what is expected and considered "correct" behavior, and concern about the costs of mistakes, creates anxiety. The incongruities, indeed, the outright contradictions, inherent in the double identity required for, and the premise underlying, their relationship (*i.e.*, equality between unequals) creates dissonance and heightens the student's vigilance in "reading" and following the professor's lead. As the relationship escalates, the student often feels increasingly burdened by the demands of the relationship, in over her head, and powerless to exit. How, after all, do you tell a professor who has trusted you, made himself vulnerable to you and valued your friendship that you are too busy to find time to talk with him? It is the power and control his position grants that nurtures this scenario, holds her captive and renders escape routes risky.

Profiles of Sexual Harassers in the Academy: Attitudes and Behavior

The five roles commonly assumed by male professors in the service of obtaining sexual intimacy with students depict how diverse behavioral styles lend themselves to sexual exploitation and provide a context for illuminating the common underlying theme of power and control, elements the professor depends on to achieve his aim.

A professor's proclivity for a particular role is a function of the behavioral repertoire most accessible to him, his self-image and the projected image he finds most comfortable or desirable. It reveals little about the underlying dynamics which motivate him to use this role to establish sexual liaisons with students. They are vehicles for exploitation, not reasons. However, within a particular role, there are a range of "attitudinal stances" reflected in the professor's behavior. These attitudinal stances dictate the parameters and requirements, define the arena, and establish the tone of the relationship. In short, they guide his actions.

These attitudinal stances are different from the professorial roles described above. They operate within a role. They are the attitudes with which the role is approached; the attitude the professor has about the sexual liaison. Attitudinal stances are analogous to personality traits. The "attitudes" (like "personality" attributions) are inferred from one's "stance" (behaviors) within specific contexts. The context, here, is relating sexually to students.

Attitudinal stances are likely to suggest some of the motivational dynamics underlying the harasser's behavior: how he feels about himself and how he views women. The attitude with which the harasser approaches his behavior may suggest how ego-syntonic the harassment (i.e., the degree to which the harasser experiences conflict and guilt around his behavior), the rationale adopted to justify or understand his behavior, and even the psychological meaning hidden in the harassment.

In order to shed further light on the psychodynamics of male faculty who sexually harass female students, we have identified four familiar themes or dimensions useful in developing profiles of these men.[4] Each is a continuum between two poles and it is likely that most harassers can be ranked on all four dimensions. They are not independent dimensions and one's position on one of them will often suggest a trend on another. The dimensions are characterized by, and labelled for, behavioral patterns representing the extremes of each pole. The dimensions are:

1. *The Public versus the Private Harasser* (Dziech and Weiner, 1984). This dimension assesses the professor's behavior of sexually relating to students along a continuum from open, "public" displays to hidden, secretive advances and encounters.
2. *The Seducer/Demander versus the Receptive Non-Initiator.* This dimension can be viewed as an "active-passive" continuum and refers to the degree to which the professor actively pursues sexual encounters with students.
3. *The Untouchable versus the Risk Taker.* This dimension refers to the degree of "entitlement" and invulnerability/vulnerability with which the professor engages in sexual liaisons with students.
4. *The Infatuated versus the Sexual Conqueror.* This dimension contrasts professors along the continuum of affection and care felt toward their student lover—how "special" she is to him.

While the two poles of each dimension appear to be opposites and to reflect different underlying needs, this is not always the case. For example, although the opinionated person is operating from a different psychological constellation than one who never has an opinion, both may be motivated by a fear of being wrong, of being exposed as "stupid." The different expressions of the same feeling reflect developmental experiences and superego constraints. If a feeling is judged unacceptable and creates anxiety, the expression may, on the surface, appear antithetical to its meaning. Another example, relevant to these dimensions, is the behavioral expression of hostility toward women. Thus, the need to denigrate women may be couched in gratuitous behavior, flattery and the bestowing of favors. Although this seems to suggest a fondness for the person, it may well be a vehicle for rendering the woman submissive, dependent and obliged.

An analysis of the psychological dynamics portrayed in these four attitudinal dimensions shed light on the emotional constellation of the male faculty harasser and the way in which the structure of the academy nurtures this behavior.

The Public versus the Private Harasser

Dziech and Weiner (1984) present a most vivid behavioral depiction of this attitudinal dimension. The Public Harasser "performs" in public. He prefers an audience. His posturing toward women is flagrant (*e.g.*, touching) and patronizing. He is quick with sexist and glib comments. This is the professor who spends a lot of time with students, often hanging out at student pubs and the like. He is available, approachable and informal.

The Private Harasser conforms to the stereotype of the academic, somewhat elite scholar. He is formal, aloof and conservative in appearance. His presentation usually makes him the last to be suspected, and as such, perhaps the most dangerous (Dziech and Weiner, 1984). While avoiding notoriety, he uses his position to gain private access to women students. Students are caught off guard and disoriented by his sexual advances.

While both the Public and Private Harasser obtain gratification from being able to use and abuse their power without censure, there are different dynamics operating for the two men. The public behavior is "showing off." It is a call for attention, an advertisement about one's manhood. It is a competitive gesture directed toward other males. His desired audience may be colleagues, but it is equally likely to be male students. Taking liberties with women is an adolescent symbol of manhood and the Public Harasser is crudely attempting to let other men know he is "one of the boys".[5] Accordingly, he prefers to be surrounded by attractive, popular students (male and female) and courts the attention of women students who, in his opinion, are highly desired by other males. The women victimized by his behavior are, in and of themselves, unimportant and interchangeable. Like stage props, they are required, but not central, except as evidence of manhood. Motivated to mask feelings of inadequacy, the Public Harasser is undaunted by the fact that his more perceptive colleagues are unimpressed. If he is at all aware, he chalks it up to their jealousy or divides the faculty into teams: those who are "in"/"with it" and those who are not. He, of course, is in the "in" crowd. The readiness of the system to tolerate his behavior permits him to maintain his illusion, while his blatant display has sufficient risks to add excitement to the role. Risk highlights his assertion about being a "real" man. Since the audience for this performance is men, the Public Harasser is actually less invested in engaging in sexual relations with students than his behavior suggests, in contrast to the Private Harasser (Dziech and Weiner, 1984).

The Private Harasser is a man with a "secret." Although it might appear on the surface that his behavior is motivated simply by the desire for sexual encounters, the dynamics are considerably more complex. The secrecy is not simply prudence, an attitude reserved for his sexual behavior. It is noticeably characteristic of the way he presents himself in all professional arenas. The Private Harasser is intensely invested in his public image. Indeed, the rigidity with which he adheres to this image suggests how excessive this investment is and its importance in maintaining an intact self-concept. Why, then, would a man who is so protective of his image risk destroying it? Clinical observations suggest several possibilities.

The very secretiveness of the Private Harassers' activities is, in and of itself, exciting and gratifying. He takes pleasure in the deception. While the Public Harasser gets gratification from what people know about him, the Private Harasser finds it in what they do not know. Just as his lectern separates him from his students, his very demeanor is a shield from the eyes of others. He guards all his secrets, not so much because he is ashamed of them (he may or may not be) but because there is power in the secret—the power of getting away with something and never being suspected, the power of deception. Needless to say, there is disdain for those deceived.

There is another aspect to the secret worth noting. It is part of a more elaborate fantasy life and the fantasy is an important source of emotional sustenance. Most fantasies are kept secret, for if no one knows them, no one can destroy them.

Power and control are all integral aspects of the dynamics underlying the behavior of the Private Harasser. He exudes these publically in his professional attire and presentation. He uses these to intimidate students and to secure sexual contact. Compensating for intense self doubts about his potency (sexual and otherwise), demonstration of his power is foremost and he selects as his objects those he has direct power over. This tactic not only avoids challenging his fantasy and fragile self-image, it is often a required component of his secret identity. As a rule, the whole scenario is part of his fantasy.

Seducer/Demander versus Receptive Non-Initiator

A popular retort to condemnations of sexual liaisons between faculty and students makes reference to the perception that not infrequently it is the female student who is "on the make" and seduces the professor. How often this occurs is difficult to assess. For one thing, it is not always clear what constitutes an "initiation." If a student responds to a professor's attentive, solicitous, personal and mildly flirtatious behavior with a sexual overture, where did the initiation begin? What is even more problematic, is the evidence that men frequently misinterpret women's behaviors and clothing as seductive and signaling a sexual invitation. This finding includes interpretations of interactions between female students and male faculty members (Abbey, 1982; Henig and Ryna, 1986). Of the 235 male faculty members who responded to the Fitzgerald et al. survey (1988), 17.5 percent reported an experience in which a student initiated an unsolicited attempt to stroke, caress or touch them (they were not asked whether these were sexual invitations) and only 6 percent believed they had been sexually harassed by a student.

Nonetheless, focusing on the ambiguities sidesteps the issue. The professor who is absolutely innocent of leading the student on, ceases to be innocent once he has sexual contact with her. The unequal power distribution in the faculty-student relationship makes his "concession" to her overtures exploitation. The fact that the female student "asked" is not an explanation for why he complied. Yet this is the very justification offered by the Receptive Non-Initiator.

In our society a woman's offer of free sex is considered a logical explanation for a man's indulgence. A woman would never get away with offering such an excuse. We may condemn a man for "asking" but not for saying "yes." The stereotype about men's pervasive sexual needs and dominating drive to satisfy them prevail to the degree that we consider such behavior normal, or at least understandable.

The Receptive Non-Initiator is the professor who, as a rule, does not initiate the first sexual overture, but is most accommodating when the student does. The Receptive Non-Initiator draws the line between morality and immorality at who does the asking. Superego constraints are operating here and are one of the distinctions between the Receptive Non-Initiator and the professor who actively sets out to seduce a student (the "Seducer") or who uses his position to demand sex (the "Demander"). However, it is not that simple and it would be an error to assume that this dimension can be characterized by degrees of conscience. Superego constraints and sources of guilt can be quite idiosyncratic. Rigid standards in one domain may find a formidable match in the guilt-free escapades in another. There is an idiosyncracy in the moral price tag people place on different behaviors that only legislation can standardize and regulate.

The Receptive Non-Initiator acknowledges the power of his position. He recognizes how the imbalance of power renders blantant overtures questionable and places undue pressure on the student. He recognizes her disadvantage in the interaction and contends with this awareness by resisting making the first move. It is a transparent rationalization but it serves to reduce his discomfort about his unethical behavior. It is true that this standard spares the student from the trauma of confronting a sexual invitation, the disinterested student is left out of the arena and direct coercion is not involved. As such, it is probably less unethical (as opposed to more ethical) than the behavior of the Seducer/Demander. Nonetheless, the roles remain intact, as does the imbalance of power and its exploitation. The Receptive Non-Initiator either blinds himself to this obvious reality, or more commonly, acknowledges it but says "so what? She was the seducer. I put no pressure on her." He claims freedom from responsibility. To him the ethics only apply to proactive behavior, not reactive behavior.

However, the Receptive Non-Initiator's inhibitions against initiating sexual contact with students are considerably more complex than a personal morality. He would experience asking for sex, or even overtly seducing the student, as diminishing and the resulting relationship would be less gratifying.

The Receptive Non-Initiator wants to be seeked out. He needs to feel "lovable" in his own right, for *who* he is, not for *what* he is. Henry Kissinger, Secretary of State under President Nixon, was much more honest about the seductiveness of status. When asked by a reporter why women found him attractive, he responded "power." Kissinger knew the "score." The Receptive Non-Initiator is aware of the lure of his position and likes it. He tends to try to appear desirable, either by tending to his physical appearance or by adopting a role that encourages trust and familiarity. Yet, he deludes himself into believing that he is truly special if he doesn't have to ask, if the student offers the first sexual invitation. Were he to be the sexual aggressor he would never truly trust that it is he and not the professor who is desirable. The fact that he and the professor are one in the same to the student is inconvenient and pushed aside.

If the Receptive Non-Initiator wants to feel loved for himself, why doesn't he just find a woman who is his equal, over whom he does not wield power? Would not this be more affirming? But the Receptive Non-Initiator does not feel particularly lovable and doubts that such women will give him the degree of acceptance he longs for. For the most part, he is right about this assessment. A peer probably would not give him what he wants and they most likely have not in his past, because his needs are excessive and his insecurities loom when he becomes involved with a woman. A partner who is an equal does not provide the unconditional affirmation of the idealized mother. And a strong and powerful woman who "mothers" her man would trigger pervasive feelings of impotence and inadequacy. A student is a promising and available alternative. Actually, some variation on this theme applies to all sexual harassers although it gets expressed differently in the interplay of power and sex. For the Receptive Non-Initiator, these feelings are compounded by an intolerance for rejection. Confronting rejection, and all it means, is avoided if one makes no requests.

Thus, the Receptive Non-Initiator is most ambivalent about power. While his professorial role is critical for his self-esteem and he capitalizes on it to establish familiarity with a student, he cannot not tolerate the suggestion that it underlies his appeal.

Power and control are at the center of the dynamics of the Receptive Non-Initiator's sexual liaisons with students. While it may appear that he is giving over control and some degree of power by his initial passivity, he is in reawlity staunchly holding on to all of it. While the Seducer/Demander makes himself vulnerable to rejection and scorn by inviting sexual contact, the Receptive Non-Initiator is in the position to give or not give what is requested of him. This carries considerable power and contributes to his "keeping the upper hand" throughout the duration of the relationship. As would be expected, given these dynamics, such men are likely to test the woman's devotion regularly as they need continuous confirmation of their power as well as "proof" that they are loved. Under such circumstances, the student is likely to find herself in an abusive relationship.

The Seducer and the Demander (*i.e.*, the "Power Broker") have been grouped together on this dimension because both actively seek and plot sexual encounters with students (in contrast to the initial passivity of the Receptive Non-Initiator). In order to obtain what they want, both men take advantage of their position and the student's vulnerability. Although the Seducer, using impressive mental acrobatics, sometimes denies the role of power in his conquests, power does not hold for him anywhere near the degree of conflict as it does for the Receptive Non-Initiator. Both the Seducer and the Demander accept sexual privilege with students as an entitlement of power and control.

There are, however, notable differences between the Seducer and the Demander, although these too may fall on a continuum. While the professor's virtual monopoly on power and control pervade all relationships with students (sexual or otherwise), the Demander literally uses his "real" power, the rights that are part of this professional duties, to "purchase" sex from students. He is the most ruthless and unethical and perverts the educational process. He views, and treats, his female students as whores.

His disdain for women is most blatant, as is his rejection of their place in the academy. The Demander reduces women students to the role of sex object and his behavior is a clear communication that they do not belong in the academy. They are bodies, not brains, and they will have to serve him as women to obtain what he controls. He needs to demonstrate to them his "real" power and render them literally under his command and at his mercy. The Demander operates from a psychological investment in "keeping women in their place." He is threatened by the advancement of women because it challenges his male privilege—and his self-definition of masculinity is tied to control over women. He seeks gratification by exercizing the limits of his power.

As is apparent from the above, the Demander's behavior is not motivated by the need to be loved or judged desirable. Although these needs may well be present, they are rigidly guarded against. Indeed, should these needs surface and enter his motivational scheme, his whole defense structure is threatened. For, if he wants a woman's affection he is vulnerable to her and she has some power. She can give or withhold something he wants and that something cannot be purchased or controlled by his position.

There is a common stereotype, frequently cited in discussions on
sexual harassment, that female students sleep with their male professors for
the purpose of improving their grades and obtaining favors. That is, the
claim is made that these students intentionally use their bodies in order to
use their professors for their own means. Such assertions are interesting in
their presentation of the faculty member as the victim and the student as the
victimizer, the one in control. The available research suggests that this is an
infrequent occurrence (14 percent of the male respondents in the Fitzgerald
et al. 1988b study indicated that a student had implied or offered sexual
favors or cooperation in return for some reward). Even introducing this
twist into a dialogue on sexual harassment reverberates with the same belief
and attitude about women students as does the behavior of the Demander:
women do not have the competence to succeed in college so they use their
femininity (bodies) to compensate.

The absurdity of viewing sexual harassment through the above lens is
apparent. Those occasions when it is descriptively accurate represent a sad
case study of the impact of gender stratification on women and gender
relationships. The male professor has all the power and control and the
female student has bought into the attitude that, as a woman, her most
advantageous asset is her body and she is intellectually inadequate. The
professor and student then play out this script. But she has little power or
control in this interaction. "Selling one's body" is not power, it is the result
of powerlessness. Additionally, the motivation, whatever it may be, that
accounts for her behavior, is not an explanation for the activities of the
professor.

This discussion is pertinent to understanding the dynamics of the
Demander. The exchange of favors for sex is the core of his script but he
does not view women as an equal negotiator in the contract. In contrast to
the stereotype of the student who plots to use her body as a term paper, the
Demander shuns perceiving the student as having even that much
autonomy and, as such, control. While acknowledging the trade-off they
make, he reserves all the power and control and would be unable to tolerate
the contention that it was *he* who was being used. He would be devastated to
learn that a student interpreted his proposition along the lines of "I really
have him where I want him. He is so 'hot' for my body, he's eating out of my
hands. This will be an easy grade." Of course, rarely is this the student's
perception. She knows the reality of the power dynamics.

The Seducer, like the Demander, targets specific students with whom
he would like to be sexually intimate and actively sets out to achieve his
goal. Like the Demander, he is willing to introduce this new twist to their
relationship. Indeed, he intends and expects to. He has taken charge from

the beginning, written the script and manipulated circumstances, for the purpose of seducing and is prepared to initiate sexual intimacy when he judges the time right. The Seducer is not, however, usually thrown off balance should the student "beat him to the punch," as this is merely evidence of the success of his efforts. Unlike the Demander, the Seducer needs to feel desired, "loved," and attractive. He is aware of his power, but unwilling to negotiate an exchange of favors for sex. To do so would negate the motivating force behind his seduction—evidence that he, the man that he is, is desirable, even irresistable.

Unlike the Receptive Non-Initiator, the Seducer does not struggle with the lure of his position. To the contrary, he cultivates it for his purpose. It is not a narcissistic blow to the Seducer that his power is part of his appeal and he does not interpret it as an abuse of power. The Seducer views his power as an achievement, as evidence of his value and worth and as proof of his specialness. It is the very thing that he believes earns him love. Doubting that he is lovable without the dressing, and feeling that one is loved for the outward expression of their successes, he is not conflicted by the role his power plays in his attractiveness.

The Untouchable versus the Risk-Taker

There is a distinction between the professor who does not worry about, or even consider, the consequences of his behavior and the one who feels he is walking on the edge and at any moment could get pushed over. The narcissism and grandiosity which orchestrates the behavior of the former contributes to the feeling of being "untouchable." It reminds us somewhat of the egocentric reasoning of the adolescent,[6] particularly as witnesses in the notion that they are special and unique. This personal fable (Elkind, 1980), which contributes to such beliefs as "it can't happen to me," "the rules are for others, not me," often guide actions. And, like the adolescent who, according to all indications short of the behavior itself, does not want to die in a car accident but nonetheless drives drunk, the Untouchable believes there are no real risks. He is in control—beyond the ranks of censorship.[7]

Whether or not the Untouchable flaunts his liaison or is intentionally indiscrete will depend on some of the other dynamics addressed elsewhere in the paper. Although his behavior is a bold challenge to the system, this is not necessarily one of the motivating factors underlying it. The distinguishing dimension of the Untouchable is his extreme egocentricity—his poor social perspective taking in this domain.[8]

Some Untouchables, bolstered by a distorted sense of self-importance and omnipotence, simply operate as though they exist outside the system, as though the rules do not apply to them and they cannot be hurt. These men appear so oblivious to the surrounding community that it seems unlikely their behavior is designed as a statement to others. Others are almost daring the system with the statement "No one will mess with me. I make my own Rules!" (Both types tend to be more vulnerable to rejection from students whose rebuffs can turn into denials and projections). Either way, the Untouchable's behavior reflects poor reality testing and judgement. For example, such men may assert, and appear most sincere when doing so, an unambivalent commitment to their wives and families and a clear and determined unwillingness to sacrifice the family for the sake of the affair. They behave like model husbands and fathers with their families and conscientiously meet all family obligations. Yet, these very same men will unabashedly escort their student lover to university events and seemingly not entertain the reality that this presents tremendous risks to their *status quo*.

Whether the Untouchable is led by the conviction that "no one will mess with me; I'm better than the rest" or merely is unable to step outside of his own inner world sufficiently to assess the situation through the eyes of others, he is egocentric and grandious.

At the opposite extreme is the Risk Taker—the professor who believes he has really stepped "out of line." He has done the forbidden, said "fuck you" to the system and may have to pay the consequences. He is being "naughty" and his naughtiness is a statement. He knows he is challenging the system by taking for himself what he is not entitled to. He believes he is playing with fire but the compulsion to do so is more powerful than the fear of the consequences. At the very least, he cannot moderate his behavior by a consideration of the possible long term consequences.

The Risk-Taker does not sleep as well as the Untouchable. He does not sleep well at all during the affair and is frequently irritable with people. He fluctuates between the "high" of his naughtiness and the guilt and fear of punishment. In this latter state he is likely to project these feelings onto the woman whom he now blames for his transgression. Since she represents his disobedience, his perception of himself as "bad" and the reason for his eventual punishment, she is viewed, and treated, as Eve, the wicked temptress. He views himself as the victim, and punishes her for the infraction. During this cycle, he can be quite cruel and the lover may find herself the object of sadistic behavior. At such times, the Risk-Taker is identifying with the system and people from whom he fears retribution as a defense against his feelings of vulnerability. While he keeps his anxiety sufficiently in check to allow him to play out some of the affair, it is not an adequate defense and the Risk-Taker level of anxiety remains quite high throughout the duration of the affair.

The Infatuated versus the Sexual Conqueror

Little needs to be said about the Sexual Conqueror. He is a familiar depiction. Sometimes referred to as a "womanizer," other times as a Don Juan, the Sexual Conqueror is only interested in numbers. He repeatedly, often compulsively, seduces one or many women. While the Sexual Conqueror may have preferences in the type of student targeted for seduction (*e.g.*, the aloof and disinterested; the shy and reticent; "party girls;" "virginal" types; married women; ethnic women), the individual woman, as a particular human being with her own unique qualities and life situations, is not only irrelevant, it is rarely processed. Women are interchangeable. While the Sexual Conqueror is often determined, amorous and focused when in the process of seduction ("conquering"), his interest wanes once he has achieved his goal. "One nighters" are common and satisfying, although he may, at any one time, maintain several lovers to fill in the inevitable gaps.

The Sexual Conqueror generally knows, and remembers little about the woman. We have heard stories from women who have approached these men several months after their sexual encounter and insist that the man seemed confused about who they were. In line with this, we have had the experience of confronting men with evidence that supported a particular woman's accusations and witnessed reactions that suggested difficulty in recalling the incident or the person. Several counselors/ therapists, consulted for this paper, reported anecdotes in which male clients/patients (examples included non-academic as well as academic settings) who fit this profile, could recall specific incidents but were not able to match the woman with the event, or who were unable, with any degree of confidence, to provide information about a specific woman. (Confusing women, *e.g.*, "She was in constant conflict with her mother, . . . I think, . . . maybe that was the girl from remedial . . ." or combining select aspects of several women in a description of one woman, were noted.)

The above examples represent an extreme and the Sexual Conqueror is often more moderate in his behavior, needs and ambitions. But the repetitive pattern of his behavior and the anonymity he imposes on these women suggest the extent of his pathology—the anxiety about, and need to document, his sexual potency and masculinity and the terror of intimacy with a woman.

The Sexual Conqueror is not, however, the typical male professor who engages in sexual liaisons with female students. Many professors enter into such relationships with an intensity and need that is the antithesis of those reflected in the behavior of the Sexual Conqueror.

It would be incomplete, and as such, stilted and misleading, to imply that all faculty who engage in sexual relationships with female students are deceptive and manipulative men who consciously use their position of power for the explicit purpose of sexually exploiting female students. There is an identifiable dimension that characterizes men who are emotionally drawn and attached to a specific female student. In short, they become infatuated. Their behavior is not designed primarily for sexual contact, but rather to establish a "meaningful" relationship. She is not an exchangeable object or part of a stable. If he is rebuffed, he does not rapidly find another—but another there will eventually be.

Sometimes these feelings evolve inadvertently out of encounters designed to be more exploitative. Often they evolve more naturally as the faculty member slowly acknowledges to himself his desire to see the student more often and recognizes that he has a "crush." Although the more impulsive and less reticent are likely to jump into a courtship once the feeling takes shape, others approach it with more forethought.

In discussions of student-faculty "dating," someone always tells anecdotes about marriages that resulted from such relationships. They do, indeed, exist, but they are the exception and make for a weak defense or explanation of the dynamics underlying student-faculty sexual liaisons. What is more, a relationship that ends in marriage is not evidence that the power element which operates in student-faculty relationships did not apply in the particular case. A faculty member's desire or willingness to marry a student does not necessarily imply equality in the relationship or erase the real and/or psychological power he wields over her. And, as the previous discussion of the academy suggests, the student may not be in a position to objectively evaluate what is in her own best interest or to resist pressure he may place on her. Actually, a faculty member's determination to marry his student may also have exploitative aspects as it raises questions about his use of power and control in obtaining what he wants.

Couples involved in such relationships adamantly deny that their academic roles are reflected in their relationship, although it is often apparent to perceptive people who are familiar with the subtleties of the academy. It "passes" in public, however, because faculty-student roles parallel male-female roles in the larger society. Such couples, however, sensitive to community opinion, generally wait until the female student graduates before they tie the knot. Sound as this may be, a September marriage following a June graduation is insufficient time to erase the psychological dynamics of the academic roles upon which their relationship evolved.

Undoubtably, many of these marriages are as appropriate and successful as most marriages and it is unwise and unjust to make assumptions and blanketly categorize individual cases or situations. The focus here is patterns—there are always exceptions—and while rules and flow charts simplify life, caution is urged in readily applying them to all professor/husband-student/wife couples (after the fact). Nonetheless, with that disclaimer in place, these couples are atypical, and raising them in response to dialogue or policy on sexual intimacy between faculty and student is a transparent and indefensible argument for maintaining a system which encourages the sexual exploitation of women. It is the rule, not the occasional exception, which must guide policy, educational programs and counseling services.

Nonetheless, those exceptional cases when student-faculty affairs end in marriage suggest the genuineness and sincerity with which some faculty may pursue and participate in a relationship with a student. The Infatuated is sincere and genuinely cares about the woman, although marriage as an outcome is unlikely to even enter the range of possibilities for most of these men. Indeed, the Infatuated, like other faculty who sexually harass women students, is often married. While his marital status makes his sincerity suspect and, as with all extramarital affairs, imposes practical limitations and additional emotional complications, stresses and pressures, the married Infatuate is quite, often intensely, attached to the woman. For the time being, he is "in love." It is not simply a sexual extra-curricula activity ("quickies" on the side) he is after. He seeks a form of emotional affirmation and gratification of needs that require greater intimacy than that supplied solely by sexual encounters. Nonetheless, for most of these men, whether married or not, the assumption that it is temporary is not only part of the appeal but also part of its justification.

In contrast to harassers that keep their emotions more in check, the Infatuated risks emotional vulnerability. He is also more likely to become dependent on the woman for he has specifically turned to her for the gratification of his needs.

The description presented so far does not seem distinctly different from the course of events that preceed most love relationships—a person is "drawn" to another, the two spend time together, get to know one another better, and "fall in love." It is natural, usually even desirable, to fall in love with someone who gratifies emotional needs and meets various other requirements for an intimate relationship. If the faculty member pursues and enters into a relationship with a student with the sincere intention of giving it a chance to develop, is not this simply the normal process of adult bonding in a love relationship?[9] Although student-faculty relationships may be judged unethical as a rule, why is not this the exception? Why would we classify the Infatuated as a sexual exploiter?

The imbalance of power and control in the faculty-student relationship is also very central to these liaisons, although the faculty member will deny it most adamantly and rarely is consciously aware of it once the relationship is established. Nonetheless, during the courtship he will use the advantage of his position, as do others, to attain her affection All people motivated to "sell" themselves (for the purpose of forming a relationship or otherwise) put their best foot forward. But the context in which this courtship occurs suggests its exploitative potential: "winning the heart" of the object of one's affection, inevitably and unavoidably (whether by conscious design or not) involves the abuse of power by capitalizing on the vulnerable state that power renders the other.

The Infatuated is not simply someone with the unfortunate luck of falling in love with a woman who, circumstantially, happens to be a student at the institution in which he teaches—a circumstance which complicates things but is irrelevant to the interpersonal dynamics. The Infatuated is particularly attracted to students *because they are students*. Their very status in the academy, *vis a vis* his, is part of the attraction. Thus, the power differential is integral to the relationship.

The Infatuated is in love with a relationship that veils a multitude of self-doubts. It allows him to be the man he feels unable to be in a relationship with a peer, or even someone who does not see him robed in his academic attire. Indeed, his relationship with the student is usually a marked contrast to his marriage or past love relationships.

The Infatuated thrives on being "looked up to;" on being able to teach and guide the lover; on being at the center of the relationship; on having greater "wisdom;" on doing "more" important things; and on pondering more "cosmic" thoughts. He takes pleasure in being identified with the powerful system she is up against and in being able to advise her from the inside and teach her the ropes. He thrives on telling her the nitty-gritty of his work day, the details of department politics, and trivial gossip about his colleagues. Not infrequently, these men are discontent with their own status or treatment in their department or in conflict with someone in the college who wields greater power. Indeed, the affair may well have been triggered by a series of such incidences and tensions which have undermined his self-esteem.

The professor finds in his lover an empathic, uncritical partner. He complains to her about his mistreatment and explains how it is a result of others' inadequacies, insecurities and jealousies. He seeks from his student-lover (and finds, if she plays her part) an ally in his defensive structure—someone who assures him he is "right," confirms his assertions and joins him in constructing an interpretation of the situation which supports his self-esteem. She may even actively reinforce it—feed it back to him in select parts—should she sense his self-doubts surfacing. Often this is subtle, other times it has a ritualistic flavor (e.g.—He: "Maybe they are right and the problem is me. Maybe I really can't . . ." She: "Stop talking that way. You know . . . And don't forget . . ."). She senses how critical this support is for maintaining the relationship. She may also, however, gradually develop some doubts of her own (particularly if unsuspecting people make pertinent comments about her lover, or if she obsesses about his plight and struggles to make sense out of information that appears unlikely and "questionable"). If these doubts are not somehow dismissed, they smolder, and the relationship begins to turn. Conflicts arise (usually about things that appear unrelated to the source of her doubts but can be reduced to her withdrawal of support or increased demands for more consideration from him) and the relationship becomes fragile. In the end, she is as likely to be the one who wants to terminate the relationship as is he.

The manner in which these men treat their student-lover varies considerably as a function of the professor's other psychological constellations. The "Malevolent" Infatuated treats his student-lover porrly, even abusively. He is likely to deny the legitimacy of her needs, as only his are important, and remind her of how fortunate she is that he chose her. He may denigrate her, either overtly by referring to her inferiority or covertly by focusing on his own superiority. He might cruely criticize her schoolwork, mock her opinions, trivialize her interests, and dismiss and discourage her amibitions. Such malevolent treatment does not camouflage his disdain for women.

The Infatuated, however, is equally likely to be "benevolent." The "Benevolent" Infatuated takes the role of nurturer and demonstrates his affection with a most reassuring consistency. He may flatter, support and praise her. The "Benèvolent" Infatuated often mentors his student-lover— guiding her through the system, providing constructive feedback, and emotionally and pragmatically supporting her ambitions, often encouraging her to set higher goals. This behavior may be based on a realistic assessment (e.g., the quality of her work warrants praise; pushing her to aim higher is supportive of her dreams but not her doubts about her ability). Or, it may more accurately reflect his own dynamics (e.g., encouraging a career direction may run counter to her own ambitions and reflect his desire to see her as, or attempt to make her into, the woman whose love is most affirming).

The "Benevolent" Infatuated's adoration of his lover may be as distorted as her image of him. He may lift her from the realm of "ordinary" woman and place her on a pedestal. He may depict her as a saint, in contrast to his wife, the "ball-busting" shrew, and view her as the "good mother" he longs for, as opposed to the depriving one he recalls. Of course, no woman can measure up to this although the student-lover may try. Her efforts will eventually leave her depleted, her humanness and needs will surface and the relationship will deteriorate.

Nonetheless, while in full swing, the "Benevolent" Infatuated has what he wants. To be loved and adored by the near-perfect woman makes him feel very special. He resists evidence of limitations. Indeed, he takes pride in her achievements and will enter into, or create for her, rationalizations about disappointments (e.g., a poor grade) which shift (i.e., project) the blame (e.g., the teacher's incompetence). Thus, she too, may be viewed as the victim and the two may play out this scenario and take turns as the victim and counselor.

There is a qualitative difference in the support and care the professor gives to his student-lover from that which she gives to him, and both differ from that observed in the mutual bonding of peers. This difference is inherent in the imbalance of power in their academic roles. These roles cannot be dismissed—the relationship centers around them. For example, there is a qualitative difference between compliments and the like, bestowed by the more powerful one onto an underling, and those offered by someone lower on the hierarchy to one higher up. (Think of the differences in the way in which a teacher praises a student and the way a student compliments a teacher; the way in which the praise is received and experienced by the teacher and the student.) The obvious parallel is the parent-child interaction. Both receive tremendous gratification from the caring affection of the other—but there is a qualitative distinction in the meaning carried by feedback (e.g., a parent does not attach the same meaning to their child's declaration "you're so smart" as the child does to the identical statement from the parent). Thus, there is a parental, often patronizing, element in the professor's support of the student. And, as is sometimes seen in parent-child dynamics, the faculty member's concern is frequently rooted in the narcissistic gratification obtained from his lover's achievements. She "belongs" to him and her achievements are his and reflect on him. She, or rather the relationship, has become part of his identity.

The above dynamics appear to work smoothly as long as he stays "on top." While he remains in control, he takes credit for her successes. He is not, however, living vicariously through her (the way a parent might when something about the child mirrors his/her unrealized desires or fantasies). To the contrary, he cultivates the reverse. If she becomes too strong or more self-confident than he, their relationship "contract" is at risk and he is threatened. This sometimes happens with a graduate student-lover who begins to accrue professional credits and is judged to have more promise than the professor-lover or when an undergraduate is accepted into a graduate school which far outshines the one the professor attended. It may also happen when the student "outgrows" the relationship—no longer needs or feels gratified by what he provides, or when she begins to see beyond the roles and becomes disillusioned with him and the relationship (which is likely to happen as she develops an independent sense of her own self-worth). When he sees the changes occurring, he may loose interest or covertly attempt to sabotage her progress. This can take the form of withdrawing support, discouraging her advancement or challenging her competence. Indeed, the "Benevolent Infatuated" may begin to demonstrate behaviors more typical of the "Malevolent" Infatuated, blurring somewhat the distinction between the two and revealing an underlying anger so well camouflaged in the previous stage. Alternatively, the Infatuated may invert the anger and embrace the feelings of inadequacy, which motivated and defined the affair in the first place. With his defenses weakened, he will succumb to depression.

One last note about the Infatuated. His ripeness to "fall in love" and readiness to enter into a relationship with a student usually occur at critical periods in his life. It generally follows some event or series of events that intensify his self-doubts, undermine his masculinity and trigger feelings of inadequacy (e.g., rejections in love relationships, professional disappointments). These feelings preceded the particular crisis and were a painful, pervasive and integral aspect of his private identity, but they were a source of turmoil that he had previously succeeded in keeping under the surface. The relationship is a band-aid designed to help heal the wound. It acts like a euphoria-inducing drug. In its initial stages and at its height the professor-lover looks like a "new man." Everyone notices. He is flying, happy and self-confident. The effects of the "drug" wear away but there is a high risk of addiction.

The Benevolent-Malevolent Dimension

The "malevolent-benevolent" pattern pervades all four attitudinal stances described above and is a useful dimension for gaining insight into the dynamics of sexual harassment—possible underlying motivations and the character of the relationship. All of the men profiled in this paper demonstrate some balance of malevolent behavior (i.e., the use of the relationship to repeat old themes of sadism, control, punishment and humiliation) and benevolent behavior (i.e., assuming the kindly, caring, protective, father-teacher role). This theme was developed within the discussion of the Infatuated to provide a context for the way in which it operates. But it is always present. As is true for all four attitudinal stances, it is never all one or the other. These men fall somewhere on the continuum between the two extremes. For conceptual purposes, however, it was necessary to depict the extremes.

As noted earlier, most men who engage in sexual relations with students can be placed somewhere on the continuum of the two poles of all of the attitudinal stances and it would have been reasonable to create a fifth "attitude" describing the "Malevolent-Benevolent" stance. However, its pervasiveness in the relationship between the faculty-lover and the student-lover and the evidence it suggests for an underlying theme which motivates these men's behavior, encouraged setting it aside for special attention.

The theme which appears to characterize almost all men who have sex with female students is anger toward women. This hostility is clearly seen in the behavior of the malevolent, sadistic pattern, but the benevolent pattern often provides a convenient example for contradicting the generalization. However, the benevolent man is also keeping the woman "in her place" and treating her as a subordinate. The need for power and control in the relationship is clear. Whether the man takes the student as a beloved protégé or whether he dominates and debases her with anger and rage, he continues to need, and feel that he has, complete control. This undercuts her autonomy and encourages dependency. It is aggressive, hostile and self-serving behavior. It mirrors and reinforces the stratified gender roles and oppressive nature of traditional gender relationships in our society. The surface behavior of the benevolent faculty-lover not only masks the likely rage and threat women trigger but presents an image easily warmed to. The frequency with which the benevolence turns nasty reforms the picture and suggests that the extremes of "benevolence" are in fact a reaction formation against underlying rage. It is a socially acceptable way of expressing anger, threat and disdain.

Sexual Harassment, Male Psychology and Cultural Norms

The attitudinal dimensions are a preliminary attempt to sketch profiles of male professors who select to have sexual relationships with students. Additionally, while this paper describes behavioral patterns and suggests underlying psychological meaning and dynamics, the analysis is somewhat surface. The data for a more in-depth analysis that traces development roots of the different profiles or even distinguishes etiologies of those who harass and those who do not, is simply not available. These ideas have been put forward for scrutiny, discussion, study and revision.

Nonetheless, the attitudinal dimensions are valuable in suggesting repetitive themes which appear as common constellations of all harassers as well as highlighting subtle differences. The profiles are useful in knowing what the problem looks like and in developing educational programs and institutional policies to discourage harassment.

While sexual harassers represent a diverse group of men, whose psychological histories are undoubtably equally diverse, all of the profiles reflect one global theme: "manhood"—what it means to be a man and how one demonstrates to oneself and others that one is, indeed, a "real" man. But what does it mean to be a real man? Why the drive to demonstrate one's "maleness"? And how does this translate into attitudes toward women?

It is easy to see how sexual conquests are considered evidence of "manhood" but this hardly explains sexual harassment. Why students? Why must there be a victim? Why the need to control another and exploit power? The sexual aspect of the behavior of the sexual harasser is really a secondary gain of a more profound statement. The emotion expressed in their behavior is one of fear and hatred of women. Doubts in one's masculinity and ability to measure up to definitions of "male" find expression in misogyny—the disdain, devaluation and oppression of women.[10]

Are these professors distinctly different from other men? Dziech and Wiener (1984) raise this question and explore the possibility that certain types of men are attracted to academia and that the academy can exacerbate self-doubts about masculinity. In a review of the research, they suggest that during their adolescence, professors tended to be non-athletic, unpopular with the "pretty" girls and low in status and power and self-esteem—all adolescent measures of masculinity and success. Additionally, they point out, in our society financial resources are a measure of success and the vehicle to power. While the intellectual, scholar, teacher role is socially esteemed, it is not congruent with our definition of masculinity. It also fails to provide the material evidence of success. It does, however, provide one with a position of power and control over more people than most men ever dream of "ruling." What is more, academics, emerged in a culture of youth, may be particularly ripe for experiencing an intense mid-life crisis (see Levinson, 1978) in which they struggle to revise their self-image, find dignity, reflect on the past and plan their futures. Regardless of the developmental stage individual conflicts about masculinity can be traced to, the professor is in a setting that provides the opportunity to exaggerate his own self-importance, confirm feelings of power and desirability and exploit female students in the process of expressing his own self-doubts and disdain for women.

However, sexual harassment is not limited to the academy. It exists in all settings (e.g., executive suites, construction sites, the military). Athletes, men with great wealth, blue-collar workers, and the like, sexually harass women if the setting provides the opportunity to do so. It cannot be dismissed as an occupational phenomenon.

Pleck (1984) maintains that the primary powers women have over men are "expressive power" (the power to express emotions) and "masculinity-validating power" (the power to make men feel masculine by adhering to their prescribed role) and that men's dependency on women for these needs is a major motivation to control and have power over women. Men need women to fill their emotional gaps. The fear that women will withhold this spurs desperate attempts to dominate women, their vehicle for feeling somewhat whole. Pleck analyzes men's power over women in interaction with men's power relationships with one another (e.g., competition) and power (lessness) within society and how these dynamics serve, and are promoted by, a competitive economic structure. Others trace the roots of this misogyny—disdain, devaluation and oppression of women—to envy of women and the masculine requirement to disown aspects of the self rooted in early experiences with nurturing, caretaking women (see for example Chodorow, 1978; Horney, 1932; Zalk, 1987).

Whichever angle one chooses to apply to the phenomenon of sexual harassment, we can speculate that these men are particularly drawn to vulnerable women (e.g., students, employees) not simply because they exaggerate the evidence of the male's own power, but because these men feel so very vulnerable themselves. In "conquering" these women, they symbolically, albeit lamely, conquer their own vulnerability. He hates in them what he hates in himself. He masters (sic!) his fear, by "mastering" them—possessing what he seeks without acknowledging it as a part of the self.

It is reasonable to hypothesize that the male dynamics which prompt harassment are much more universal and operate in diverse settings. The psychological costs of being a "man" are great. The rewards for the price paid are power. The greater the damage, the more that power is asserted, embraced and abused in an attempt to compensate for the losses. Some men are most vigilant in protecting themselves from exposure and that vigilance, along with poor coping skills, can easily lead to "acting-out."[11] Sexual harassment is acting-out and acting-out serves to avoid confronting and constructively addressing the conflict.

All men are forced to confront the perverting influence of pressures to conform to the demands of a gender stratified society. Why some men rise above, or somehow seem to side-step, its influence and others are shaped by it in ways that stunt their development, remains in the domain of speculation and theory. But men certainly fall on a continuum in their perspective on, and comfort with, being a "man."

Male sexual harassers in the academy and the academy itself may well be a model institutional structure to study for an understanding of the multiple factors which promote the exploitation of women. Male faculty, in general, may be an ideal sample for gaining insights on male development and the psychology of men. It may be that the academy has a tendency to attract men whose emotional development resulted in pervasive self-doubts about their masculinity, intense disdain and fear of women and the need to exert and witness the evidence of their power. And the unique nature of the academy, with rewards that do not measure up to stereotyped evidence of male achievement and success, its power hierarchy which distorts and agrandizes the image of the professor, disempowers students and "minds its own business" in the arena of faculty-student interactions, encourages the abuse of power. Certain men may be attracted to the academy both because it shields them from the highly competitive world of men outside its walls while providing a profession in which they are surrounded by people over whom they have power and control.

Male Faculty Who Defy the Profiles

The above indictment of male faculty is unfair and one-sided. Not all male professors sexually harass women students. Our experiences with sexual harassment programs and the male faculty who have been our partners in these efforts (as well as other men we have worked with) leave no question in our minds that there is another, very different profile of the male professor. Many men pursue a career as an academician for psychologically "healthy" reasons and the choice is evidence of maturity and ego strengths. These professors have not been scarred (or the scars have long since healed) by the dissonence and conflict created by gender roles and demands. They have rejected stereotypical definitions of masculinity and its expression. They are comfortable with themselves as people and men, and with the multiple dimensions of their identity. They have chosen to pursue knowledge and to contribute to society through intellectual pursuits and by nurturing the intellectual development of others. The challenge of stimulating ideas, the excitement of witnessing change, the satisfaction of producing something others judge worth reading, and institutional involvement designed to enhance the educational environment are their sources of gratification and evidence of success and achievement. Such men are more comfortable empowering students than dominating them. They are a marked contrast to the sexual harasser.

There is much we can learn about male psychological development and the function of institutions in perpetuating an oppressive society from these men, working alongside of the sexual harasser, as well as the harasser, and much to be learned from studying their behaviors within the organizational structure of the academy.

Conclusion

How can the information provided in this chapter serve the campaign to stop sexual harassment in the academy? If the pervasive practice of sexual harassment is an outcome of the impact of gender stratefied roles, demands and limitations on male psychological development, how can it be stopped? Of what use is this perspective? While the transformation of societal structures is the ideal, it is hardly a realistic tactic for eliminating sexual harassment.

However, the institution of the academy can be changed and can be changed in ways that will discourage the exploitation of women. The very fact that sexual harassment is one of many culturally ingrained and promoted expressions of women's oppression and serves to perpetuate that oppression, means that academic institutions *must* take responsibility for programs, policies and structural revisions that will discourage and create a hostile environment for the exploitation of women.

Other chapters in this book address the needed institutional reforms and methods and policies for confronting sexual harassment. The material presented in this paper underscores the need for institutional responsibility and suggests directions for reform. It is essential that *all* students be empowered, that they know their rights and the parameters of appropriate behaviors for all institutional roles. The empowerment of female students, in particular, is essential. Women, more than men, experience the academy as hostile and disempowering (Belsky *et al.*, 1986). While some pedogogical techniques and teacher attitudes may empower women more than others, an institutional atmosphere, promoted and supported from the top, that publically and consistently endorses gender equality and reflects it in curriculum, projects, programs, policies and the like, is a most effective and implementable vehicle for the empowerment of women students. Empowered women are much less likely to tolerate abuse and faculty will find an environment much less conducive to exploitation. Women students who have been exposed to Women's Studies and are knowledgeable about and supportive of women's rights are more likely to report incidences of sexual harassment than those who are not (see the Preface to this book).

Sexual harassment *must* be an open issue on campus. It must be publically dissected for both students and faculty. While peer support groups are valuable for the victims of harassment, students will only feel safe reporting incidences if they are supported and protected at all levels of the system. Faculty and administrators need to educate students about sexual harassment and must guarantee, through policies and procedures, that they will not let the student down. We cannot encourage students to "blow the whistle" and leave them open and vulnerable by inaction.

While we cannot hire or retain faculty based on "types," the forms and shapes in which harassment gets enacted should be part of the educational campaign. Faculty evaluations can include questions about gender discrimination in the classroom and students' reports should be considered in hiring and tenuring decisions. Indeed, interviews for faculty positions should include issues pertinent to attitudes toward women students and women's advancement.

Most importantly, the veil of secrecy must be lifted. Colleagues frequently know who among them is harassing students. It is not only through the grapevine; students often confide in trusted professors. But it usually stops there. It is risky to turn one's colleague in, and the student accurately learns "what's the use?" "nothing will be done," "I'm on my own." Everyone must take this seriously.

Notes

1.   The focus is on male faculty-female student sexual liasons as these represent the preponderance of harassment incidences in the academy as well as the workplace (e.g., Fitzgerald et al., 1988a, 1988b; Gutek and Morash, 1982; Lott, 1982; Sandler, 1981).

The gender stratification of most societies is such that it hardly strikes us as surprising or even unacceptable whe the older, more accomplished male professor is attracted to his younger, eager, often admiring female student. Although this is, in and of itself, worthy of critical analysis, it is not an explanation for sexual harassment. There is a large, qualitative jump between feeling something and acting on those feelings. Yet for some, the former is sufficient justification for the latter and requires little consideration of the context and the consequences.

That it is not simply a function of the two roles (i.e., student and professor) but an interaction of roles and gender, is evident by the fact that women professors rarely sexually harass male students. Indeed, we would find it curious, at best, if a female professor invested time and energy, took risks and used the power of her position to secure sexual encounters with younger male students. She would undoubtably be the object of considerable speculation about "her problem." The male faculty/female student affair is sufficiently frequent and compatible with social roles that its existence elicits little surprise.

2.   There are many fine publications that provide a historical perspective on the status of women faculty and students in higher education (e.g., Chamberlain, 1988; Simeone, 1987). Additionally, the Project on the

Status and Education of Women of the Association of American Colleges (Washington, D.C.) has a publication which regularly addresses these issues and the interested reader is encouraged to obtain this material and take advantage of the valuable service they provide.

3.   I am disregarding maintenance workers, support staff and the like. While their work is essential, their role is not part of the definitional purpose of the academy.

4.   While these psychological profiles, based on attitudes and behavior, draw upon the research and writings of others, the substance of this material comes from personal experiences with sexual harassment and harassers. This material was based on information provided from the following sources: colleagues' observations of, and interactions with, sexual harassers; sexual harassers' perceptions of encounters and affairs; stories told by students who were the object of harassment; anecdotes and perceptions shared by people who were confidants of harassers, many of whom were privy to (often witnessing) the details of one or more sexual encounters with students (usually as they enfolded) and several of whom had established a relationship with the student and socialized with the couple; and clinical material provided by counselors and therapists who treated men with a history of sexual liaisons with students or employees. Thus, the "data" were subjective reports. Patterns appeared to emerge and were subject to a psychodynamic theoretical framework. Undoubtably, when viewed through a different theoretical lens a different picture is likely to emerge.

5.   In speculating on the psychological roots motivating male professors to sexually harass female students, Dziech and Weiner (1984) explore the possibility that this behavior reflects unresolved adolescent crisis. In their review of other research on adolescent males' definitions of masculinity, power and status and histories of male professors, they note that as adolescents, professors were "outies," not part of the in-group (an experience which negatively effects self-esteem), lacked the adolescent markers of status (*e.g.*, athletics) and, like their more popular peers, wanted to date the best looking girls rather than the smartest.

6.   Egocentrism is also descriptive of the functioning of the infant and preschooler. The egocentrism of the infant stems from the lack of awareness of self as distinct from others. As such, they experience themselves as the center of the universe—their needs, perceptions, feelings and so forth are absolute. The egocentric reasoning of the preschooler entails an inability to take the perspective of others, to be simultaneously aware of themselves and the outside world (Piaget, 1969). Elements of both

these stages may also be operating, in a somewhat developed form, for the Untouchable.

7. It is recognized that reckless, life-threatening behavior by adolescents may represent a "death wish" but the point pertinent here is the element of egocentric reasoning.

8. Pryor (1987) found that male college students who scored high on his paper and pencil measure of "likelihood of sexually harassing" a woman, given a risk free opportunity to do so, also scored low on the measure of perspective taking (*i.e.*, they had difficulty taking another's perspective).

9. Disregard, for the moment, the possibility that the faculty member could be married. While this fact certainly throws suspicion on his sincerity and intentions, it is not germane to the argument being presented.

10. Pryor (1987) found that male college students who scored higher on his "likelihood to sexually harass" measure also scored higher a rape proclivity and authoritarian measure, and had negative feelings about sexuality. Additionally, these men were more likely to describe themselves in socially undesirable masculine terms or masculine terms that strongly differentiated them from the stereotypical female.

11. "Acting-out" is a psychological term for expressing emotional conflicts through a series of behaviors which are symbolic of the conflict. That is, rather than recognize the conflict or tolerate the anxiety it elicits, the individual plays out some version of it. An example would be the adolescent who runs away from home in response to struggles around separation issues.

References

Abbey, A. (1982). Sex differences in attributions for friendly behavior: Do males misperceive females' friendliness? *Journal of Personality and Social Psychology, 42,* 830-838.

Belenky, M.F., Clinchy, B.M. Goldberger, N.R. and Tarule, J.M. (1986). *Women's Ways of Knowing: The Development of Self, Voice and Mind.* New York: Basic Books.

Chamberlain, M. (1988). *Women in Academe: Progress and Prospects.* New York: Russell Sage foundation.

Chodorow, N. (1978). *The Reproduction of Mothering.* Berkeley, California: University of California Press.

Dziech, B.W. and Weiner, L. (1984). *The Lecherous Professor: Sexual Harassment on Campus.* Boston, Mass.: Beacon Press.

Elkind, D. (1980). Strategic interactions in early adolescence. In J. Adelson (ed.) *Handbook of Adolescent Psychology,* 432-444. New York: Wiley.

Fitzgerald, L., Shullman, S., Bailey, N., Richards, M., Swecker, J., Gold, Y., Ormerod, M., and Weitzman, L. (1988a). The incidence and dimensions of sexual harassment in academia and the workplace. *Journal of Vocational Behavior, 32,* 152-175.

Fitzgerald, L., Weitzman, L., Gold, Y., and Ormerod, M. (1988b). Academic harassment: Sex and denial in scholarly garb. *Psychology of Women Quarterly, 12,* 329-340.

Gutek, B. and Morash, B. (1982). Sex-ratios, sex-role spillover, and sexual harassment of women at work. *Journal of Social Issues, 38,* 55-74.

Henig, S. and Ryan, J. (1986). Sex differences in levels of tolerance and attribution of blame for sexual harassment on a university campus. *Sex Roles, 15,* 535-549.

Horney, K. (1932). The dread of women. *International Journal of Psychoanalysis, 13,* 348-366.

Levinson, D. (1978). *The Seasons of a Man's Life.* New York: Ballantine Books.

Lott, B., Reilly, M.E., and Howard, D.R. (1982). Sexual assault and harassment: A campus community case study. SIGNS, 8, 296-319.

Piaget, J. and Inhelder, B. (1969). *The Psychology of the Child.* New York: Basic Books.

Pleck, J. (1984). Men's power with women, other men and society: A men's movement analysis. In P.P. Rieker and E.H. Carmen (eds.), *The Gender Gap in Psychotherapy.* New York: Plenum Press.

Pryor, J. (1987). Sexual harassment proclivities in men. *Sex Roles, 17,* 269-290.

Sandler, B. (1981). Sexual harassment: A hidden problem. *Educational Record, 62,* 52-57.

Simeone, A. (1987). *Academic Women: Working Towards Equality.* Mass: Bergin and Garvey.

Tangri, S., Burt, M. and Johnson, L. (1982). Sexual harassment at work: Three explanatory models. *Journal of Social Issues, 38,* 33-54.

Zalk, S.R. (1987). Women's dilemma: Both envied and subjugated. Presented at the Third International Interdisciplinary Congress on Women, July, Dublin, Ireland.

Handling Complaints of Sexual Harassment on Campus

IV

Editor's Notes

In the previous section, Sue Rosenberg Zalk as well as Louise Fitzgerald and Lauren Weitzman pointed out the need for educational interventions on sexual harassment on campus. They also recognized the fact that education, however successful, is not sufficient in itself to prevent sexual harassment or offer remedies when it occurs. Because sexual harassment occurs in the context of institutional power, individuals who have been victimized are often, understandably, reluctant to use the ordinary channels in the college or university for resolving complaints. This is especially true because of the humiliating and disorienting impact of sexual harassment, where the victim may experience the sort of self-doubt, self-blame, and sense of degradation common to victims of rape, incest, and battering.

It is important, as Paludi and Barickman (in press) have argued, that the means of hearing and resolving complaints of sexual harassment be distinct from the regular departmental and administrative hierarchies. They described the succes of a Sexual Harassment Panel that is independent of the administrative structures of the President's office and the Office of Student Services. This structure is described in detail by Dorothy O. Helly in "Creating a sexual harassment panel on a college campus." Dr. Helly discusses major issues in establishing a Sexual Harassment Panel on a college campus, including handling informal and formal complaints by students, faculty, administrators, and staff, the establishment of an explicit policy against sexual harassment on campus, and the make-up of such a Panel. Dr. Helly also discusses the issue of confidentiality in resolving complaints.

Mary Kay Biaggio, Deborah Watts, and Arlene Brownell, in "Addressing sexual harassment: Strategies for prevention and change," also address interventions on a college/university campus that can be implemented by a Panel or other designate. These interventions include: (1) placing items relating to sexist comments or sexual invitations on teaching evaluations; (2) publishing articles on sexual harassment in student newspapers; (3) disseminating information about institutional policies that prohibit sexual harassment at new student orientations and dormitories; and (4) setting up community activist strategies to raise public awareness and to protest particular instances of sexual harassment.

Helen Remick, Jan Salisbury, Donna Stringer, and Angela Ginorio, in "Investigating complaints of sexual harassment," aptly point out that educational interventions concerning sexual harassment increase the likelihood that complaints will be brought on campus. They offer suggestions for working with unions and how to handle investigations of sexual harassment and the effects of these investigations for individuals as well as the campus climate.

And, unlike Dr. Helly, Drs. Remick, Salisbury, Stringer, and Ginorio argue against one Panel as the investigative body in sexual harassment cases. They describe several alternatives, including relying on the Ombudsperson in the college/university setting as well as the Affirmative Action Officer. Sandra Shullman and Barbara Watts, in "Legal issues," discuss the legal implications involved in handling complaints of sexual harassment on campus, whether the complaints are handled by a Panel, Dean of Student Services, Ombudsperson, and so forth.

In "In her own voice: One woman student's experiences with sexual harassment," Lela Demby shares her experiences as an undergraduate student trying to establish policies and procedures against sexual harassment at her university. She addresses the difference in perspectives on the role of relationships in the academic environment.

Each of the authors in this section support Bond's (1988) plea for an ecological perspective for handling sexual harassment on campus: educational, psychotherapeutic, legal, and sociocultural. As Bond argued:

> The use of an ecological perspective can move beyond finger-pointing to a more comprehensive understanding of a complex social problem that has been a critical barrier to women's professional development for many years. . . . Continued development of an ecological approach will provide a more solid basis for developing policies and preventive interventions to reduce the negative impact sexual harassment has on women's professional development. (6)

And, as Lela Demby states:

> If I had to choose one thing to leave you with . . . it would be the plea to listen to student input when formulating your own policies on dealing with sexual harassment and assault. We all want policies that are the most optimal and efficient, addressing the needs of the

survivor and the community. We will tell you some of the most important things you need to know, because we've been there. We know.

References

Bond, M. (1988). Sexual harassment in academic settings: Developing an ecological approach. *The Community Psychologist, 21*, 5-6.

Paludi, M.A., and Barickman, R. (in press). *Sexual harassment of students: Victims of the college experience.* In E. Viano (Ed.), *Victimology: An International Perspective.* New York: Springer.

9

In Her Own Voice:
One Woman Student's Experiences with
Sexual Harassment

Lela Demby

A few days ago, when I told a friend that I had been asked to speak at a conference on sexual harassment, he jokingly said, "So, how does it feel to be the foremost authority on sexual harassment and assault in the world today?" I smiled, because that was the same type of question that I had been asking myself lately: "How can I speak for unknown but countless survivors? How can I act as a voice for so many women, when I am not an expert, nor a professional, nor a counselor or any kind of authority on the subject?" So I came to the conclusion that I could only base my comments on my own experiences, both as a member of a student task force on administrative procedures and policies on sexual harassment and assault, and as a survivor.

I also can draw on the events of the past two years at Princeton University, and the incidents that split that campus community. So my aim is to recount what actually *has* happened, to real people in real crises. This is *not* a hypothetical situation, or a "what-if," for that was the major flaw in how the following cases were dealt with: the policy and procedure that had been formulated by the administration had had no previous student input, and so were not influenced by the persons they were supposed to help, the victims and the survivors. They were the ones who could have told the administrators what was needed in a procedure for handling cases like their own, because they knew what they had to do without in their own specific instance. Many of the measures did more to protect the interests of the offender rather than the survivor, as in the university's reluctance to act formally against the man in a reported incident. Very rarely is anything put on his transcript for fear of jeopardizing his chances of getting into another good school or getting a job. But is there not a responsibility to the survivor to punish the offender? And is there not a responsibility to notify other institutions that they may have a rapist or a harasser on their hands when they admit this man?

For instance, there is the case of the man who had been harassing many first-year women repeatedly. But the system was so fragmented that each dean knew only of one or two reported incidents. It was only when he had done some other offense and was brought before the committee that people started talking to each other and realizing that between them, they had a considerable list of names of women who had come to them complaining about this man. He was asked to withdraw. But the same decentralization of processing incidents like that one, and the tendency to try to handle it in ways that are quiet, informal, and unobtrusive were responsible for the next true example. A woman had been raped by her boyfriend, and filed a complaint against him in the university. A dean met with the two parties, and convinced the man to voluntarily withdraw from the university. However, since nothing was put on his transcript, he was re-admitted when he applied to come back the following year. He proceeded to enroll in the same courses that the woman was in, and harassed her until she was driven to seek outside counseling. She had no support when trying to get her classes changed after the deadline, no support when trying to explain her poor academic performance to her professors. No survivor would have had any support if she had tried to have her room changed because her assailant lived down the hall, or delay exams because she was under too much pressure to concentrate. No one responsible for structuring the system had foreseen the myriad different situations in which being sexually harassed or assaulted could—and did—affect one's life.

Statistics are published every semester on how many offenses of what kind were reported, but never the numbers on cases like these. So many students and faculty did not know that sexual harassment and assault could occur at a place like Princeton. They were recently brought face-to-face with the real situation.

For the case that started the major student awareness, two women were visiting an eating club, which is of the nature of a fraternity or sorority, but co-ed. They were upstairs when one of the women got into a verbal altercation with a male member of the club. The two women then went downstairs and met with another friend whom they had come to see. The same two women were beginning to go up the stairs when the man and some of his friends came down the stairs. He said to the same woman that she had better get out of his way "or he was going to rip her titty off." She refused to back down, so he shoved her back, hard enough to slam her against a wall that was 15 feet behind her. (Later on that night, as she was undressing, she was to find bruises from where she had impacted.) The man then left. The women tried to look at a club membership face-board hanging by the side of the front door to identify the man, but other club members escorted the women out of the club, refusing to permit them to look at it. The women then went next door to another club and called the police and campus security, who came to take reports. The police caught the man and a friend exiting the club through the back door, and took reports from all persons involved.

Throughout the next couple of days, the woman debated whether to press charges through the local police or to utilize the university's procedures; she opted for the latter, since both she and the assailant were students. However, she and her friend had to go through several different administrators before they could locate the ones who handled sexual assault. When he was notified of her action against him, he filed a counter-charge of sexual assault against her.

Throughout the next months, a complicated series of events happened that even now few people understand. However, the woman was not told what the procedure was nor how it was going to be carried out. The meetings were disorganized, and members had not received briefings of the case beforehand. When it finally did convene, reports had been distributed only the day before. Questions were asked on the lines of, "Why were you two women there in the first place?" "Why didn't you two just back down when he got violent?" "What did you say to him for him to be so violent?"

Meanwhile the campus newspaper had carried the details of the story, and the campus itself was rife with similar speculations. The fact that this was being termed a "sexual assault" was a cattle prod to the community. The majority of the doubt was placed on the woman's actions and intentions. During the proceedings, the man's story came out to be that she had been drunk and was antagonizing him and his friends all night, and that on the stairs she had a lit cigar, waving it in his face, trying to burn him. He was trying to protect himself, and just happened to brush her shoulder, knocking her down. His friends corroborated his story. Another friend of his who was there that night had a letter printed in the newspaper, saying that she had been going around to all of the men in the club that night, asking them to show her their genitals. He signed the letter, and his name was printed in the paper with it. However, *no mention of drunkenness or cigars* was in any of their original statements to the police. She only had her one friend as a witness. During the proceedings, no one was required to take an oath of honesty nor do anything to swear that he or she was telling the truth.

About a month later, a decision was finally handed down from the committee: the man *and the woman* were to receive equal official reprimands, he for his behavior, she for "use of provocative language." They had judged her actions to be of the same caliber as his, physical or non-physical. The student body and many faculty were in an uproar. There were two totally different stories to what really happened; it was clear that someone was obviously lying. But one top official was quoted as saying that the burden of proof that real courts have is not the same as the one the university follows. There was no "beyond a reasonable doubt" requirement; furthermore, the university could not ascertain who was telling the truth. In a news conference, the same official was forced to admit also that the university could be sued for its decision in a disciplinary matter if it was too harsh in its decision against one party.

The students' reaction was instantaneous. No one could believe that it was going to be left at that. Someone was lying, and should be punished for it. Many felt as if the university were punishing both parties, innocent and guilty, simply because it did not have the resources to find the truth. Students organized discussion groups with administrators who were open to what they had to say, in order to air their frustrations about how the case was handled. Someone was victimized, someone got away with physical abuse. What if the man was innocent, shouldn't his name be cleared? The disciplinary committee had gotten so hung up on the term "sexual assault" that it forgot the basic points of the case: human being A physically injured human being B out of spite; was this institution going to tolerate that type of behavior? The message was, "yes, if you the victim can't prove that you were totally innocent." The woman was punished for not backing down from a man, for causing his wrath to go out of control. This believe is of the same sexist train of thought that says that a woman asks to be raped when she wears "provocative" clothing, or that if a woman had agreed to have sexual relations with a man before, that she really has no right to deny him further relations.

The controversy turned into an "us against them" debate, with the man, other club members, and those who felt that the woman brought it on herself on one side, outraged students on the other. The club felt that they were being singled out, that everybody always takes the woman's side of a story, that they were being victimized. They felt that people's reactions against them were simply anti-male, and they became defensive as a group. At open forums, the discussions got aggressive and accusatory, often out of control. The question came up, "What is sexual harassment? How do we define it?" The men started to wonder if their actions were going to be misconstrued as such, and women began to wonder if they had experienced the same thing but had not realized it as such. No matter what, the message had been sent out by the institution that, no matter what it says, it was not prepared to handle cases like these, that you could end up punished just as much as the offender if you report sexual harassment. People began to feel almost as victimized by the system as the actual survivor did.

The students' and faculty's response, coupled with the glaring inadequacy of the university's disciplinary measures in the sexual assault case, led the then-president of the university, William Bowen, to call for an investigation led by the then-provost, Neil Rudenstein, to see if the university had implemented all of its policies and procedures. Mind you, not to re-open the case and solve it, but to see if the university could be held liable for its decision because its procedures were not carried out in full.

It was at this time that I and a group of concerned women students with two women deans formulated the Women's Center Task Force on Sexual Harassment, and began corresponding with the provost through letters and in meetings. We submitted a paper to him with suggestions to keep in mind for policy review and change. These suggestions were based on our own and other women's experiences and victimizations by offenders and "the System." We knew that the foundation to the policy already in existence at that time was flawed from the start. It had had *no student input*, and no survivor input, when it was being formulated. Therefore, it overlooked the basic requirements of perception needed by a procedure that could efficiently handle incidents of that nature.

The people judging the case were not sensitive to the issues surrounding sexual harassment or assault. But then again, they cannot be blamed because the university itself was not sensitive to it. Some students still did not believe that there was such a thing as date-rape. There was a sentiment of "Boys will be boys," and alcohol played a major role as scapegoat in most of the incidents. You could get away with anything as long as you and some friends stuck together in your stories.

In our memo to Provost Rudenstein, we asked him to implement new procedures such as forming a smaller, better trained committee to handle reports of sexual harassment, and the hiring of an individual whose sole responsibility would be to coordinate the policy and procedure involving sexual harassment and assault, including training of designated individuals, and acting as advocate, counselor, and intervening official for survivors, and ensuring that all aspects of the formal process are consistently implemented.

Along with the actual procedure and its stages, the university disciplinary committee's standards of evidence needed to be clarified. For both parties' sakes, the mudslinging that occurred in the earlier case had to be prevented. Many men were worried that opportunities for false accusations would now arise due to the heightened awareness of what was going on. But in our group discussions, we tried to convince them that, by revamping the policies, their rights would be protected, too. A lot of the negative response that the Women's Center received was because many men perceived all of the hype as being *anti-male* simply because it was coming from the Women's Center.

In this memo, we also were sure to point out that, while using the pronoun "she" all throughout the paper, *all students*, male and female, are to be included in consideration of this matter. Race, ethnicity, disability, and sexual preference and orientation all influence the type of sexual harassment being perpetrated, and how it will be judged. Gay, minority, or other non-mainstream students are in danger of having cultural prejudices and stereotypes interfere in the resolution of their cases. But every single one of our suggestions was based on encounters that all of us had either gone through ourselves or had to help a friend. We knew what worked, and what did not work, because we had been there.

A month later, the Women's Center had a "Take Back the Night" march, consisting of about thirty people. It ended violently when the march proceeded down the street where the social clubs were located, and many clubs' members, some drunk, were waiting outside to verbally abuse the marchers and throw beer cans at them. They shouted, "The night belongs to Michelob." Several men exposed themselves to the marchers, and were photographed on videotape doing so. This event touched off a wave of severe dissension among the student body. Most were horrified at what happened, but some felt that it was just "another Women's Center plot to get at the Clubs," since some of them were all-male. Specific participants in the march were continually harassed and threatened by phone, and a group of male students went through a section of campus yelling, "We can rape anybody we want."

However, the administrative and student response to this incident was much different than the one before. We had all become more sensitive and aware. The University was asked to officially make a statement about the incidents, and the dean of students circulated a letter condemning the student reaction to the march. Another march was scheduled to take place, and even the faculty showed their support by signing a petition supporting the cause and urging administrators and officials to attend this next march. Nearly 400 people showed up for it, including top administrators and people from the town community who wanted to show their disgust at the previous march's reception. Even a few of the offenders from that first march were there to apologize publicly for what they had done. That night, a catharsis occurred that had been building up since people finally decided that it had gone too far when an effort by survivors to empower themselves and to express their constitutional rights to free speech and assembly had been negated so brutally. Students began saying that, no matter what they thought previously, they did not want to be associated with an institution that tolerated intolerance. These same students finally forced the university to state its stance on this kind of behavior. The second march proceeded down that same street again, this time in silence, bearing candles, and being greeted by the clubs with candles of their own. People realized that this was bigger than an "us-against-them" battle; this was struggle for human dignity and decency.

It is regrettable that it took the extremes of the continuum from sexual harassment to rape to bring this kind of awareness to the student body, but finally, at last, the problem has been recognized for what it really is: an insidious crime that totally alters the academic and social atmosphere on a campus, where environment is extremely important to be able to concentrate and learn. Already, women at Princeton are at a disadvantage due to the male:female ratio (3:1). In classroom situations, I have been the only woman and the only minority out of a class of 20, and have had to sit through sessions of man-talk and jokes such as "Men only put women up on pedestals so that they can look up their dresses," or that a man isn't really a man until he has had sex with a black or hispanic woman. I'm supposed to laugh at this coming from a teacher or assistant, or femininely demur from as being too off-color for a woman's tastes. I've talked with second and third-year women who, in their first year, had been at a party at a social club, and had had her breast squeezed by a drunken male student on the dance floor. Others around her said "he's drunk; he didn't mean it" and she finally put it out of her mind. But years later, it came back to disturb her because of the recent incidents. So if you want to talk impact of sexual harassment and assault on the college campuses, I've got something to talk about. If you want to talk about lasting effects and hindered communications, I've got things to talk about. Because the impact of those experiences last has also made progress.

Many of the suggestions from the memo that the Women's Center Task Force on Sexual Harassment sent to the administration were acted upon, and Princeton University has hired a Sexual Harassment/Sexual Assault Counselor. The policies and procedures for responding to an incident have been changed to a great extent, from the time that campus security may be involved on up to the actual committee meetings and formal hearings. A more centralized and efficient system, sensitive to the complexities of the incident, is being formulated. But first of all, before any of this restructuring took place, the institution had to be convinced to listen to student input. Tragically, it took extreme cases to make that point clear, but at least now it has been made, and realized as valid.

10

Investigating Complaints of Sexual Harassment

Helen Remick, Jan Salisbury, Donna Stringer, and *Angela Ginorio*

Sexual harassment is a major problem in higher education. While promulgation of policy and good educational efforts on sexual harassment are effective responses to sexual harassment, they increase the likelihood that complaints of sexual harassment will be brought. How complaints are handled determines whether others will bring complaints and whether legal action will follow. If complaints are handled fairly and in a timely manner, virtually all complainants and alleged harassers will accept the process. Word will circulate that complaints are taken seriously and handled well. An effective complaint process will encourage genuine complaints, discourage complainants from going to outside agencies, and deter potential harassers. Bungled complaints will discourage potential complainants from seeking on-campus relief, sending them to outside agencies, and signal harassers that they can continue their behaviors with impunity. When cases go to court, everyone loses (McMillen, 1987, 1, 13-15).

Sexual harassment is a type of gender based discrimination and must be understood within the context of power and inequality of opportunity (Walker *et al.*, 1985; see also Shullman and Watts in this volume). Because it involves sexuality, the investigation of sexual harassment complaints presents a number of challenges. Sexual harassment is not like other forms of discrimination; the offending behaviors are seen as intimate and sexual, therefore difficult to discuss. While other forms of discrimination often involve rejection of a person, accompanied by a refusal to interact, sexual harassment is typified by a refusal to leave someone alone. Each case is unique, requiring a specially tailored response; it is important to be sensitive to the differences in each situation and to avoid trying to use exactly the same response to each complainant. This emphasis on the need for individualized responses does not preclude an understanding of sexual harassment as discrimination against an entire class of people.

This chapter proposes investigative and organizational strategies to address sexual harassment complaints in the context of sex discrimination. The practices have evolved over a decade, and the authors have applied them in a variety of settings.

GENERAL ISSUES

Confidentiality

Investigations need to be confidential, with information transmitted outside of the investigation on a need to know basis only. The need for confidentiality is essential to protect the rights of those claiming discrimination as well as those of the alleged harasser. This need may appear to conflict with the need of the institution to publicize its willingness to take active steps in resolving sexual harassment complaints; informal information systems, however, are very effective in disseminating information about the existence of and response to sexual harassment complaints. These same informal systems pass the word when complaints of harassment are not acted upon and keep complaints from being made in-house, forcing them to outside agencies.

Those with responsibility for hearing complaints of sexual harassment must at the same time be mindful that in the face of a lawsuit, all notes, reports and other written materials are likely to be open to discovery (that is, must be produced when subpoenaed and are then part of the court record). Institutional lawyers may be able to argue successfully that: such materials should be kept confidential because of demonstrable physical danger to those who made reports; that people are often only willing to make reports under assurances of confidentiality (documentation probably would need to exist that the person interviewed said that he or she needed confidentiality); and that a breach of that confidentiality will interfere with the ability of the institution to address civil rights violations (Cole, 1987). However, the general trend recently in cases involving higher education has been towards discoverability of most documents. Further, in some states and for public institutions, there may be a question as to which records are accessible under public disclosure or freedom of information laws. For these reasons, persons taking complaints should indicate that they will assure confidentiality to their best ability, and should make sure that information kept in files is in a form that they could defend to others.

Working with Unions

If any part of your workforce is unionized, administrators with responsibility for sexual harassment should carefully read and understand the union contracts. Notification rights should be identified. Typically contracts give members the right to have a union representative at any meeting, including investigatory interviews, which could lead to a disciplinary action.

In sexual harassment cases, it is important to keep in mind that the role of the union is to represent its members in disciplinary actions taken by administrators. Investigations take place *before* any disciplinary action and have as their purpose to ascertain whether discipline is appropriate. Union members can certainly have a union representative present during the investigatory interview, but there is otherwise no role for the union until disciplinary action is proposed. At that point, administrators should be sure to follow the processes outlined in the union contract, as it would be to follow procedures determined by a faculty senate, civil service rules, or other formal procedures (Olswang, 1987).

Most unions will examine both the facts and the procerss used in a case. If the union believes a member has been guilty of sexual harassment it would most likely advise the member not to pursue an appeal or a grievance. If, on the other hand, the facts clearly indicated that the union member had committed sexual harassment but had been disciplined too severely or without appropriate process the union would defend the member in an appeal of the discipline or process. If the member wishes to pursue an appeal against the advice of the union, the union is obligated to defend the member.

Sexual harassment charges put unions in a difficult role. Unions represent members in disputes with employers; this means that the union is bound to represent the alleged harasser. Other union members, especially women, are often outraged when the union takes this position in a sexual harassment case. Unions need to take special care in explaining what their role is and to take other actions, such as special training for shop stewards, to indicate that they oppose sexual harassment in the work place.

Administrators should work with union leadership to establish relationships such that the union will bring sexual harassment issues to management's attention when reported first to the union. Some unions may wish to handle complaints of sexual harassment of members like any employee grievance. This approach has several important drawbacks. First, the persons charged with responsibility for union grievances are unlikely to have the special sensitivities necessary in many sexual harassment complaints. Second, grievance procedures usually have very short limitations on timeliness of complaints; very often complaints must be made within 15 or 30 days of the time of the alleged offense. Experience with sexual harassment complaints indicates that many are not brought that rapidly. Third, to limit complaints to such a short time period creates a conflict with the federal laws allowing for complaints of discrimination within 6 months of the alleged offense. Administrations would do best to negotiate with the unions to allow sexual harassment complaints to go through institutional, not grievance, procedures.

Institutional Placement

The person with responsibility for hearing and/or investigating charges of sexual harassment must have sufficient credibility and access to power so that appropriate actions can be taken. It is helpful as well if they are in jobs where students and others are likely to look for them. Metha and Nigg (1983, 11) found that members of the educational community saw affirmative action and deans' offices as the most likely places to go to report sexual harassment. Biaggio et al. (1987) indicate that affirmative action offices are usually the offices with these responsibilities, and suggest widespread efforts on campus to let others who might get reports of sexual harassment know which office has responsibility.

Affirmative action officers are appropriate to receive complaints against faculty only if they have responsibility for faculty matters, and have enough credibility within the system that a finding of sexual harassment would be taken seriously and result in appropriate action. Where affirmative action officers do not have responsibilities for issues related to faculty or are otherwise not appropriate, a tenured faculty member or senior administrator, with appropriate release time to meet these additional responsibilities, should be appointed to deal with complaints against faculty.

It may also be appropriate to have separate persons or offices responsible for informal as opposed to formal complaints. At the University of Washington, for example, a faculty member with 25 percent release time listens to informal complaints against faculty members. The affirmative action officer, who reports to the provost, is responsible for taking all other complaints. See discussions below on formal and informal complaints.

GENERAL APPROACHES

Committees

We recommend against the use of committees to deal with sexual harassment complaints (Remick, 1986). Committees are a familiar part of campus life and seem to be preferred for dealing with sexual harassment where some groups on campus do not trust the administration to handle complaints effectively. A committee can be useful in identifying administrative policy problems and solutions, but should not be used for individual complaints.

Committees have several drawbacks. First, such a process assumes that no special skills are needed to counsel those with complaints or to investigate them. Second, committees never respond rapidly to complaints: meetings must be arranged to deal with cases, people are busy and have schedules which are difficult to coordinate, and meetings may seem impossible during semester breaks, summers, etc. Third, since the committees function outside of the proper chain of command for disciplinary actions, they are not in a position to take appropriate actions when harassment is found. Fourth, too many people know what has happened or is allged to have happened, and it is very difficult to maintain appropriate levels of confidentiality. Dziech and Weiner (1984, 159-160) give an excellent example of pitfalls of committees.

If the campus community does not trust administrators to address sexual harassment, then that is the issue to be addressed. If the fault lies with an affirmative action officer who is not trusted, then that person should be replaced. If an investigation can be competently conducted but no action taken, then look for ways to make the top administration more responsive to the issue.

Administrators who have groups clamoring for a committee should appoint a responsible person or persons to investigate sexual harassment complaints. They should then be prepared to support these persons when they investigate a complaint and take appropriate action if there is a finding that harassment has occurred. In order to build campus trust, administrators should make periodic informal reports to an appropriate group (*e.g.*, faculty senate or committee on status of women), recognizing the need for protection of names but letting them know that action has been taken. These steps will relieve pressure for committee structure by establishing trust that administration will take appropriate action.

Use of Investigators

Investigations take special skills. In-house complaints may or may not end up at an outside enforcement agency or in court. Whoever conducts investigations should be aware of the standards applied by outside agencies and the reasons for them and should be aware of when and why he or she deviates from the standards. (Lebrato, 1986; CUPA, 1986).

Each complaint and investigation brings something new to one's knowledge of sexual harassment and investigative techniques. If possible, the same persons should have responsibility for investigation so that they can learn from each experience and improve their methods. Small campuses may want to assign these duties to the same person for each complaint, while large campuses will probably want to have full time investigators.

Formal and Informal Complaints

Many institutions appear to consider complaints to be informal if they are not committed to writing, and to require a written complaint for formal action. In this approach, institutions may take the position that they cannot act on a sexual harassment complaint unless the victim is willing to submit a formal written complaint. The reasoning given is that if the victim is not willing to come forth and have his or her name attached to the complaint, then the institution has no grounds for proceeding. To act on an unwritten complaint, it is assumed, would violate the rights of the alleged harasser.

This reasoning ignores the legal guidelines. The U.S. Equal Employment Opportunity Commission (EEOC) guidelines on sexual harassment make clear that in the employment area, the employer is liable for any harassment by a supervisor, whether or not the employer has knowledge that it has occurred. Further, the employer is liable for harassment by co-workers or outsiders when the employer knows or could reasonably be expected to know that the harassment has occurred. (EEOC regulations do not always apply directly to relationships between faculty and students because there may not exist an employment relationship; however, it can be assumed by analogy that such laws as Title IX of the Education amendments would apply similar standards.) This means that once a situation is brought to the attention of the institution, whether to an affirmative action officer, someone in personnel, or a department chair (among others), the institution then knows of the situation and legal liability exists. Should a person refuse to sign a statement, then later sue, claiming that the institution knew of the situation but did nothing to keep it from continuing, the institution would be hard pressed to say that it has a policy on the issue, knew of this complaint, but did not act because their procedures for formal complaints were not exactly followed.

Legal requirements do not rule out the possibility of informal actions. We would differentiate instead informal and formal actions by their outcome and whether there is an investigation. Informal complaints may or may not be written, are not investigated, and do not result in formal disciplinary actions. Persons complained against may agree to actions such as apologies, demotions, or voluntary resignations, without going through formal disciplinary procedures. Formal complaints, on the other hand, must be written whether by the complainant or by someone else and agreed to by the complainant, require an investigation, and result in formal disciplinary action if it is found that harassment has taken place. Price Spratlen (1987) says that informal complaints can best be characterized as educational in intent for both the complainant and the alleged harasser, while formal complaints are more legal in nature.

Institution Initiated Complaints

If the complainant hesitates to proceed with a complaint but all indications are that a serious problem exists, consider an institution-initiated complaint. In cases of serious allegations where we had difficulty getting an individual to bring a complaint, we have initiated complaints on behalf of the institution. These were cases in which we had reason to believe there was a problem, and the investigation took place on the institution's behalf, in order to assess whether liability existed. This shift of responsibility for the initiation of the investigation from the individual to the institution relieved the fears of alleged victims such that they fully cooperated with us even though they had been reluctant to bring a complaint. This procedure protects the institution in those situations where a problem has been brought to its attention, thus creating potential legal liability. If a problem exists, the institution then has sufficient information to proceed with corrective action, and if the allegations are unfounded, the institution can demonstrate that it has investigated the situation and has reason to believe no action is necessary.

Ombudsman

Johnson and Shuman (1983) and Meek and Lynch (1983) found that students will avail themselves of informal complaint mechanisms, while they are hesitant to bring formal complaints. An ombudsman can play an important role in listening to and resolving informal complaints against faculty. We offer the following as a model which has been very successful for us (Price Spratlen, 1987). Such a person should be a female tenured faculty member with a background providing counseling skills. The ombudsman can be available by phone or in person to talk about possible sexual harassment situations. Some complainants will choose to use phone contact only in order to preserve their anonymity. The ombudsman helps the complainant clarify the issues surrounding the harassment, defines terms, listens, and provides advice. At the time of an in-person meeting, the ombudsman may ask the complainant to write down what has happened, so that the complainant and the ombudsman can better understand what happened.

Most often, when the harassment is not of a serious nature, the complainant will only want to talk to a knowledgable person and plan what action to take herself or himself. In these cases, the ombudsman will give advice; she also will follow up by phone in several weeks to be sure the situation is resolved.

When more intervention is needed, the ombudsman will agree to talk to the faculty member and his or her chair. In this procedure, the ombudsman calls the faculty member to her office; she explains the behavior that has been described to her and asks whether the faculty member agrees that it occurred. In our experience, faculty members agree on the stated behavior about 90 percent of the time, though there is usually disagreement on what the behavior meant.

The ombudsman may ask the faculty members to write down their version of the situation as well; some are willing to do so, while others may agree to read the statement made by the complainant and signed that they agree that the situation was as described. The ombudsman looks for resolution of the situation, as appropriate: sometimes nothing more is required than this conversation, and sometimes she holds meetings bringing together the faculty member, the complainant, and the chair of the department or dean. In the latter meetings, the ombudsman offers the complainant a "safe" place to let the faculty member know how he or she feels about the behavior and what effect it had on his or her well-being. If serious harassment is described or the harasser is a repeater, official disciplinary action might be called for, and the ombudsman turns the case over to the provost for formal investigation.

Formal Investigations

Formal investigations are necessary whenever: (1) a formal complaint has been received; (2) the complaint (formal or informal) is about an alleged harasser against whom previous charges have been filed; or (3) when the nature of the complaint (formal or informal) is of such a nature that the alleged sexual harassment may lead to disciplinary actions. Because higher education institutions often have little experience with formal investigations, this topic is treated in detail below.

CHARACTERISTICS OF A GOOD INVESTIGATOR

Institutional Considerations

The investigator or investigative unit should report directly to the person who will determine the institutional response. It is essential that the investigator be aware of and try to minimize his or her departmental loyalties or dislikes when carrying out investigative responsibilities. At the same time, the investigator must also be sensitive to the "culture" of the institution and recognize that persons in certain kinds of jobs or at certain levels will need to be treated differently to get to the same end (*i.e.*, resolution of a complaint). For example, an investigator can usually get pictures of nude women off the walls in the motor pool by going to a supervisor who can order the pictures removed, but will need a different approach to get a faculty member to remove from his door an art print showing people in fifty coital positions.

Investigator Credibility

A key to effective investigations is the credibility of investigators. Investigators must conduct their inquiries, write their reports and make recommendations in objective, clear language so that the institution, the alleged harasser and the alleged victim can trust that they are being treated fairly.

Credibility will be achieved largely by remaining neutral while providing necessary support to all involved. This means that an investigator cannot allow any of the parties to pressure her/him to reveal confidential information, to become an advocate for anyone involved, or to "take sides" in a final report or recommendations. Language in written material should be based on findings as they relate to the law and the facts, not to an investigator's personal feelings.

The investigator must also be honest. If the institution has failed, management must be so informed. If the investigation yields information that an employee has experienced poor treatment but not discriminatory harassment, the complaining employee should be told this in straight-forward language which does not lead her/him to believe or hope that allegations will be supported in a final report. While employees never like being told their allegations are without support, our experience is they prefer to have this information as early and as candidly as possible so they don't continue pursuing a "lost cause."

The need for credibility suggests that a primary criterion for good investigators is the ability to be fair and candid, without allowing personal feelings to interfere with effectiveness. Once an investigator has achieved a reputation for fairness, both the investigative office and the institution will become a place where members of the university community will go to resolve sexual harassment situations.

Sensitivity to Hierarchy

Dealing with complaints of sexual harassment requires a delicate approach. Some may argue for egalitarian treatment, where all complaints are handled in the same fashion. This will not work. The rules associated with disciplinary action against faculty are different from those against staff or students, and treatment of sexual harassment must parallel existing procedures. It is difficult enough to approach someone who has been accused of sexual harassment because of th personal nature of the complaint and the need to watch for false accusations; one does not need to compound the situation by breaching the written code and social etiquette of the institution. Faculty members should be approached on these topics by other faculty members, persons with Ph.D.s, or others seen as peers, because status inequality can have subtle but strong effects. For example, if the investigator is too deferential to faculty and does not ask hard questions, the investigation will be hampered because essential information may not be uncovered. On the other hand, a faculty member who feels educationally superior to an investigator may accuse anyone questioning his or her authority of being a bully or violating his or her civil rights; likewise, an investigator who feels inferior to a faculty member might try to bully him or her to demonstrate power. Thus an investigation may be hampered either by friction or deference resulting from status inequality.

Persons investigating complaints against or by staff persons must be aware of any civil service or other personnel rules. These rules will set limits on possible remedies.

Sensitivity to Issues

Investigators *must* be able to relate well to a wide variety of persons, so that complainants and respondents will talk to them. First, they should have the ability to think and talk about sexuality and deviant behavior. Because of the high incidence of sexual abuse in our culture and the associations sexual harassment brings to this abuse, the investigators must be prepared and able to listen to stories about incest, rape and battering. Second, the investigator must not: criticize the complainant for not being aggressive enough in response to the alleged harassment, openly identify with the complainant, or apologize for or criticize the behavior of all men. Third, a knowledge of psychological theory appears helpful, though those with counseling training must exercise care not to become a "counselor" to persons who clearly need help. Investigators must maintain a distance from all parties so that they can make a reasoned judgment about the nature, legal issues, and resolution of the complaint, *and* be upheld as objective by others such as judges, hearing officers, etc.

Men or Women as Investigators

The question inevitably arises as to whether males or females should do the investigating. Sexual harassment is about sexual behavior, attitudes and beliefs about sex. There is a strong reluctance on the part of many women to discuss sexual matters with men, especially ones they do not know. We found this reluctance to be so strong that it interfered with the investigation. For example, women are likely to tell a man that another man has propositioned her; she is more likely to tell another woman that the harasser repeatedly asked her "if she wanted to fuck." Propositions come in many forms and are more or less socially acceptable. If the complainant is unwilling or unable to tell an investigator what actually happened, the investigator cannot judge the seriousness of the event.

In addition, men and women do not necessarily share the same sense of how severe or damaging a behavior has been (Gutek, 1985). For example, in one case the harasser had on several occasions grabbed a woman's hand and placed it on his erect penis. On another occasion, he had propositioned a woman in an elevator, she had said no, he had followed her to her room, grabbed and forcefully kissed her, and then left. Men tended to see the first behavior as the more offensive, while women tended to react to the second as a scenario for rape and therefore far more serious and frightening.

When staffing and workload permit, we have concluded that the best approach to investigating sexual harassment is to have an interview team of a male and female, which provides the benefit of both perspectives simultaneously. Outside of the interview situation, each can use the other for occasional reality checks and for support. "Mixed" teams do not seem to interfere with reporting; the interviewee simply tends to make eye contact with the same sex person while answering sensitive questions. For the female complainant, the team approach offers a "safer" environment than talking about sex to a strange man.

Personal Needs

Investigators must not go into this kind of work if they have a strong need to be liked or to have their work appreciated. No matter what the outcome of a case is, someone and possibly everyone will be angry. The alleged harasser may continue to deny that he or she did anything wrong and may accuse the investigators of being overzealous, on witch hunts, man haters, etc. The complainant may be satisfied with the outcome but anxious to forget everything about the situation, including the work of the investigator. The complainant may not be satisfied with the outcome and may blame the investigator for not doing more. Sometimes the final outcome determined by the institution will be less than the investigator recommended. The investigator must take comfort in knowing that he or she did the best that could be done. If the investigator finds that he or she too often does not get management support in these cases, the investigator should consider why: has the investigation been badly done; are reports clear enough; does management have a poor understanding of the psychological and legal aspects of harassment; or does management not care. In cases where management remains unresponsive, the investigator may need to consider a new employer.

Investigation of sexual harassment complaints, especially where the complainant has a past history of victimization and/or the alleged behavior of the harasser is far beyond acceptable bounds, can take a high toll on investigators. The investigators as well as the complainants are often forced to relive past traumas. It is common for women to experience anger not only at the alleged harasser, but also for any harassment or sexual trauma they had experienced in the past. We found that women investigators tend to take their anger home, and to experience varying levels of difficulties in relationships with men in their personal lives. This effect seems to be more pronounced in heterosexual women than lesbians. Men often become confused by what cultural heroes like Burt Reynolds, Errol Flynn or Don Juan have modelled as manly and what the law now defines as illegal. Male investigators may therefore experience a kind of "collective guilt" for the destructive behavior of men; they may feel guilty for past actions or fantasies. As with women, this guilt is taken home and complicates personal relationships. The men in the lives of the women investigators sometimes experience the same kind of guilt as do the men investigators. For these reasons, using a supportive team approach to investigating and resolving sexual harassment is helpful for personal survival and professional effectiveness.

INVESTIGATIONS

Investigator Autonomy

Institutional leadership must be prepared to give investigators the autonomy and power they need to do a good investigation. It is important for the investigator to remember his or her role: on behalf of the institution, the investigator is trying to find the facts and remedies in order for the institution to make the best possible decision as to how to respond to the complaint. Institutional interests include maintaining morale and productivity as well as limiting legal liability; decisions to cover up incidents of sexual harassment, or failure to find or take seriously existing problems are not in the best interest of the institution. While he or she works on behalf of the institution, the investigator does not represent the complainant or the respondent (the person accused of discrimination). In the gathering of facts and assessment of the situation, the investigator should strive to be seen as a fair, neutral third party; it may be necessary to remind others involved in the investigation of this neutral role.

Complaint Intake: Part 1

If an investigator knows from initial phone contact that a person with a sexual harassment complaint is coming in, he or she should set aside a two hour period for the first interview. If two persons will be investigating the complaint, both should be present at the initial interview. This interview should ascertain: what behaviors occurred and approximately when; who else knows about the behaviors or may have experienced similar incidents; who in management or supervision has been notified of the situation and what they did; and what the complainant expects as an outcome (*e.g.*, for the behavior to stop, counselling, back wages). The investigators should be prepared for this session to be very emotional. This emotional level may be the result of trauma created by the sexual harassment. The complainant may also have concerns about the effects of reporting on work place interactions, the responses of friends and family, and the possible impact on his or her career and personal reputation.

Complainants may have other experiences which add to the trauma of sexual harassment. Because the incidence of sexual abuse is so high in the general population, many complainants, especially women, may have been sexually abused at some previous time in their lives. Sexual harassment of a person who has previously experienced abuse will often cause that person to relive those traumas. In addition, many harassers seem to choose vulnerable persons as their victims. It is very common to find that complainants are in the midst of such major life changes as divorce, a recent death in the family, or a move to a new town and/or job with the accompanying isolation from friends and relatives.

Investigators should ask complainants not to discuss the complaint with others in order to lessen the probability of retaliation and to avoid influencing other witnesses. Even after such advice, the complainant is likely to talk to others. This breach may have several outcomes. First, other victims and/or witnesses often come forward after they hear that someone else has initiated a complaint. Second, the emotional effect on other witnesses is often lessened if they are expecting to be contacted as a witness and have had time to prepare themselves to talk about the alleged harassment.

Most complaints are serious, yet complainants will often conclude their recitation of facts with a request that nothing be done—they don't want to hurt the harasser or endanger their own situation (Gutek, 1985). Investigators should make it clear that the institution has an obligation to make the environment free of such situations and that legally the investigators cannot ignore the complaint nor can they ignore their knowledge of the situation even if a complaint is not brought formally. The parties may decide at this time whether to pursue the complaint as a formal one requiring a written resolution, or as an informal complaint.

Complaint Intake: Part 2

The complainant will often call the next day to say that she or he has thought about it overnight and wants to withdraw the complaint. Again the investigator will need to explain that he or she takes the complaint seriously, the alleged behavior is not acceptable to the institution and should not be occurring in the work environment, and the institution wants it to stop and will proceed with an investigation, either formal or informal. The legal liabilities of the institution do not give investigators the option of ignoring a complaint once it has been brought to their attention. If the investigator assures the complainant that the issue is important and that the investigator will offer as much protection as possible against retaliation, the complainant will usually agree to proceed and be willing to attest to the discriminatory acts. This reluctance to follow through on the complaint may occur several times.

Notification

Notification should be limited to a need to know basis. For example, the appropriate supervisors of the complainant and alleged harasser should be notified that a complaint has been received and an investigation is taking place because he or she need to know why the complainant's performance or emotional state may not be up to usual standards, that no disciplinary actions should be taken against the complainant or alleged harasser without consultation with the investigators, and that investigators may be talking to other members of the department. Should the immediate supervisor be the person accused of harassment, then that person's supervisor should be the person informed. If the alleged harasser is in a different department from the complainant, his or her supervisor should be notified as well. This notification is essential because the supervisor should know the complainant and alleged harasser will be absent for interviews and may have changes in their performance; watch for further situations of harassment; prevent retaliation against the complainant; and be given a chance to give to the investigator any information of other incidents of harassment.

The respondent should also be notified that a complaint has been lodged against him or her. He or she should be asked to meet with the investigators at the investigators' office as soon as possible. The investigators should prepare for the meeting by reviewing the material from the intake interview and making a list of items to be covered. The list should include that the institution takes complaints seriously and that a complaint has been brought against the respondent. Describe the behaviors alleged by the complainant and ask the respondent whether the described behaviors occurred. In our experience, the respondent often admits that the behaviors occurred, though there may be some difference in interpretation of intent or severity. After the behavior has been described and possibly agreed to, *then* it should be labelled as sexual harassment and unacceptable.

Interviews

Interviews are rarely as straight-forward as the above descriptions might indicate. Investigators should be prepared to take the time to establish rapport with whomever they are talking to and to allow the conversation to "wander" on occasion. The idea is to get the needed information at some time, not to get it as fast and "efficiently" as possible. These interviews will be stressful to all involved. In order to reduce the stress and improve the effectiveness of the process, the investigators should allow time for getting acquainted and should expect a limited amount of small talk.

The investigator should contact other persons named by the complainant as possibly having information about the harassment. A list of items to be covered should be prepared before the interview, so that no important issues are missed. Again, however, the investigator should avoid overly structured interviews; important new information can come out during the discussion if the interviewer is able to establish an open, safe forum for conversation. Others in the environment should be interviewed as well, to see whether they have observed or experienced any harassing behavior. When asking questions, do not ask whether they have seen or experienced sexual harassment; the definition is so different to each individual, that specific behaviors should be referred to instead. For example, in interviews we have had persons say that they had not experienced sexual harassment from a certain person, while at the same time stating that he had regularly propositioned them, touched them or others, or told offensive jokes. The interviewer should be sure that by the end of the interview the interviewees understand the legal definition of sexual harassment and which behaviors are not acceptable; this is best done by giving the interviewees a written definition and taking time to explain any part of it that may not be clear.

The use of tape recorders is not recommended; they make most persons self-conscious and uncomfortable even under the best of circumstances, and these interviews will be tense enough without an added impediment. Acceptability of note-taking depends on institutional culture, the perceived status of the interviewers and the type of person being interviewed. For example, note taking is routine in many professional settings and may not be noticed, while in blue-collar settings a notebook might be viewed with mistrust. With two interviewers, it is possible for one to be asking questions while the other is taking notes without being too obvious; it is important that they alternate in these roles so that the notetaker is perceived as a professional part of the investigative team, not a secretary. Be sensitive to what is acceptable and appropriate.

Referrals to Counseling

The complainant is likely to be very emotional and in need of strong support. The best support an investigator can provide is information on the process, acknowledgement of the legitimacy of emotions felt, and referrals to appropriate resources. The investigator may wish to ask the complainant whether she or he has people outside of the institution to talk to and may suggest that the person seek emotional support, even including counseling, if necessary—making it clear that she or he is not crazy but will need support because of their feelings about the harassment and because the investigation and resolution process will be stressful. Investigators should be very careful that this referral is not seen as validation that illegal sexual harassment has occurred, since at this point no conclusion has been reached. The investigators should be sensitive to the response of the complainant to the suggestion for counseling. There are wide differences in acceptability of counseling as an aid to problem-solving, based on such factors as education, race, age, social class, religious background and individual preference. Complainants who are not interested in counseling should not be pushed to receive it.

Institutions with employee assistance programs (EAPs) or student counseling programs may wish to make referrals of complainants and/or respondents to these services. Before this is done, evaluate whether the program is qualified to handle sexual harassment cases. For example, if the primary purpose of an EAP is alcoholism counseling, the staff may not be sensitive to the issues surrounding sexual harassment.

Commitments to Complainants

Investigators should beware of making commitments to the complainant. During investigations, investigators should not commit their institution to specific actions. Investigators will rarely have the authority to make such decisions, and those who can will want to wait until they have assessed whether sexual harassment has actually taken place and, if so, what the appropriate remedy is. An early commitment may be difficult to undo even should the investigators find later that the complaint has insufficient merit. If the investigation leads to the conclusion that counseling, for example, is appropriate, the employer can always pay for the counseling already received. While one may want to do what is best for all as rapidly as possible, one is dealing with a legal issue with potential liability. At the same time, should the early stages of investigation indicate that a serious problem exists and immediate corrective action is needed, it should be taken. This early commitment to solution will very often mitigate further economic and psychological damages and head off legal action by complainants.

Commitments to the Institution

Institutions must be willing to stay out of the way of the investigation and avoid pressuring the investigators to find no discrimination. The results of the investigation should be evaluated with an open mind, and no retaliation should be taken against the investigator for finding evidence of sexual harassment. Ignoring the situation after an investigation has shown harassment increases employer liability, and actions against the investigator can result in suits by the investigator as well as the complainant. In a recent case in Idaho, a personnel director who had been fired after finding that the owner of the business had sexually harassed an employee was awarded $1.4 million in a law suit (Shepard, 1987).

A good investigation lays the groundwork for a good resolution. An institution with the facts can clearly determine whether a problem exists and what, if any, actions are appropriate. Should corrective actions be needed, the institution can determine what to do for the complainant and with the respondent. Whether or not the institution concludes a discriminatory act has occurred, administration may want to take actions to lessen tension in the department.

Complaint Resolution

External investigators are motivated to find the facts and make a clear finding of guilt or innocence that will hold up in a court of law. Their process tends to be to accumulate every fact, talk to every possible witness, and then to make a judgment. Internal investigators also need to know the facts, but only need to know enough to move to in-house resolution of an institutional problem. If resolution is not possible, then internal investigators must proceed to exhaustive external standards.

It is expedient to resolve complaints before a formal finding must be written. After several interviews, it usually becomes obvious whether there is a problem of sexual harassment. If the alleged harasser agrees that certain behaviors or incidents took place (even if he or she does not label them as harassment), or if the harasser disagrees but several other credible persons say that they experienced the same behaviors or saw them directed at someone else, then there is enough evidence to go forward (and too much not to act). If there is a situation of an allegation of one-on-one harassment which cannot be verified, then one can still act, but in a different fashion, usually by educating the alleged harasser as to what behaviors of his or hers may be open to misinterpretation and by warning the person as to what will happen if further reports are received. In these cases, the exact response made often depends heavily on the investigator's intuitive feeling about the merits of the complaint.

Each complaint should be treated on its own merit and in its own context: there is no formula or standard way to solve a problem. The investigators should assemble the facts and present them to the person in the position of authority. If all agree that they should proceed, they have several choices, depending on the severity of the harassment, the level or kind of complainant (e.g., civil service, unionized, management employees, student, or user of services), the institutional culture and the damage if any to the complainant and/or the institutional environment.

The nature of the harassment is an important factor in determining the damage to the complainant. The role power of the harasser to the complainant can also make a big difference in how hurt the complainant is by the harassment. The attitude of others, both in the institution and of acquaintances, and personal factors such as sources of stress and past history of sexual abuse add to the impact of sexual harassment. A harassment situation can be devastating or merely annoying. The investigators must listen and observe closely and be prepared to see very different reactions to seemingly similar situations.

DISCIPLINARY ACTION AND FOLLOW-UP

Disciplinary Action

If the situation is characterized by offensive remarks, with no threats implied, and a complainant who is annoyed but not damaged, one may act rapidly and simply. Tell the harasser to stop. Tell him or her that further reports will result in disciplinary action. Warn against any retaliatory action directed at the complainant. Follow up the conversation with a letter saying the same thing. In such a situation, this is the outcome which most complainants want and, in our experience, is very often enough. Sometimes this action can take place in the interview with the respondent; he or she agrees that the incidents took place (though, of course, there was no intent of harassment). There is then no need for further investigation, since there is no conflict over what took place.

If there are multiple victims of harassment or someone who has been badly hurt, stronger actions are called for. Consider suspension, transfer, or termination for the harasser and paid counseling or transfer for the victim.

The courts have taken a dim view of solutions which require all of the change by the victim (*e.g.*, the victim is put in a new, perhaps less desirable job, while the harasser stays put). Careful documentation is in order for disciplinary situations, to protect against legal action by the harasser and to show positive actions taken should there be legal action by the complainant.

Do not be driven by fear of legal action, especially by the alleged harasser. In our experience, they frequently threaten to sue; with many Americans, this threat has replaced the threat of bodily harm. No one can be stopped from suing. In dealing with the alleged harasser, the goal is not to avoid suits, but to avoid losing them. If an institution has done its homework well and has good documentation, it is not likely to lose a suit by a harasser.

If the serious harasser is also famous or a high producer, don't protect him or her. Other famous persons or high producers are in the labor market who are not harassers and therefore do not create a liability for the institution. The adverse publicity and the legal expenses of a sexual harassment case can far outweigh any other positive contribution of an individual.

In situations where the institutional culture prefers resignations, either because firing is difficult or "not done," call a meeting with the harasser, the investigators, and the responsible administrator. Suggest that the harasser bring along his or her attorney. Tell the harasser that the purpose of the meeting is to discuss the allegations informally, before a final report is prepared, and to review what has been discovered to date. Present the harasser and his or her attorney with a summary of findings: three promises of promotion in return for sex, five threats of failed examinations, one forced kiss and fondling, etc. There is no need to mention names. We have found this approach to be very successful. The harasser may or may not continue to deny the situation, but his or her attorney will be able to make a judgment as to what is in the best interest of the client. Resignations have followed these meetings.

Our resignations are not without ramification. During this session, we present to the harasser and the attorney a draft of a statement which we will give whenever asked for a letter of recommendation. The text is "You should know that at the time Dr. X resigned, he/she was under investigation for a charge of sexual harassment. Because of the resignation the investigation was terminated and there was no finding." Attorneys have agreed with this wording. The statement has two effects: it protects the organization from legal liability should an ex-employee go on to harass at a new job, and it protects the harasser by limiting what will be said to prospective employers. That is, we instruct the harasser's immediate supervisor and others likely to be asked for recommendations, that the statement is *all* that should be said; they are not to discuss any details about any allegations of harassment.

The investigator may find that the department or institution wants to take action against a harasser that appears disproportionate to the harassment incident. This most often occurs when the harasser has many deviant behaviors and work related problems, only one of which is sexual harassment. Alcoholism, drug abuse and/or mental illness are often involved and make these cases very complex. In these cases, the manager has been observing problems for a long time but has taken no action, usually out of a lack of information or ability with disciplinary actions. The harassment charge involves investigators from outside the department and gives the manager something specific on which to take disciplinary action. It is important that the sexual harassment program not get labelled as too punitive, overzealous, etc. because disciplinary actions are out of proportion. One should limit the discipline to that which is appropriate to the case in hand, and initiate separate disciplinary actions against the person for other non-harassment problems.

The Effects of the Investigation

Any investigation, and especially one involving discrimination such as sexual harassment, disrupts the particular setting. The act of interviewing sensitizes people to the general issue of sexual harassment and to their work or educational environment. They are forced to think about their attitudes and behavior and report their perceptions about the specific situation. They often feel obliged to "choose sides." It may be unavoidable that people will question the character, motivations and competence of both complainant and respondent.

Initiating an investigation raises the expectations of the complainant. While the person who complains knows intellectually that the outcome of the investigation may or may not support his or her allegations, there is an emotional expectation that the complainant's needs will be met. Even if the complaint is validated and appropriate actions are taken, the actions may not be enough for the complainant to feel vindicated.

In the course of conducting an investigation, the investigators may have disappointed, outraged and offended some people. For instance, some people look at sexual harassment as a purely interpersonal conflict and they feel that a formal legal investigation only serves to blow a small personal problem out of proportion. At the very least, many people resent outsiders investigating their group and take the asking of questions as an accusation of collective guilt. Professors are especially likely to see any questioning as inappropriate infringements to their autonomy and perhaps their academic freedom.

The effects of an investigation process on the alleged harasser vary greatly. The response may vary from social withdrawal to resignation or leave of absence. The person may also aggressively lobby for himself or herself and against others now identified as disloyal trouble makers.

Investigative contacts can include education about sexual harassment, investigations, and legal responsibilities and can do a great deal to help those involved to have realistic expectations and amore cooperative attitude. Moreover, it is important for interviewers to give specific guidelines to interviewees about what can be said about the interviews, to whom and why.

Investigators cannot solve all of these problems. However, they can be prepared and should report to appropriate administrators the kinds of problems they uncovered and suggest that steps be taken to solve them. Each institution will have its own approach to such issues, sometimes depending upon available funds, other times upon local customs. Actions can include bringing in organizational development specialists to look at unit functioning, referring individuals to counseling, bringing in counselors to work with the unit, special training programs either for individuals or the unit, or unit meetings to discuss problems. What is most important is that people surrounding an investigation be aware that problems will arise and that an effort be made to restore group cohesiveness and effectiveness.

CONCLUSION

Handling a complaint of sexual harassment in an institution of higher education requires a complex set of investigative organizational procedures and resources. This chapter describes a system of investigation which may be most likely to resolve a situation fairly, prevent further harassment, and mitigate harm to a complainant and liability to the institution.

References

Biaggio, Mary Kay, Watts, Deborah, and Brownell, Arlene. (1987). Contending with sexual harassment on campus: issues and impediments from a faculty and student perspective. Unpublished paper presented at the National Conference of the Association for Women in Psychology, Denver.

Cole, Elsa Kircher. (1987). Assistant Attorney General, University of Washington. Personal communication, December 3.

Dziech, Billie Wright, and Weiner, Linda. (1984). The Lecherous Professor. Boston: Beacon Press. (159-160)

College and University Personnel Association. (1986). Sexual Harassment: Issues and Answers. Washington, D.C.: College and University Personnel Association.

Gutek, Barbara A. (1985). Sex and the workplace. San Francisco: Jossey-Bass.

Johnson, Michael P. and Shuman, Susan. (1983). Sexual harassment of students at the Pennsylvania State University. Unpublished paper, Department of Sociology, Pennsylvania State University.

Lebrato, Mary T., Editor. (1986). Help yourself: a manual for dealing with sexual harassment. Sacramento: Sexual Harassment in Employment Project of the California Commission on the Status of Women.

McMillen, Liz. (1987). The residue from academics' lawsuits: Often anguish for everyone involved. *The Chronicle of Higher Education*, April 1, 1987, 1, 12-15.

Meek, P.M. and Lynch, A.Q. (1983). Establishing an informal grievance procedure for cases of sexual harassment of students. *Journal of the National Association for Women Deans, Administrators, and Counselors.* 46(2):30-33.

Metha, Arlene and Nigg, Joanne. (1983). Sexual harassment on campus: an institutional response. *Journal of the National Association for Women Deans, Administrators, and Counselors.* 46(2):9-15.

Olswang, Steven. (1987). Vice Provost, University of Washington. Personal communication, December 21.

Remick, Helen. (1986). Issues in implementation of a sexual harassment policy. In *Prevention of Sexual Harassment in Academe*, Lois Price Spratlen, Editor, 17-25. Seattle: University of Washington Office for Equal Employment Opportunity.

Price Spratlen, Lois. (1987). Ombudsman for Sexual Harassment, University of Washington. Personal communication, December 21.

Shepard, Ira Michael. Personnel director recovers $1.4 million for wrongful discharge. CUPA News, July 10, 1987, 3.

Walker, Gilliam, Erickson, Lynda, Woolsey, Loretta. (1985). Sexual harassment: ethical research and clinical implications in the academic setting. *International Journal of Women's Studies*, 8:424-33, September/October.

11

Addressing Sexual Harassment:
Strategies for Prevention and Change

Mary Kay Biaggio, Deborah Watts, and *Arlene Brownell*

Recent studies suggest that sexual harassment is a significant problem on university campuses. Dziech and Weiner (1984), after reviewing available surveys, conclude that 20 to 30 percent of female students report sexual harassment during their college years, though rates vary according to specific categories of harassment, such as generalized sexist remarks, seductive behavior, sexual bribery, sexual coercion, or sexual assult (Fitzgerald and Shullman, 1985). Whilte ample evidence indicates that sexual harassment is a serious and widespread problem (Till, 1980), the majority of instances of harassment go unreported (Swecker, 1985). In fact, victims are likely to report only severe levels of harassment (Sullivan, Redner, and Bogat, 1985), even though harassment at any level of severity is not likely to stop without some action taken on the part of the victim (Benson and Thomson, 1982; Sandler and Associates, 1981). Further, when instances of harassment are confronted or when complaints are filed, it is often difficult to satisfactorily redress the problem or prevent similar reoccurrences.

Benson and Thomson (1982) note that harassment has numerous adverse effects on female students: self-doubt, loss of confidence in academic ability, disillusionment and cautiousness with male faculty, and suspicion of male instructors. Unfortunately, many victims report that they cope with harassment by avoiding or dropping classes, avoiding the perpetrator, bringing friends to meetings with the professor, mentioning boyfriends or partners to demonstrate lack of interest in the harasser's actions, attempting to ignore the behavior, switching majors, or dropping out of the program (Adams, Kottke, and Padgitt, 1983; Benson and Thomson, 1982; Dziech and Weiner, 1984). Thus, harassment may result in

significant costs to female students—often limiting their academic opportunities.

This chapter discusses several issues raised when university faculty
and student affairs staff address occurrences of sexual harassment of female
students on university campuses. (It is recognized that males may be victims
of sexual harassment; the focus here is on female victims of harassment.)
Sullivan et al. (1985), in a survey of 219 undergraduate women, found that
women believed that victims of harassment were more likely to report to a
woman versus a man, and were more likely to report problems to someone
outside of the perpetrator's department. It has been our experience that this
is generally true. Thus, it behooves university personnel at all levels, and
especially women, to be prepared to deal with reports of harassment. In
order to responsibly and effectively address the occurrence of sexual
harassment on campus, possible actions must be thought through carefully.
In this chapter we will examine issues and possible strategies that can be
employed to effectively contend with the problem of sexual harassment as it
affects university students. Though the focus here is on strategies that can
be employed in the university setting, many of the strategies may be
applicable to other settings as well.

Sexual harassment has been defined in a variety of ways. The Equal
Employment Opportunity Commission defines sexual harassment as
unwelcome sexual advances, requests for sexual favors, and other verbal or
physical conduct of a sexual nature and asserts that such occurrences
constitute unlawful sex discrimination under certain circumstances. The
National Advisory Council on Women's Educational Programs argues that
"Academic sexual harassment is the use of authority to emphasize the
sexuality or sexual identity of a student in a manner which prevents or
impairs that student's full enjoyment of educational benefits, climate or
opportunities" (Till, 1980, 7). Indiana State University's official policy
states that "sexual harassment is definfed as: (1) sexual contact of any
nature which is not fully and mutually agreeable to both partiets; (2) any
verbal, written, or pictorial communication of a sexual nature, which has
the effect of intimidating the person or persons receiving the communication; and (3) unwelcome sexual advances, requests or contacts of any
nature, when such acts are intended to be or have the effect of being the
basis for either implicitly or explicitly imposing favorable or adverse terms
and conditions of employment or academic standing" (Indiana State
University, 1981, AH-11). Each of these definitions focuses on the sexual
nature of the advance, whether it be physical, pictorial, or verbal, though
the extent to which the definitions address legality or possible outcomes
varies.

THE EFFECTS OF UNIVERSITY POLICIES
ON REPORTING AND PROCESSING

There are a number of ways in which policies can impede or facilitate fair disposal of harassment complaints. For instance, restrictive and technical definitions of sexual harassment may not take into account the more subtle and insidious forms of harassment. The way in which harassment is defined will affect the institution's policy and procedures.

> Definitions of sexual harassment are important because they can educate the community and promote discussion and conscientious evaluation of behavior and experience. Students learn that certain experiences are officially recognized as wrong and punishable; professors are put on notice about behaviors that constitute sexual harassment; and administrators shape their understanding of the problem in a way that directs their actions on student inquiries and complaints. A definition can set the tone for the university community's response to sexual harassment. (Crocker, 1983, 697)

For a comprehensive analysis of university definitions of sexual harassment and the implications of these definitions for policy, the reader is referred to Crocker (1983) and Somers (1982).

According to the Equal Employment Opportunity Commission it is the employer's responsibility to prevent and redress sexual harassment. On the university campus, the Affirmative Action Office is usually charged with the execution of this responsibility. However, level of commitment to affirmative actions principles varies widely, and many affirmative action officers have lost status and influence during the past five years because of the Reagan Administration's civil rights policies (Evans, 1985). Further, since it is typically faculty, staff, or counselors who first learn of specific occurrences of harassment, it behooves them to be aware of university policies and the Affirmative Action Officer's role in the system. It must be recognized that not all universities appoint an Affirmative Action Officer and, among those institutions which do appoint an officer, she/he may be vested with little authority. A further issue is that the Affirmative Action Officer is an employee of the university administration, which is responsible for structuring the officer's role and responsibilities. Thus, Affirmative Action Officers may be perceived as having, and may experience, conflicting loyalties in their role which may conspire against their effectiveness.

Legal precedent has been established for hearing sexual harassment grievances under the stipulations of Title IX (*Alexander vs. Yale*, 1977; 1980). Further, in 1981 the Office of Civil Rights of the U.S. Department of Education determined that sexual harassment of students is a violation of Title IX of the 1972 Educational Amendments, thereby serving notice that universities are liable if they do not have adequate grievance procedures to handle students' complaints (Adams *et al.*, 1983). Many institutions have responded by articulating policy statements defining harassment and formalizing procedures for processing complaints. Administrators of universities which have not yet formulated policy statements might be more inclined to do so if administrators viewed the policies as protecting the institution as well as its students and employees.

However, the mere presence of a policy is not sufficient evidence of its effectiveness. The U.S. Merit Systems Protection Board (1981) recommends specific procedures for addressing harassment: A memorandum from the university president condemning harassment should be distributed; materials should be designed to educate people about their rights, definitions of sexual harassment, and procedures for dealing with complaints; adequate procedures must be developed to handle complaints; and a system to monitor and evaluate these procedures at all levels should be implemented. Policy statements should thus provide a clear understanding of harassment, possibly including examples of different types of harassment, and should spell out procedures for filing complaints and persons to whom inquiries or complaints should be directed.

University policies may impede rather than facilitate processing of harassment complaints. If, as the U.S. Merit Systems Protection Board recommends, a good monitoring system is in place, then there is a means to document inadequacies in the policy and to revise the policy accordingly. If a monitoring system is not in place, then the responsibility for evaluating the policy is diffused and there may be no clear means to address inadequacies in the policy. The implementation of an objective monitoring body with sufficient credibility and support to be effective in changing policy may be critical to achieving an effective policy.

Further, university procedures may conspire against effective disposal of complaints. It must be recognized that harassment charges are embarrassing to institutions, and administrators may wish to suppress reports even though such suppression potentially places institutions in greater legal jeopardy than a direct response to complaints.

There are a number of ways in which procedures might obstruct remediation. For example, procedures may fail to protect the confidentiality of either the victim, the accused perpetrator, or both. It is difficult to establish reporting and grievance procedures that contain sufficient safeguards for confidentiality to both encourage their use by students and assure the rights of the accused while simultaneously discouraging false allegations (Adams *et al.*, 1983). For instance, The Alliance Against Sexual Coercion, an organization whose sole purpose is to counteract the sexual harassment of women, suggests that a credible grievance procedure will provide four guarantees: confidentiality, impartiality in investigating, protection from retaliation, and an assurance of a viable administrative remedy if the allegation is proved. In addition, the name of the complainant should be known only to the individual investigating the complaint and the person accused during the investigation (Alliance Against Sexual Coercion, 1980). This degree of confidentiality theoretically protects both the rights of the complainant and the accused during the investigation. Yale University has a "limited identification" policy that in certain circumstances allows the student to protect her/his identity from the professor named in a complaint (Dziech and Weiner, 1984).

Students face a number of risks in reporting harassment, for example, retribution, identification as a "troublemaker," etc. Procedures that are insensitive to the risks a student takes in bringing forth a complaint may fail to protect the student's interests during the proceedings. For instance, we know of one university where procedures called for the complaint to be placed in the student's academic file rather than in the accused perpetrator's file. Such practices may promulgate revictimization of the student while protecting the perpetrator. There should be a clear statement that the university does not allow any retaliatory actions to be taken against people filing complaints, and this policy should be strictly enforced (Alliance Against Sexual Coercion, 1980). A student who requests to transfer course sections or drop a course should be allowed to do so.

Unfortunately, the prevalence of harassment far exceeds the incidence of reports (Sullivan *et al.*, 1985). Students may believe that their complaint will not be taken seriously, that they will be blamed for the harassment, or that they will be retaliated against (Adams *et al.*, 1983). Yet, it has been found that students who complain to appropriate persons or to the harasser about being harassed are more effective in ending the incidents than those who do not (Benson and Thomson, 1982; Sandler *et al.*, 1981). Institutions must provide clear and safe means of reporting harassment and must widely disseminate this information to students as well as to faculty and staff. The reporting of sexual harassment will serve to change the university climate over time, by alerting university officials to the extent of the problem and by demonstrating to students that their complaints will be taken seriously (Sullivan *et al.*, 1985).

Grievance procedures should spell out remedies and disciplines for proven charges of harassment. "A clear statement that disciplinary action or remedial action will be pursued if the charge is proved is a clear statement that the university thinks that sexual harassment is wrong and is willing to back up their words with actions" (Alliance Against Sexual Coercion, 1980, 18). Further, disciplinary or other actions should not focus on the victim (*e.g.*, allowing the student to leave a course or obtain a grade change), but on the harasser, specifying what disciplinary action will be applied. The range of disciplinary measures—from a reprimand to dismissal—should be spelled out.

Meek and Lynch (1983) and Diamond, Feller, and Russo (1981) recommend that, in addition to formal grievance mechanisms, an informal grievance procedure be made available to students. When such an informal procedure was instituted at the University of Florida more students reported instances of sexual harassment. Apparently, many students simply wanted to make their experience known and to have someone ask the perpetrator to stop the offensive behavior. However, it is not clear how effective this informal procedure would be in preventing future occurrences of harassment by the same perpetrators or in protecting the students who may find it necessary to have continued contact with the perpetrator from retribution.

> Ironically, successful informal mediation deceives the campus community into not knowing or acknowledging that there are harassment problems. Files are not kept, public knowledge is minimal, and sanctions for an offender are limited. Without some form of record keeping, the same professor can abuse individual students one at a time and be given the same "second chance" over and over again. Without an attempt to document the frequency of problems on a campus, the institution can deceive itself into believing that sexual harassment is only a minor issue. (Dziech and Weiner, 1984, 175)

Still, the benefits of an informal procedure may make it worth considering as an additional, but not sole, means to address harassment. Meek and Lynch (1983) recommend that certain professionals in student affairs be responsible for dealing with complaints. They contend that speaking to student affairs personnel is less threatening than reporting the problem in the offender's department. They strongly suggest that these professionals be women, since they assume that female students would be more comfortable talking with women about harassment, an assumption borne out in research by Sullivan *et al.* (1985).

An effective policy against harassment will not place all the responsibility on victims to report and thus stop harassment. Clearly, persons with low status are at risk when they report offenses by persons with higher status. Thus, perpetrators must come to understand the inappropriateness of harassment and the harmful effects it can have on victims. Universities might institute preventive or educational approaches in an attempt to increase awareness of the problem among faculty, staff, and students. Workshops or guest lectures that address the specialized concerns of deans, department heads, and faculty can be useful preventive devices (Dziech and Weiner, 1984), particularly if units or departments with high incidents of harassment are targeted. These may deal directly with the problem of sexual harassment, or they may approach it as part of the larger issue of the "chilly classroom climate" to which women students are subjected (Hall and Sandler, 1982). Though such programs can be coordinated by the administrative offices on campus, e.g. Affirmative Action, faculty and staff who are familiar with the extent and nature of the problem can serve as valuable consultants or workshop leaders, particularly if they are knowledgeable about effective means to raise awareness about the problem.

ATTITUDES ABOUT HARASSMENT

Dissemination of information will not necessarily affect attitudes that perpetuate victimization. We know that victims' responses to harassment vary as a function of their attributions and attitudes about harassment and sex roles. Even if students recognize the inappropriateness of sexual advances, they may fear that their report will not be taken seriously or that they will be blamed for the event. In fact, Jensen and Gutek (1982) found that women who evidenced behavioral self-blame were less likely than other victims to either report harassment or talk to someone about it. Similarly, women with traditional sex-role beliefs were more likely to blame themselves and other women for harassment. Jensen and Gutek thus suggest that only by changing people's general sex-role beliefs can one affect a change in the attitudes toward harassment.

In recent years researchers addressing victimization have called attention to the relationship between attitudes regarding sexual victimization (e.g. adversarial sexual beliefs, rape myth acceptance, etc.) and tolerance of sexual victimization (Burt, 1980; Diamond, 1980; Weis and Borges, 1973). In effect, such attitudes perpetuate the occurrence of victimization by minimizing its significance, blaming the victim, recognizing only extreme forms of victimization, and conspiring against the reporting of victimization.

Harassment is a pervasive phenomenon, and failure to recognize or report even "mild" occurrences increases the probability it will continue. The provision of a clear definition of the many forms of harassment, however, increases the probability that individuals will recognize and report such behaviors. On most campuses, there is no clear mechanism for disseminating information about problems such as sexual harassment. Thus, universities must not only address the nature of the information to be provided but also the means or forums for dissemination of this information. The Alliance Against Sexual Coercion (1980) recommends the following means of making university policy public: distribute the grievance procedure annually to all students and include the procedure in the faculty code book; have a committee that specifically reviews the work of the grievance committee or officers; and generate public discussion by annually placing the issue of sexual harassment on the agendas of governing bodies of the university.

Several myths about harassment serve to minimize the problem. According to one view, a woman should be complimented, not incensed, if confronted with male sexual interest and should accept the fact that men have been genetically selected for sexual arousal (Hagen, 1979). Others hold that women use their attractiveness and sexual wile to gain favors from male professors. However, as Benson and Thomson (1982) point out, these views neglect the formal role relationships between superiors and subordinates, and thus fail to recognize the coercive nature of these "attentions." "Rather than having a unilateral sex advantage, female students face the possibility that male instructors may manipulate sexual interest and authority in ways which ultimately undermine the position of women in academia" (Benson and Thomson, 1982, 240). Another myth is that female students unjustly accuse their professors of harassment, thus ruining their professors' reputations and endangering their livelihood. We know that most victims do not report harassment (Swecker, 1985); contriving a complaint is an even less likely occurrence.

Evans (1978) points out a number of myths about harassment, including sexual harassment is fun, harassment is trivial, sexual harassment only affects women in low-status jobs, and sexual harassment is easy for women to handle. These contentions generally ignore, trivialize, or discount the seriousness of the problem for women. Evans cites survey data from the Working Women United Institute (1978) indicating that women experience negative emotional reactions to harassment; harassment can have serious economic repercussions for women; harassment is pervasive across various employment settings; and women faced with harassment are placed in a double bind or no-win position. Research on the effects of harassment occurring on university campuses reveals that female students experience reactions and difficulties similar to those reported by female employees (Benson and Thomson, 1982).

Three constellations of attitudes and beliefs which foster acceptance, and thereby prevent the elimination, of sexual harassment have been identified by Swecker (1985). The first is the point of view which accepts and extends stereotypical heterosexual relationships to the environment at large. According to this belief, men and women are naturally attracted to each other, it is natural for men to pursue their attractions, and men and women both enjoy this "pursuit." This belief leads to a tacit denial of harassment as a problem. The second recognizes a power differential by which superiors gain sexual favors from subordinates. Though this view acknowledges sexual harassment as a power issue, it narrowly defines harassers as superiors and views harassment as normative. The third barrier involves the unquestioning acceptance of sex-role norms which maintain male dominance and female powerlessness. According to this standard, women who react negatively to harassment are stepping out of line and creating problems. To alter the context in which harassment is allowed to occur, systemic prevention, rather than case-by-case remediation, will be necessary to prevent sexual harassment. It is not sufficient to have the proper policies in place. "Administrators must recognize that they are a part of a system which perpetuates the conditions allowing sexual harassment to occur" (Swecker, 1985, 6).

A variety of interventions can be implemented in order to challenge attitudes that perpetuate harassment:

1. Key individuals within organizations can be targeted (e.g., residence advisors in dormitories, student government officials, department chairs, unit supervisors, sorority and fraternity presidents, etc.) for attendance at workshops; these persons can be informed about the institutional policy against harassment and can be given responsibility to disseminate the information. Swecker (1985) describes a project that was directed toward training administrative personnel both to define and recognize sexual harassment and to effectively respond to sexual harassment. The training approach was interactive and experiential; administrators responded to video vignettes and rehearsed responses to various situations. Unfortunately Swecker did not report on the effectiveness of this project. At the very least, however, we hypothesize that periodic exposure to such workshops would sensitize university administrators to the problem of sexual harassment.

2. New student orientations are another arena for disseminating information about institutional policies that prohibit sexual harassment. Diamond et al. (1981) recommend that pamphlets defining sexual harassment and advising students of their rights as well as how to avoid, when possible, and how to handle harassment should be distributed to all incoming students. Materials on sexual harassment should be included in student handbooks.

3.   Such classes as Psychology of Women or Human Sexuality are excellent arenas in which in-depth discussions about sexual harassment can occur. Persons who are not employed by the university are likely to be valuable resources for special presentations in such classes. However, because this strategy obviously reaches only a small proportion of students, it should not be the sole means to provide information to students.

4.   Items relating to sexist comments or sexual invitations can be placed on teaching evaluations. This format would provide the opportunity for students to anonymously report their perceptions of such classroom behavior, and would serve as a mechanism for feedback to instructors wishing to monitor their own behavior.

5.   Student newspapers can be urged to publish articles on sexual harassment.

6.   The names of persons who are known to be chronic harassers can be made public or passed through the student grapevine. Embarrassment over such exposure may motivate change. In addition, some students do avoid taking classes from people known or rumored to make inappropriate overtures to students (Adams et al., 1983).

7.   One interesting tactic comes from the experience of a graduate student. Several women students in a small graduate class discovered upon comparing notes that they had each been sexually harassed by the same professor. They decided to collectively tell him that they found his behavior discomforting. They waited until the next occurrence and then as a group nondefensively but firmly confronted him and requested that he not repeat such behaviors. Apparently the group strategy was effective in this case; the women felt empowered by working together and their strategy nullified any protests of innocence. Obviously not all professors will respond positively to this intervention, but the group process provides support and allows for a collective assessment of the probably outcome prior to taking action.

8.   Community activist strategies can be used to both raise public awareness and to protest particular instances of harassment. The strategies suggested by the Alliance Against Sexual Coercion (1980) include: having a speak-out or protest with press coverage; picketing offending faculty member's classes and using other public humiliation/confrontation tactics; conducting a survey showing the prevalence of harassment at the university and widely publicizing the results; sending warning letters to harassers informing them that they are engaging in illegal sexually-discriminatory behavior and listing the ways they can be legally prosecuted; and blitzing the media with stories and flyers. Women's Forum Quarterly, a publication of Seattle Central Community College in Washington, publishes the winner of the "Sexist Remark of the Quarter Award"; the purpose is to increase awareness of sexism and bias in the classroom (Dziech and Weiner, 1984).

Hall and Sandler (1982) similarly recommend that local statistics be developed to promote recognition of the specific institution's problem while counteracting the tendency to avoid or deny the problem.

It is generally more desirable to employ preventive, proactive attitude and behavioral change strategies than to simply confront individuals. When university employees and students become fully aware of the problem and the inappropriateness of harassment then they will be more likely to monitor their own behavior and the behavior of those around them. Thus, if a critical mass of people in a unit or department do not condone harassment, they may be able to exert pressure to conform on those who fail to recognize or take the problem seriously.

PROCESSING COMPLAINTS

It is not unusual for university faculty, staff, or counselors to become aware of instances of harassment either through observation, hearsay, or the self-reports of victims. Many complicated issues arise at this point.

1. If a student reports being the recipient of sexual overtures but does not define them as harassment, should these events be defined as harassment by the person to whom they are reported? It would seem appropriate to label this experience harassment for the following reasons. Victims typically experience humiliation, embarrassment, and guilt following harassment; a turning point in their feelings and approach to the harassment occurs when they recognize that they are not to blame and that the harasser is violating their rights (Salisbury, Ginorio, Remick, and Stringer, 1986). Further, Fitzgerald and Shullman (1985) found that 50 percent of the female students they surveyed reported having experienced at least one incident of harassment when specific behaviors meeting legal definitions of harassment were described to them without the use of the term harassment. However, when asked directly if they had been harassed, only one percent indicated that they believed they had been sexually harassed. Thus, naming the problem can validate the victimization experience and facilitate the victim's understanding of the harassment, as well as encourage receptivity to a range of support services available to counteract the isolation typically experienced by harassment victims.

2. Is it appropriate for a faculty person or student affairs staff member to advise the victim or to intervene on the victim's behalf? Victims are likely to confide in persons that they trust when reporting incidents of harassment. Thus, even though university employees may not be formally designated for this role, they may become involved in harassment cases by virtue of advice being sought by the victim. In such instances, we believe

that persons confided in should serve as advocates for the victim, even if only to counsel the victim on whom else to approach for further advice.

If there is no established grievance procedure or if the designated procedure thwarts the process and has been ineffective in remedying harassment, then how should the advocate proceed? Eventually the advocate may decide to work for institutional policy reform. Initially it is important to help the victim cope with the harassment. The advocate may be able to suggest a range of adaptive strategies found in the literature or refer the victim to someone who is kowledgeable about coping with specific types of harassment (*e.g.*, the Affirmative Action Officer, an appropriately trained counselor, or someone who has coped successfully with harassment experiences). In addition, the student can be referred to support groups available at the student counseling center or the campus women's center. If there is an effective grievance procedure (formal and/or informal) in place at the institution then advocates can inform the victim on how to proceed. If the victim wishes to file a formal grievance, then acting as an advocate means determining how this can be accomplished with minimal risk to the victim. It may be necessary for the advocate to consult—confidentially, and with the permission of the victim, of course—with others on campus who are knowledgeable about how to effectively use the system. If the victim wants the advocate to informally help to prevent further harassment, then the advocate must determine how to affect this end. If the advocate happens to be the administrative superior of the perpetrator, then the advocate can discuss the problem directly with the perpetrator. However, if this is not the case (and it is not likely to be because women, who are most likely to be sought out for assistance by victims, are most concentrated in the lowest academic ranks), then the advocate should encourage the victim to solicit help from a superior who might be sympathetic to the difficulty and who would confront the perpetrator. If the victim is reticent, then the advocate can offer to go with the victim to the superior. If the victim is unwilling to verbally request assistance from another person, then the advocate might suggest that the victim put her request in writing. If the victim refuses to act further on her own behalf, the advocate must decide whether or not to proceed. However, the advocate's case would be quite tenuous unless armed with the victim's complaint. Of course, all of these possibilities should be discussed with the victim before any action is taken.

3.   Several other practical issues must be considered if a university employee becomes aware of instances of harassment. Should the victim be urged to lodge a formal complaint? To what extent should the possible costs and benefits to the victim of pursuing a formal complaint be presented (*e.g.*, see Adams *et al.*, 1983)? What is the role of the advocate in protecting the victim from further harassment? Obviously, it is important that the victim

understand the grievance procedure and its probably impact on her/him. Complaints and lawsuits increase the stress on the complainant and usually do so until final resolution (Salisbury *et al.*, 1986). Victims need to have as much information as possible in order to make an informed decision about filing a formal complaint. Of course, it may not be possible to anticipate all the possible outcomes or problems but advocates should be thorough in exploring these issues.

If the victim is in a position to be harmed by the perpetrator, steps should be taken to remove the threat of conctinued harassment or of retaliation for reporting the harassment. The possibility of continued harassment or retribution should be examined in a manner that communicates to the victim that her/his well-being is important. It is not uncommon for victims to worry about retribution, and a sensitive discussion of such a possibility is likely to validate the victim's reactions to the harassment.

Taking steps to minimize negative consequences for the victim usually requires the cooperation of the head of a unit or department. This necessitates disclosure of the harassment and, therefore, must be acceptable to the victim. However, the victim should be made aware of the options and their likely consequences and then be allowed to make the final decision. Special arrangements may sometimes be necessary in order to avoid limiting the victim's access to the same educational opportunities as provided to other students. For instance, if the student is taking a required course that is only taught by the perpetrator and does not wish to continue with this instructor, then an alternative should be developed by those who can affect such actions.

4. Should the person to whom harassment is reported urge the victim to gather evidence or document specific events? How can the desire for confidentiality or discretion be balanced with the necessity of providing clear evidence? Diamond *et al.* (1981) recommend that a written and dated record of all incidents, with witnesses noted, be kept. Gathering information does not mean that a report must be filed, though the investigation of a report is facilitated if specific instances have been documented. Victims can be urged to document instances of harassment but keep the documents in their own possession until they decide whether or not to file a formal grievance.

Some (*e.g.*, Sullivan *et al.*, 1985) recommend that results of hearings in which someone has been found guilty of sexual harassment be made public. This would communicate to students that such charges are taken seriously and that the university administration is handling complaints to the satisfaction of students. Alternately, the numbers and dispositions of complaints could be publicized, without disclosing identities of involved parties. In any event, if harassment is proved, one potential benefit in releasing the outcome of the investigation is that such publicity sends a clear message about the unacceptability of harassment and it might deter subsequent harassment.

DEALING WITH THE CONSEQUENCES OF HARASSMENT

Victims often suffer serious consequences of harassment (Benson and Thomson, 1982) or are adversely affected by the proceedings when complaints are filed. Numerous stress reactions have been reported in surveys and in therapy: physical aches and ailments, confusion and self-blame, feelings of humiliation and alienation, reduced ability to concentrate, loss of self esteem, decreased self-confidence, lessened ambition, sleeplessness, fear, anxiety, depression, anger, and disillusionment with male professors (Benson and Thomson, 1982; Safran, 1976; Working Women's United Institute, 1978). It is important that advocates understand the negative effects of harassment; even if victimsn do not seek counseling, advocates can help them to understand the link between the experience of harassment and their stress reactions, thus normalizing their experience.

While evidence suggests that harassment will not stop without some counter-response on the part of the victim or an advocate, the act of filing a complaint in itself is stressful and may generate adverse consequences (Boring, 1978). Following the filing of a report victims should be prepared to be questioned, blamed, and possibly transferred from the situation in ways that may call attention to them (*e.g.*, having an advisor or course section changed). Advocates should be aware of the possible consequences of filing complaints and should expect to be called upon to provide victims with support during this process. It is not uncommon for victims to experience social isolation from classmates not wanting to be associated with a "troublemaker," or even from friends who are inexperienced in helping others cope with such stress. There are little data on percentages of victims who receive professional counseling as a direct consequence of harassment, though Ginorio (1982) reports that nine percent of all student victims talked to a counselor or psychologist about sexual harassment. It may be helpful to refer the victims of harassment for counseling, though this should be done in a way that does not imply blame or disturbance on the part of the victim. Salisbury *et al.* (1986) found that group support was more effective than individual counseling in aiding individuals to cope with the specific effects of sexual harassment, especially in the initial, acute stages of the harassment experience. They report that the group provided validation of the victim's feelings, understanding of the victimization experience, and support, and that the group process was related to changes in self-image, radicalization, activism, and healing.

It must also be recognized that advocates of victims may suffer adverse consequences as a result of supporting victims during either informal or formal complaint proceedings. Advocates may be asked to testify on the victim's behalf, adding a quasi-legal component to their role. Since women are more likely than men to become privy to reports of harassment, and since women are more heavily represented in the lower ranks and are less likely to be tenured (Sandler, 1986), they may be more vulnerable than employees who are in higher tenured ranks.

> Academic women find themselves in a Catch-22. They cannot function as responsible professionals and women if they ignore the sexual harassment of students, but they cannot confront it or be advocates without great risk to their own credibility and status within the institution. (Dziech and Weiner, 1984, 154)

When formal complaints are investigated there will be disruptions in the department or unit. Those who profess ignorance about harassment as well as those who have long observed and come to tolerate mild occurrences of harassment are likely, at a minimum, to experience feelings of ambivalence. They may question the validity of the charge, minimize or rationalize the perpetrator's responsibility for the occurrence, or lapse into victim blaming. Even if they do not want to vindicate a colleague when serious harassment has been charged, they may experience a sense of loyalty to the person they have worked with for years, which further distorts their objectivity. The advocate's role in the process may become suspect, and she/he may be perceived as encouraging a "trouble-maker" or being one herself.

Advocates may also find that some colleagues, in an attempt to resolve their own ambivalence, will want to discuss the charge with them. Questions of confidentiality arise here and the victim's requests must be honored. Advocates should be aware that judicious discussions of the issues are important because they may shape the course that any hearings will take and they may influence future policies in that unit.

CONCLUSION

Faculty and student affairs staff who are in the position of observing and being told about instances of sexual harassment must consider a multitude of issues in determining how to effectively address the problem. It is important that advocates understand the institutional policies regarding harassment and know how to use the grievance procedure that is in place at their university. Many victims may not want to pursue a formal complaint and may simply request the support and guidance of the advocate to whom they are reporting the incident. In either situation the advocate must consider the extent to which she/he can be effective without engendering the resentment of the accused or others. When significant risks are involved for the advocate, she/he may be most effective by requesting that the student also report the harassment to a superior or another colleague who would be sympathetic to the victim and who might be in a better position to act on the complaint. The decision to actually file a complaint should be an informed one; victims have the right to understand the complaint process and difficulties they may encounter. Similarly, the investigation should be carried only as far as the complainant wants it to go (Alliance Against Sexual Coercion, 1980).

References

Adams, J.W., Kottke, J.L., and Padgitt, J.S. (1983). Sexual harassment of university students. *Journal of College Student Personnel*, Nov., 484-490.

Alexander v. Yale University, 459 F. Supp 1 (D. Conn.), 1977.

———— . 631 Fed. 2d. 178 2nd Cir. (D. Conn.), 1980.

Alliance Against Sexual Coercion. (1980). *University grievance procedures, Title IX, and sexual harassment on campus*. Boston: Alliance Against Sexual Coercion.

Benson, D.J., and Thomson, G.E. (1982). Sexual harassment on a university campus: The confluence of authority relations, sexual interest and gender stratification. *Social Problems, 29*, 236-251.

Boring, P.Z. (1978). *Filing a faculty grievance*. Washington, D.C.: Women's Equity Action League.

Burt, M.R. (1980). Cultural myths and support for rape. *Journal of Personality and Social Psychology, 38*, 217-230.

Crocker, P.L. (1983). An analysis of university definitions of sexual harassment. *Signs: Journal of Women in Culture and Society, 8*, 696-707.

Diamond, I. (1980). Pornography and repression: A reconsideration. *Signs: Journal of Women in Culture and Society, 5*, 686-701.

Diamond, R., Feller, L., and Russo, N.F. (1981). *Sexual harassment action kit.* Washington, D.C.: The Federation of Organizations for Professional Women.

Dziech, B.W., and Weiner, L. (1984). *The lecherous professor: sexual harassment on campus.* Boston: Beacon Press.

Evans, G. (1985, November 6). Affirmative-action officers say their influence on campus is waning, blame Reagan's policies. *The Chronicle of Higher Education, 27,* 31.

Evans, L.J. (1978). Sexual harassment: women's hidden occupational hazard. In J.R. Chapman and M. Gates (Eds.), *The victimization of women* (203-223). Beverly Hills: Sage Publications.

Fitzgerald, L.F., and Shullman, S.L. (1985, August). *The development and validation of an objectively scored measure of sexual harassment.* Paper presented at American Psychological Association, Los Angeles, Ca.

Ginorio, A. (1982). *The sexual harassment of University of Washington students.* Unpublished manuscript.

Hagen, R. (1979). *The bio-sexual factor.* New York: Doubleday.

Hall, R.M., and Sandler, B.R. (1982). *The classroom climate: A chilly one for women?* Washington, D.C.: Project on the Status and Education of Women, Association of American Colleges.

Indiana State University. (1981). *Indiana State University Handbook.* Terre Haute, In.: Indiana State University.

Jensen, I.W., and Gutek, B.A. (1982). Attributions and assignment of responsibility in sexual harassment. *Journal of Social Issues, 38,* 121-136.

Meek, P., and Lynch, A. (1983). Establishing an informal grievance procedure for cases of sexual harassment of students. *Journal of the National Association for Women Deans, Administrators, and Counselors, 46,* 30-33.

Safran, C. (1976). What men do to women on the job: A shocking look at sexual harassment. *Redbook, 149,* 217-224.

Salisbury, J., Ginorio, A.B., Remick, H., and Stringer, D.M. (1986). Counseling victims of sexual harassment. *Psychotherapy, 23,* 316-324.

Sandler, B. and Associates. (1981). Sexual harassment: a hidden problem. *Educational Record, 62,* 52-57.

Sandler, B. (1986). *The campus climate revisited: Chilly for women faculty, administrators, and graduate students.* Washington, D.C.: Project on the Status and Education of Women, Association of American Colleges.

Somers, A. (1982). Sexual harassment in academe: legal issues and definitions. *Journal of Social Issues, 38*, 23-32.

Sullivan, M., Redner, R., and Bogat, G.A. (1985, August). *Sexual harassment of university students: Students' perceptions and responses.* Paper presented at American Psychological Association, Los Angeles, CA.

Swecker, J. (1985, August). *Straightening out the power curve: Eliminating sexual harassment in institutions.* Paper presented at American Psychological Association, Los Angeles, CA.

Till, F. (1980). *Sexual harassment: A report on the sexual harassment of students.* Washington, D.C.: U.S. Department of Education.

U.S. Merit Systems Protection Board. (1981). *Sexual harassment in the federal workplace: Is it a problem?* Washington, D.C.: U.S. Government Printing Office.

Weis, K., and Borges, S.S. (1973). Victimology and rape: The case of the legitimate victim. *Issues in Criminology, 8*, 71-115.

Working Women's United Institute. (1978). *Responses of fair employment practices agencies to sexual harassment complaints: A report and recommendations.* NY: Working Women's United Institute.

12

Institutional Strategies:
Creating a Sexual Harassment Panel

Dorothy O. Helly

General Background[1]

In 1981 a process began at Hunter College of the City University of New York which brought together faculty, counselors, staff, and students to discuss and propose ways of dealing institutionally with sexual harassment on campus. That process was affected by the federal legislation making sexual harassment illegal and by directives from the City University to come into compliance with such legislation. The result was a Policy Statement and Guidelines and a Sexual Harassment Panel representing all sectors of the Hunter College academic community. The process was neither easy nor swiftly accomplished, but in the course of pursuing it, the participants educated themselves and began to educate elements of the campus community to increased sensitivity to the meaning of sexual harassment. Sexual harassment has long been a phenomenon in which the victims have been blamed for their victimization, the most subtle and pervasive exercise of power over the structurally subordinate that has made even the victims doubt their own right to accuse their victimizers and claim justice for themselves.

To understand the context in which the Sexual Harassment Panel was created at Hunter College, it is necessary to know some general facts about the college itself. Founded in 1870 as New York City's first public normal school for women, Hunter College by 1914 was a free-tuition municipal women's college offering a liberal arts degree. Into the 1960s its undergraduate student body numbered between four and five thousand; and though it became coeducational in 1964, women students have never made up less than seventy percent of its enrollment. From the mid-1960s to 1980, however, the percentage of women on the faculty and in positions of faculty and administrative leadership declined, despite the appointment of its first women presidents.[2]

From the early 1960s Hunter College became part of the City University of New York, one eventually of ten senior (four-year) colleges, seven community (two-year) colleges, a Graduate School for Ph.D. programs, an affiliated medical school and, more recently, a law school. With the inauguration of a City University policy of "open admissions" in 1970, the size and composition of the student body at Hunter College radically changed from under 5000 students, predominantly white and white ethnic in background, to between three and four times that size, sixty percent representing African-American, Hispanic and other Caribbean, and Asian heritages. The imposition of tuition and further modification of "open admissions" in the mid-1970s did not alter this trend.

Hunter College, situated in the heart of Manhattan, is representative of a complex urban society, for which it serves, as it has traditionally done, as an important avenue of social advancement. Surveys in the late 1970s indicated that forty percent of its students were not born in the United States. By the 1980s records also indicated that twenty-five percent of Hunter College students are older, returning women students.

From 1980 to 1988, affirmative action in the Hunter College presidency of Donna E. Shalala increased both the number of women and the number of African-Americans, Hispanics, and Asians on the faculty. By 1985 her leadership and a college community responsive to affirmative action guidance had resulted in women faculty again numbering some forty-one percent of the total. When Karen Bogart visited the college in 1983, as part of her preparation of *Toward Equity: An Action Manual for Women in Academe*, she found seventeen programs and policies she could include in her list of "Exemplary Programs and Policies that Promote Sex Equity in Postsecondary Education." Taken together, these programs and policies made Hunter College an outstanding example of equity at the university level. One of these seventeen policies was its Sexual Harassment Procedures.[3]

History of the Panel

Student unrest in the spring of 1970 led to changes in the college governance system. The new academic senate at Hunter College was composed of faculty, students, and administrators, and an office of ombudsman was instituted. The third incumbent in that office sent out a memorandum in October 1981 addressed "To All Who Expressed Interest" in meeting to consider a policy and procedure for sexual harassment. What had precipitated it? In May of the previous spring term, when making his annual report to the senate, the ombudsman commented on a special category of case he had dealt with that year. A student had sought the ombudsman's help in difficulties she was having with one of her professors, and had cited among her troubles with him his general denigration of women in the classroom. What sort of remark had the student complained about, the ombudsman was asked. He replied, the professor referred to women by such stereotypes as "dumb blondes." In response, there was an outburst of laughter among the members of the senate.

As an associate dean at the college in charge of the evening session and graduate services, I was an *ex officio* member of senate. My reaction to the senate response elicited by the ombudsman's report was anger and dismay. I made an appointment to see him. We had worked on many committees in the past and I trusted his common sense and integrity completely. Since I could be forthright with him in expressing my concerns, we shared a frank discussion about what we both knew about the issue of sexual harassment at the college. We then agreed to explore the question further, each promising to talk with others among the faculty and staff who might share our concerns. The ombudsman followed up with a memorandum, raising the question of forming a working committee on the subject. I suggested doing so early in the fall term.

The ombudsman's October 22 memorandum invited recipients to meet in his office early in November and included two enclosures. The first was a copy of the Standford University *Campus Report*, dated January 14, 1981; the second was an article from *The Chronicle of Higher Education*, dated May 4, 1981. The Stanford *Campus Report* announced a recently adopted formal policy on sexual harassment. Previously announced informal procedures had been formalized to meet the requirement of a federal Equal Opportunity Employment Commission policy for universities announced in 1980. A committee made up solely of college officials had formulated Stanford's policy, which defined sexual harassment as "repeated and unwanted sexual behavior, such as physical contact and verbal comments or suggestions, which adversely affects the working or learning environment." The policy included informal and formal procedures to be used by faculty, staff, and students "subjected to offensive sexual behavior."

The *Chronicle* article ("Accused of Sexual Harassment, Male Professor Sues Female Complainants for $23.7-Million") dealt with a Clark University sexual harassment charge made by two women faculty against a member of the sociology department. The complainants complained that university officials were not dealing with the specific issues of sexual harassment and sex discrimination they had raised. The university's resolution of the case was to settle it out of court with the accused faculty member. That left him free to enter his own suit against his accusers. The issues of institutional responsibility and the rules under which the Clark administration operated were central of the concerns of the women complainants.

At Hunter College, the concern at this stage among those discussing sexual harassment was specifically the nature of responsibility of the institution to set up procedures to protect those who believed themselves sexually harassed. This focus brought help from the new chair of the department of Romance Languages, recently hired from Yale University. At Yale, as the head of a residential college, he had taken part in the university discussion of procedures for handling sexual harassment cases. Learning of our concern to familiarize ourselves with what other institutions were doing, he shared with us materials that explained what had precipitated the Yale "Advisory Committee on Grievance Procedure." He was also able to supply us with a written record of how Yale went about setting up a committee to pursue the various issues involved in establishing a statement of policy and procedures. We also examined the resulting handbooks for the faculty and students, which were aimed at dissemination information on Yale's policy.

The chair of Romance Languages also put me in touch with the associate dean at Yale who was convener of their committee. In a long telephone call in mid-December 1981, she outlined her experiences in introducing these issues into the Yale community. She agreed to visit Hunter College to speak on this topic.[4] When she came, she explained in her role in setting up a sexual harassment procedure at Yale to interested administrators and faculty members.

Examing the Issues

In response to the ombudsman's October 1981 memorandum, four of us began a discussion of the materials already in hand. This core group included the ombudsman, a member of the Counseling Staff—another Hunter colleague with whom both the ombudsman and I had often worked and on whose judgment we could depend—a woman student who was a psychology major working with the ombudsman and interested in this topic, and myself. In addition to the Stanford University and Yale University Sexual Harassment Procedures (including working notes on the Yale committee's work), we had available a "Sexual Harassment Fact Kit" assembled by Robin Diamond, Lynn Feller, and Nancy Felipe Russo for the Federation of Organizations for Professional Women (1981).

In our discussion, we raised the following points for consideration in terms of our policy and procedures and our overall strategies for dealing with sexual harassment at the college: (1) counseling victims of sexual harassment; (2) educating faculty to the implications of the power they wielded in their relationships with students; (3) disseminating the legal definition of sexual harassment as coercion and threat involving sexual behavior; (4) investigating what official college actions might follow if an allegation of harassment were substantiated; (5) finding out what must be done to protect accusers and to insure due process for the accused; (6) and finding ways of informing every sector of the academic community about this issue. This working committee included, from time to time, the department chair with the Yale experience and the new counsel to the president. As the work of the committee took focus, we kept the dean of students apprised of our progress.

We decided that Hunter College needed formal guidelines and procedures. Not only were they required by law, we believed they would also be essential for dealing with the problem at the college. We further decided that these guidelines could be initiated by our group so long as it had the full support of the president of the college, the personnel office, the faculty union, and the student governments. The question remained, at what point should these other individuals and agencies be brought into the process? Our initial decision was to formulate draft guidelines as the basis for discussion.

The ombudsman prepared a preliminary "cut and paste" set of draft guidelines, culled from the available sources. His initial model included: (1) a general introduction to the problem; (2) a definition of sexual harassment; (3) informal procedures—Step 1; (4) informal procedures—Step 2; and (5) formal disciplinary procedures: (a) the Yale version; (b) the CUNY Board of Trustees disciplinary policy for students; and (c) the faculty union contract on disciplinary procedures. The committee used this draft to discuss whether there should be available both informal and formal procedures, the latter leading to formal action when necessary.

As we worked and discussed this issue with members of the office of student services, there was considerable interest in making sure counselors were prepared to handle problems connected with sexual harassment. The principal concern among counselors was the effect sexual harassment had on those who experienced it. At Hunter College one of the members of the counseling staff is designated as the college Psychologist; in mid-January 1982, he arranged a workshop for the staff and trainees on counseling victims of sexual harassment. The speaker was a social worker and therapist in analytic training who worked with rape victims at a hospital center in New York. She was also an activist in a rape intervention program. What is clear in retrospect is how little research had been done specifically on the victims of sexual harassment.

A City University of New York Policy Statement

As these consultations took place on January 25, 1982, the Board of Trustees of the City University of New York adopted a formal policy prohibiting the harassment of employees or students on the basis of sex, calling for prompt, confidential investigation of allegations "to ascertain the veracity of complaints and [take] appropriate corrective action. . . ." The Board made it violation of university policy to engage in sexual harassment or to take action against any individual for reporting sexual harassment. The definition adopted included: "unwelcome sexual advances, requests for sexual favors, and other verbal or written communications or physical conduct of a sexual nature" when submission implicitly or explicitly became a condition of an individual's employment or academic standing, when submission or rejection became the basis for employment or academic decision, or when "such conduct has the purpose or effect of unreasonably interfering with an individual's work performance or creating an intimidating, hostile, or offensive working environment."

The Board guidelines charged the presidents of the colleges of the university with implementing their policy, directing all deans, directors, chairs, administrators, and supervisors to undertake responsibility for both implementation and dissemination. The Board suggested that students report harassment to the dean of students who, after informal confidential investigation, should report findings to the president, consulting the Title IX coordinator in the process. Employees covered by collective bargaining procedures "which include gender discrimination as a ground for grievance" were to use them; those who did not were to have recourse to a panel instituted by the president. The first efforts by such a panel were to be both informal and confidential; if no informal resolution were achieved, the panel member was to submit written recommendations to the president, who was to take appropriate action, including initiating disciplinary proceedings. Allegations were to be made within 30 days of alleged occurrence, "except for extenuating circumstances." Two days after the Board issued these procedures, the counsel to the president sent a copy to the ombudsman for distribution to the working committee.

By this time the Hunter College working committee had formulated a working draft of its own statement on sexual harassment, including a definition, and the beginning of a set of procedures that might be proposed through the informal stage. Aware of the Board of Trustees statement of policy, they proceeded on the assumption that their work supplemented the university procedures and could readily exist within the framework established by them. By late March 1982 the committee had a first draft of a statement of policy of procedures for the college and realized that once they had come to some agreement it would be necessary to confer with the dean of students and the legal counsel to the president.

The Final Stage of Writing the Guidelines

The discussions of the draft guidelines for policy and procedures went slowly, but some fundamentals were established. It was decided the panel should consist of faculty, staff, and students, both undergraduate and graduate, so that individuals in each segment of the community would find someone on the panel they would feel comfortable approaching. Taking this further, it was decided that the panel should include a mix that reflected the variety in the campus community in terms of gender, ethnicity, race, and sexual orientation as well as different disciplines and areas of campus life, such as the clerical pool, counseling, and the library. Not every panel could have every possible type of member, but an effort to maintain a mix was clearly important.

Deliberations moved at an academic pace: slowly and with complexity. In the fall of 1982, the president issued an "Open Line" to the college community, citing the elements of the resolution passed by the Board of Trustees the previous winter and formally establishing a Sexual Harassment Panel. The terms of membership were two years and the panel members' additional responsibilities were: "to consult regularly with the counsel, the vice president for student affairs and the president about the effectiveness of the policy in preventing sexual harassment" and "to recommend methods for educating the campus community about sexual harassment." Eight faculty and staff and three students were appointed to the panel, with the college ombudsman serving as an advisory member.[5] There were five faculty, consisting of one male faculty member in the English Department, two women faculty in Anthropology and Educational Foundations (a psychologist), a woman instructor from Academic Skills, and myself (an historian), listed as "Evening." The three staff members were one librarian, one counselor, and one secretary, all women. The students were all women: one sophomore and two juniors. One of these members was Black and one was Hispanic; none was identified with a homosexual orientation. Three were closely allied with the women's studies' program. The panel's make-up was not yet ideal, but we now existed.

Our first problem lay in the wording of the president's "Open Line," which followed the Board of Trustee's resolution closely, directing students to report sexual harassment to the vice president for student affairs and "employees covered by collective bargaining agreements which include gender discrimination as a ground for grievance" to use the grievance procedure provided under those respective agreements. Thus the panel's existence seemed to be only for "employees not covered by a collective bargaining agreement or covered by an agreement which does not include gender discrimination as a ground for grievance." The members of the working committee had conceived of a Hunter College panel as a body which would function in the first instance for all three categories of the campus community, students, faculty, and staff.

Related to this problem was a proposal from the counsel to the president that the students on the Panel serve only "when student claims are involved." Within a few weeks a protest had arisen jointly from all the students who had been consulted about being nominated to the panel. They cited the Hunter College practice of including students on all administrative search committees and in the evaluation of administrators and protested the implied creation of two standing committees or panels instead of one if the student members were restricted to which cases they might serve on. The initial procedure suggested by the working committee, which treated all members of the panel equally, was adopted.

The First Sexual Harassment Panel

On October 1, 1982, the vice president for student affairs requested that I convene the first meeting of the Sexual Harassment Panel. On October 7, the counsel to the president sent a memorandum to the vice president with some literature she thought the panel might find useful. She also indicated that she wanted to meet with the panel "to discuss the legal issues of which they should be aware." Her concluding remarks indicated that, like the initiators of the process at Hunter, she was concerned about introducing this matter to the academic community: "We should also schedule a series of workshops (1) to educate chairs and deans as to their responsibilities and (2) to educate students and faculty about preventive measures and reporting procedures."

I invited to the first meeting of the Hunter College Sexual Harassment Panel the members named by the president, the vice president for student affairs, and the counsel to the president. The agenda I listed reflected the three areas that needed to be sorted out before the panel could begin its business: to set its policy and procedures in light of the "Open Line" from the president; to allow the counsel to the president to raise legal issues; and to take up the issue raised from the beginning of our discussions, that of educating the college community about sexual harassment.[6] In the interim, one of the students appointed indicated that she could not serve and she was replaced by a member of the financial aid staff, an Hispanic man who was also homosexual. Thus when we met we better approximated the kind of representative spread of the college community that we had hoped the panel would achieve in our earlier discussions.

At our first meeting, October 28, 1982, the instructor in Academic Skills, a black woman who had some interest in academic administration, was elected chair of the panel for a two-year term. For the benefit of new members, there was a brief review of the history of the panel. The counsel to the president presented a number of procedural and policy issues for the panel's consideration and distributed a set of proposed procedures; she also shared with the panel a copy of Rutgers University's policy on sexual harassment issued in July 1980. The ombudsman shared with the panel a clipping of a sexual harassment case at Harvard University, reported in the *New York Times* for October 21, 1982, in connection with which Harvard's Board of Overseers received a confidential report. The report urged that victims of sexual harassment be informed of the details of the resolutions of their cases, an action not previously required. The confidential report had been occasioned by student dissatisfaction over this issue, and by the lack of an appeals process, a timetable for an investigation, and an automatic procedure for examining a student's grade in a course where she or he had suffered sexual harassment.

The panel agreed that its members needed to educate themselves about a number of issues involved in procedures and to discuss ways in which to bring them to the attention of the college community. A subcommittee was formed to complete the draft of a statement of policy and procedures, using the working committee's version as its basis and dealing with the issues raised by the counsel to the president. The work of this drafting committee took a long time and involved consultation with existing formal grievance and disciplinary bodies that dealt with issues involving students, faculty, and staff. Out of the process emerged guidelines that ensured everyone's rights to confidentiality and due process while pressing for speedy action. What also emerged was a Hunter College model of procedure that allowed the panel to investigate cases raised by students, faculty, and staff. The panel sent the product of their labors to the counsel to the president in mid-January 1983. The review process continued until mid-April 1983. The college counsel suggested a system of investigation of complaints, informal and formal, by subcommittees, which could then report to the full panel for final action. This was the system adopted.

A final version of the Statement of Policy and Procedures of the Sexual Harassment Panel of Hunter College emerged April 13, 1983. It was not almost two years since the issue was raised by the ombudsman in the academic senate. The first two introductory paragraphs declared:

> An atmosphere of mutual respect among members of the academic community is necessary for the university to function as a center of academic freedom and intellectual advancement. Any

violation of mutual trust, any form of intimidation or exploitation, impairs the institution's educational process because it undermines the essential freedoms of inquiry and expression. Students and teachers must feel personally secure in order for real learning and intellectual discovery to take place.

As a place of work and study, the college must be free of sexual harassment and all forms of sexual intimidation and exploitation. All students, staff, and faculty must be assured that the college will take action to prevent such misconduct and that anyone who engaged in such behavior may be subject to disciplinary procedures.

The procedures encouraged any student, staff member, or member of the faculty to discuss incidents of possible sexual harassment with any member of the Sexual Harassment Panel and indicated a choice of informal or formal complaint procedures that might be initiated to bring about resolution of complaints. The difference between the two lay essentially in the emphasis in the informal procedure on ending the situation complained about through informal discussion and, in the formal procedure, on the requirement of a written statement and formal investigation. In the latter case, after investigation, the decision of the panel was to be referred to the president when the case involved a faculty or staff member and to the vice president for student affairs when it involved a student. Basically, the findings of the panel were advisory to the president, to whom, after investigation, the circumstances and action recommended were forwarded. The intent was always to resolve the complaint by correcting or remedying the injury, if any, to the complainant and to prevent further harassment. Any action taken by the president would be governed by CUNY bylaws.

Educating the Panel; Educating the Community

While the draft process continued, the panel members attempted to learn how to conduct an interview with a complainant. The counselor on the panel distributed some written suggestions and undertook some role play for the benefit of the members. She emphasized the need for a quiet place without interruptions, the importance of body language, the use of silence and the right pitch of voice, the way it was possible to listen nonjudgmentally, and how to ask one question at a time. She also made clear the need to assure the complainant of the confidentiality of the interview, to let the complainant know what her or his rights are according to the informal and formal procedures, to explain the role of the panel, and to discuss the complaint in terms of when, where, witnesses, and the usefulness of keeping a journal to record details. Eventually the panel evolved a uniform recordkeeping form to aid in the process.

One of the primary goals in the setting up of the Sexual Harassment Panel was that its members should be representative of the campus community in order to encourage all with concerns and complaints to come forward and make them known. Very early in the discussions of the newly constituted panel in the fall of 1982, therefore, it was decided to design a flyer to acquaint people with the panel's existence and the names and telephone numbers of its members. As a beginning, the counselor in the office of student services demonstrated how a simple one might be put together on her own typewriter. By folding an ordinary sheet of paper twice, we created a front panel with the words "SEXUAL HARASSMENT IS A PROBLEM" in large type face. Underneath came: "Now there is something you can do to stop it!" Inside, under the title "WHAT IS SEXUAL HARASSMENT?" came a definition drawn from our Policy and Procedures. The middle panel was devoted to: "WHAT TO DO ABOUT IT," which referred readers to the panel's informal and formal complaint procedures, urging the reader to explore the issue with a panel member. The third inside panel summarized information about sexual harassment in brief terms, and on the last side was listed the names of the panel members with identification and college telephone numbers. A thousand of these could be duplicated immediately and piles of them placed in appropriate places around the college where they would be noticed and picked up. It was a beginning.

Other kinds of educational techniques were developed as the panel continued in existence. The president agreed to issue an "Open Line" on the college policy concerning sexual harassment at the beginning of each semester, listing the panel members. The dean of students enabled the panel to buy a videotape produced at the University of Indiana at Bloomington, called "You are the Game," illustrating sexual harassment incidents on a college campus. This was shown and flyers on common myths about sexual harassment distributed on several occasions. The electronic bulletin board in the student cafeteria was employed to advertise these showings. Students working for the student newspapers were encouraged to write articles about the sexual harassment panel and the issue of sexual harassment on campus. Several such articles were written over the ensuing years. At one point a questionnaire was devised by some of the panel members, including the ombudsman, to establish to what extent our students believed themselves involved in situations that are legally defined as sexual harassment.

Although these efforts yielded some results, the panel members continued to feel that they had not yet found the way to raise the consciousness of the college community as a whole to the issues involved. A brochure directed toward students evolved from the first simple flyer and one directed toward faculty, the idea for which was borrowed from work done by a similar committee at California State University at Northridge. When later members of the panel, both faculty and students, made sexual harassment the focus of their scholarly research, however, these efforts took on a new dimension and greater visibility began to be achieved.

From the first members of the panel, though responsible as a group for shaping the policy and procedures to guide effort against sexual harassment, understood that individually they had much to learn about handling cases. To aid this first group, the vice president for student affairs brought forward one of the women administrators who reported to her. She was willing to talk with us about an incident of sexual harassment involving a male administrator in order to allow us to use her remarks as our first testing ground for issues. The counselor in student services who had been on the committee since its first formation facilitated the interview at which the entire committee was present. The discussion proved important. It raised such issues as how to deal with incidents that had no witness, how to evaluate information from a complainant in a nonjudgmental way, and what to advise those who came forward about keeping records of further incidents. In their discussion, the panel members raised classic questions about "enticement," "unconscious provocation," and power relations. It was important for the group to discuss their views in order to discover the areas about which disagreement might arise among them in implementing the policy and procedures they had just completed. It was also important to understand the way society, and especially an enclosed community such as a campus society, had made it easier—and more comfortable—to blame the victim of sexual harassment than to make difficult decisions against peers and colleagues. It was also important to discuss where the priority of the panel lay: upon the rectification of "wrongs" or upon the penalties and sanctions to be invoked against "wrongdoers."

These early discussions led to the decision not to include the names of persons involved in complaints in panel minutes. Similarly, panel members considered how to identify patterns of behavior on the part of particular members of the campus community on the basis of repeated incidents. As a matter of recordkeeping, this idea proved troublesome. Records of names meant confidential files and if the files were truly confidential, by whom and when would they be seen in order to establish that such a pattern of behavior existed? In the end, no such formal record keeping was entertained; instead, the long-term members of the panel became the memory of the panel. It was not an ideal solution, but no better one presented itself. Individual panel members saw students, staff, or faculty who wished to speak with them informally. Since the object of the discussion was to resolve whatever was bothering them, if that goal could be accomplished without recourse to anything as structured as an informal complaint, the matter ended there.

Categories of Cases Handled

The most common case the panel expected was some form of sexual harassment experienced by female students at the hands of their male faculty. For many reasons, this has not been borne out. First of all, it has become increasingly evident that many students who are sexually harassed do not know that the behavior that leaves them so uncomfortable may be so defined. In addition, students at urban, commuter schools bring into the classroom an expectation about dominant male behavior which accepts their responsibility for learning to maneuver around obstacles like sexual harassers. Such attitudes work against holding harassers accountable; instead the message handed along the student grapevine about potential faculty harassers is, "if you want to take their courses, just make sure you keep out of their way." This leaves the most unwary, unselfconscious, more readily victimized student available as target. Such students are convinced that they, not the harasser, are at fault and are more likely only to blame themselves should they find they have a problem. Such students are the least likely to come forward for help, which they equate with more personal humiliation.

The cases that do materialize, therefore, are often those brought by the maturer student, one whose life experiences or academic courses in women's studies have made her more self-confident and of her rights to equity of treatment in and out of the classroom. At Hunter College, it is noteworthy that the larger number of female student-male faculty cases handled thus far have involved at least slightly older woman students. An interesting subset of such cases involves what the Sexual Harassment Panel now calls "gender harassment," using a term introduced by Michele Paludi. In these cases, the more mature woman student, often in her mid- or late twenties, refuses to put up with behavior that her younger female colleagues do not openly question.

For example, a returning woman student came forward to a member of the panel to complain about the climate in a science classroom that was exemplified by a "joke" that the instructor told, the butt of which was the size of his penis. The joke was met by guffaws by the male students. The protesting woman student, however, was angered, because she believed such a joke gave permission to the men students in the class to exhibit "jock" behavior. As evidence, she cited the fact that shortly after this incident of the "joke," she observed the men at the back of the class whistling at the return of a young woman who had temporarily absented herself. The protesting student spoke to her instructor, trying to tell him that his remarks offended her, but he did not take her seriously. She therefore appealed to the Sexual Harassment Panel and the coordinators interviewed the instructor and, at his request, arranged a meeting between him and the protesting student. Together, in the presence of the two members of the panel, they struggled to clarify for each other their differing perceptions of the situation. The instructor acknowledged his surprise and slightly wounded feelings: to be told that what he had intended as "putting the class at ease" had come across to one woman student, and perhaps others in the class as well, as productive of tensions, not easing them. Once he listened and established the gap between his intentions and the act, he indicated a willingness to revise his behavior.

Another case brought to the attention of the panel involved more explicit classroom behavior. It was handled by a subcommittee, which reported their findings to the panel. A woman student complained that the climate of learning in her humanities class was disrupted for her by the instructor's insistence on paying special attention to her in the classroom, exacerbated by asking her to visit him in his apartment, which he used as an office. She had withdrawn from the course without completing it and brought her case in hopes of being allowed to take the course with another instructor, without penalty, because of the sexual harassment she had experienced. The subcommittee investigated her complaint and discussed her charges with the instructor. His response was that he was only showing keen interest in her that he exhibited in all his students, and he made clear he believed that, by his attentiveness, he was being a good, supportive teacher. In this case, what occurred looked different to the less powerful person, who was faced with the choice of either "appreciating" a degree of attentiveness that she did not want or resisting it, and opening herself to whatever retaliation her instructor chose, since he retained the power of grading her work. She resolved her dilemma by dropping the course and appealing to the Sexual Harassment Panel for redress. The subcommittee recommended that the student be allowed to take the course again with another instructor, without penalty, and that the instructor be informed that his actions were deemed sexual harassment and asked to confine his advisement of students to the college premises.

In a third instance, the older woman student bringing a charge of gender harassment against a full-time faculty member, a department chair and senior professor at the college, was deemed twice to have failed to uphold her charges. In this case, striking because it went through both unofficial and official procedures pursuing the same bill of complaint, a further novel element dealt with the use of tapes. These class discussions were entered as prime evidence, on the grounds raised by the complainant that transcripts alone failed to capture the tone of voice that conveyed the sexist nature of remarks which she alleged conveyed the pattern of gender harassment. On advice of college counsel, the panel subcommittee handling the case allowed the use of the tapes because the professor had originally allowed them to be made by the student in the class. The case posed difficulties for the panel because the complainant herself broke confidentiality and made various members of the college administration aware of her complaint, necessitating an unusual procedure once the judgment had been reached on each occasion, of informing those administrators of the nature of the Panels's negative advisory recommendation.

Although at least two cases involving staff members only were brought to the panel, they were matters that were clearly part of issues being handled in other adjudicatory bodies as well and the one that proceeded to the formal complaint stage was not found to have evidence to sustain it. No case involving a faculty complainant about other faculty has come before the panel. There are many possible reasons for this failure. Michele Paludi has suggested some of them in a series of workshops for faculty and staff at Hunter College in spring 1988. Women faculty facing a specific problem of sexual harassment are more likely to ask advice from friends and colleagues or attempt to deal with the problem themselves, rather than bring it to the college panel. These issues may be particularly stressful for women faculty, as Darlene DeFour suggests elsewhere in this volume, who are African American, Asian American, or Hispanic, conscious of the toll their marginality in the professoriate takes on them in so many other ways. Women faculty in general tend to believe that it is part of their professional task to cope with such problems informally and on their own. Certainly my own discussions with women faculty colleagues bears out this predilection. Women faculty are concerned that any action they take of a formal nature to counter sexual harassment will harm their careers because they will be labelled "boatrockers." They do not expect support from other women on the faculty, and their realistic appraisal of their situation at most institutions can not be denied. It takes courage of a high order and perhaps just plain grit to take on personally the established male hierarchies of academic life. What is needed is a well-established female support system, as many male faculty sympathizers as possible to back one's cause out loud, and a powerful, respected, administratively supported Sexual Harassment Panel in place.

One final category of case, that which occurs between female and male students, has many faces. Date rape may be a straightforward issue, but the emotional stakes are complex and on them depend whether the woman is willing to pursue her complaint. Similarly, when women students experience "hassling" at the hands of male students, most decide that it takes less energy simply to avoid the hassler. Most notably for our panel, however, was a case involving gender harassment which flourished in a climate of outright misogyny and sexism among some of the population at our dormitory. A woman student protested the graffiti-filled posters which covered the outside of a bedroom door and investigation showed how poorly the college's own guidelines on sexual and gender harassment were understood by the administrators and resident assistants in this area of campus life. Her protest led directly to instituting workshops at the residence hall to better acquaint personnel there with their responsibilities regarding harassment issues and the availability of members of the panel for consultation.

Some Problems of Implementation

Implementation of Sexual Harassment policy and guidelines remains difficult in academe. The expectations of those in subordinate and powerless positions about the prerogatives and privileges of those in power in the academic community work against it, whether we focus on the professor in the classroom, the administrator supervising staff, or the male student who reflects the privilege of being part of the dominant group in society. Those in power give grades, write recommendations, hire, fire, and can by all these means fundamentally affect careers and future lives. Those who occupy the lower steps on a clearly marked hierarchically defined pyramid of power *expect* to be treated as lesser beings. They are socialized to believe in the system that so defines them, and they play to the roles assigned them as dependent creatures, supporters of and subordinate to the greater beings whose lives they often admire and whose words they obey. This is a heady atmosphere and rare is the senior faculty member or administrator who does not succumb to its blandishments and its pitfalls of easy arrogance. (And too few are the male students who resist these models of behavior offered to them.) As Sue Rosenberg Zalk points out elsewhere in this volume, too few are the male professors who can resist the ease with which a man may be either or both a sexist or sexually-exploitative tyrant, depending upon his psyche. Since he is expected to exercise his will at the expense of lesser mortals (and whatever else they are, lesser mortals are generally female), he is rarely held accountable when in doing so he harasses them sexually or creates a classroom climate that harasses them because of their gender.

This same academic climate breeds complaisance among peers and colleagues, female as well as male. The practical result runs the gamut of attituders from "There but for the grace of God go I" and "Don't blow the whistle" to "Live and let live," "No harm done," and "That's life" to a more cheaply cynical "She was probably asking for it" and "What are pretty women for, anyway?'' Such views represent the urge of those at the top to keep the boat from rocking in order to continue to enjoy the "perks" of power, such as they are in academe. They also imply a conviction that the fate of those in positions at the top affects others similarly placed, threatening to bring them all down like a house of cards if too many whistles are blown from too many sides. This point of view is critical when chairs are asked to discipline senior faculty or deans are asked to discipline chairs. All would deny it, but there is an element of the life raft: it is important to pull together lest all go under in the storm.

Finally, there is the real and realistic concern by the person involved in bringing charges against someone higher up in the hierarchy that the results will not be worth it. The deep conviction, based on a sense of the academic hierarchy and the academic climate, is that the culprit will not suffer for his actions in the end, but rather that the victim will be still further victimized. As I have already noted in discussing some cases dealt with by the Hunter College Sexual Harassment Panel since its inception, it is more often the older, more mature woman student who is willing to undertake the arduous task of bringing charges against someone in power. Such a student either from life experience or from learned analysis of the structures of society in Women's Studies courses has a fair understanding of both the power realities facing her and her chances of success. Younger women students, as Vita Rabinowitz points out in another chapter in this volume, tend to resist labeling themselves as victims and therefore avoid circumstances where this will occur. Thus the most vulnerable woman student, the younger and less sophisticated ones, are the most exposed to the potential of sexual harassment and the least likely to take any useful recourse against it, including seeking aid from a member of the Sexual Harassment Panel.

The most difficult problem of implementation may have to do with the restrictions necessarily invoked to safeguard the rights of the accused. At CUNY, this means that after the panel has completed its investigation and submitted its findings to the president and/or the vice president for student affairs, any decision by the president to take disciplinary action against a faculty or staff member must go through two more stages of disciplinary procedure under union contract and Board of Trustee guidelines. These of course are important in safeguarding the rights of the accused, but they also mean that the complainant, even after initial investigation has sustained her, may have to be prepared to face repetition of her bill of particulars to yet other bodies of investigators. If she is the least bit vulnerable, and who is not in such circumstances, the problem becomes whether the results are worth the toll they take on her emotional constitution.

Possible Solutions: Future Work

To deal with the problem of Sexual Harassment and the academic complexities which make work in this area generally a slow process, it is necessary to begin with institutionalized procedures. Institutionalization means written procedures, setting out clear, well-defined, and judicious actions to be taken by the complainant and those in charge of investigating the complaints made, ensuring that the institution meets its obligations to protect the rights of the accused as well as to pursue the rectification of the wrongs done victims of harassment.

To deal effectively with the charges made, such procedures must be undertaken by a cross-section of respected members of the university community whose judgment can be relied on to press cases on behalf of the victimized and to guard their interests without creating "*cause celebres* which might polarize the community. These panel members must be trained to be able to handle problems, to resolve them if possible short of bringing charges, and to aid any complainant who wishes to bring charges to do so. Panel members must always act as intermediaries who are investigating a situation and only after investigation should they express an opinion as to whether the charges brought should be sustained. It is necessary when a panel acts as an advisory body to recall that its members have no power other than advisory and to make sure that the complainant and accused are aware of this as well.

To make the panel's work effective, however, it must have two essential supports. One is an available counseling system to which complainants may turn for the kind of psychological support necessary in going through the hazards of "bucking the system," and the other is the absolutely reliable support of higher administration. A counseling system ideally might include peer counseling for students, faculty, and staff which might be attached to student services, employee assistance programs, and faculty organizations. If panel members must maintain a neutral, open stance, it is critical that they can recommend to complainants who are finding the process difficult specific counselors who will be able to give them emotional support. Similarly, if the panel's findings are not upheld and those found guilty of misbehavior not disciplined in some appropriate way, the panel itself loses all effectiveness. Only a close working relationship between this advisory panel and the administrator to whom it gives advice can ensure that actions taken will constitute a real warning to would-be sexual harassers that such actions will no longer be tolerated at that institution. The panel cannot tie the hands of the administrator to whom it is advisory, but it can expect the kind of support that will make its work effective rather than the reverse.

Finally, what is needed throughout the university community, in the professorate, among administrators and staff members, and in the student body is carefully planned out education to inform each and all of the issues involved in sexual and gender harassment. This is much easier said than done. A few institutions have produced films and videotapes concerning sexual harassment, but none yet addresses the problems of a large heterogeneous student body in an urban commuter college. Even if they did, the resistances to hearing the messages involved are legion: students do not define what happens to them as sexual or gender harassment unless they really make an effort to understand the process by which these phenomena work. The larger number of faculty and administrators similarly wish the issue would go away, and do not see the need to spend their own time dealing with it.

A few faculty consider the whole issue an invasion of their "academic freedom." It is a stance rarely taken in the academic community when the issues deal with equity and race, but still openly made when the subject is equity and gender. It is critical, therefore, to raise the consciousness of the entire academic community to the way sexual and gender harassment—sexism not less than racism—can poison the learning climate for all women students and comprise a threat to their right to an equal education. Effective change in an academic community occurs when the balance is tilted in favor of it; therefore, we must educate the academic community about sexual and gender harassment. We at Hunter College hope our experience will prove helpful to efforts elsewhere. Our current emphasis on sexual harassment research may hold the seeds to greater success for us all. The more we understand about what we are up against the better we can devise strategies to counter it.

Notes

1. I wish to thank Professors Richard Barickman, Sam Korn, Sally Polakoff, and Ruth Smallberg, members of the first Sexual Harassment Panel at Hunter College, who read an earlier draft of this chapter and offered corrections and comments of a very useful nature. Sam Korn and Sally Polakoff formed that earliest discussion group out of which this institutional response to sexual harassment took its shape. My co-coordinator on the panel from 1984-1988, Richard Barickman, worked from its formal inception on the shaping of its guidelines. Ruth Smallberg has long acted as our "memory bank."

2. Dorothy O. Helly, "Coeducation at Hunter College: Curricular

and Structural Changes since 1964," in *Towards Equitable Education for Women and Men: Models for the Next Generation*, Saratoga Springs, N.Y.: Skidmore College, 1985: 51-62.

3. The seventeen programs and policy were listed in eight areas in Karen Bogart, *Toward Equity: An Action Manual for Women in Academe*, Association of American Colleges: Project on the Status and Education of Women, Washington, D.C., 1984: (1) ADMISSIONS (Career Explorations: Summer Employment for Minority High School Students, 74); (2) FINANCIAL AID (Financial Aid for Returning Women Students, 84); (3) ACADEMIC PROGRAMS (Women's Studies Program That Produced a Textbook, 90; Faculty Development to Integrate Scholarship on and by Women into the Curriculum of Introductory Courses, 104; and Public Service Careers for Women and Minority Students, 133); (4) STUDENT DEVELOPMENT (Hunter College Women and Housing Seminars: A Mentorship Program for Students, 139); (5) SUPPORT SERVICES (Ellen Morse Tishman Women's Center, 160; and the Hunter College Child Care Center, 165); (6) EMPLOYMENT (Affirmative Action at a City University, 177); (7) PROFESSIONAL DEVELOP-MENT (Stipends for Writing Grant Proposals in Women's Studies, 184; Promoting Women in Higher Education Administration, 186; Women and Minority Faculty Development Program, 190; Humanizing the Personnel System, 193; Employee Assistance Program, 195; and Career Mobility Program for Clerical Staff, 196); and (8) OVERCOMING SUBTLE DISCRIMINATION (Formal and Informal Procedures for Addressing Sexual Harassment of Students by Faculty, 216).

4. I invited her to speak at a monthly meeting of the Hunter College chapter of ACENIP (American Council on Education's National Identification Program for Women in Higher Education Administration). For the way this group formed part of a larger strategy of women's equity programs at Hunter College, see under PROFESSIONAL DEVELOPMENT in note 3 above.

5. The ombudsman raised with the president the question of whether his membership on the formal Sexual Harassment Panel was as a faculty member or in his official capacity. She stated that it was the latter and named him as a special advisory member.

6. Specifically, my memorandum of October 14, 1982, listed the proposed agenda as: Election of a chair; Panel Procedures; Legal Issues; Publicity; and Workshops for college administrators, faculty, and students.

13

Legal Issues

Sandra Shullman and *Barbara Watts*

Two federal statutes apply to sexual harassment in higher education: Title VII of the Civil Rights Act of 1964[1] and Title IX of the Higher Education Amendments of 1972.[2]

The law under Title VII is discussed first and at some length. Many more harassment cases have been decided under Title VII, partly because it has been in effect longer and partly because the incentives to pursue a private action are better under Title VII than under Title XI.

THE UNIVERSITY AS EMPLOYER: LIABILITY UNDER TITLE VII FOR SEXUAL HARASSMENT OF FACULTY, ADMINISTRATORS AND STAFF

Title VII addresses the educational institution in its role as employer and prohibits discrimination based upon sex in the terms, conditions, and privileges of employment.

Several important federal cases interpret and define sexual harassment as discrimination in employment. Though none of them was decided in the context of an educational institution, the principles they stand for are nevertheless relevant to harassment of a college or university employee.

Williams v. Saxbe,[3] decided in 1976, was the first federal court case in which sexual harassment was found to be a form of illegal sex discrimination under Title VII. Prior to that, even though Title VII had been in effect for more than ten years, courts said that sexual harassment was merely disharmony in a personal relationship *(Barnes v. Train*[4]*)* or the result of personal urges of individuals, not part of company policy. *(Corne v. Bausch and Lomb, Inc.*[5]*)* The courts justified their decisions, too, by suggesting that if women could sue for amorous advances, ten times more federal judges would be necessary to handle the upsurge in litigation. *(Miller v. Bank of*

America,[6] *Tomkins v. Public Service Electric and Gas Co.*[7])

In 1976, however, the District Court for the District of Columbia found that Dianne Williams was the victim of sex discrimination based upon the job-related punishment her Department of Justice supervisor inflicted after she refused his sexual advances. This was the first in a line of cases accepting the *"quid pro quo"* definition of sexual harassment.

In a *quid pro quo* case, the employer or the employer's agent expressly or impliedly ties a "term condition, or privilege of employment" to the response of the employee to unwelcome sexual advances. The Equal Employment Opportunity Commission (EEOC), the governmental agency charged with enforcement of Title VII, has published guidelines which define this type of sexual harassment as:

> unwelcome sexual advances, requests for sexual favors, and other verbal or physical conduct of a sexual nature . . . when (1) submission to such conduct is made either explicitly or implicitly a term or conditoin of an individual's employment, or (2) submission to or rejection of such conduct by an individual is used as the basis for employment decisions affecting such individual.[8]

Failure to receive a promotion, to be assigned to preferred working hours, or retaliatory behavior, such as unjustifiably negative employment evaluations or elimination of job duties, are an important part of the evidence the employee must present to prove *quid pro quo* harassment. In *Barnes v. Costle*[9], for example, the employee's job was eliminated after she refused her supervisor's sexual approaches.

An originally troublesome aspect of this type of case was the argument that an employer should not be liable if it knew nothing of the harassing behavior perpetrated, even by a supervisory employee. Fortunately, the Supreme Court of the United States has put this argument to rest. In its opinion in the recently decided *Meritor Savings Bank v. Vinson*[10] case, discussed in further detail below, the Court strongly suggested that *quid pro quo* harassment of an employee by a supervisor results in automatic liability of the employer. This means that in future *quid pro quo* cases, a victim can win her case without showing that her employer knew, or should have known, or approved of the supervisor's unwelcome actions.

One element crucial to an employee's *quid pro quo* case is the loss of a tangible benefit of employment. Often, however, no such loss accompanies the harassing conduct. Another line of cases is therefore equally important to the definition of sexual harassment as unlawful sex discrimination by an employer under Title VII. *Bundy v. Jackson*[11] was the first case to hold that sexual harassment could exist without the loss of a tangible job benefit. This type of sexual harassment is called offensive environment harassment, defined by the EEOC Guidelines as:

> Sexual advances, requests for sexual favors, and other verbal or physical conduct of a sexual nature . . . when such conduct has the purpose or effect of unreasonably interfering with an individual's work performance or creating an intimidating, hostile, or offensive working environment.[12]

The Guidelines recommend automatic liability for the employer in offensive environment harassment cases, but federal courts deciding offensive environment cases have not always followed the Guidelines.

One important case, *Henson v. City of Dundee*,[13] said that an employee could not establish offensive environment harassment against her employer unless the employer knew or should have known of the intimidating, hostile or offensive work environment. Other circuit courts found the reasoning in *Henson* persuasive (*Katz v. Dole*[14]). Adopting the EEOC position that the employer should be automatically liable were the D.C. Circuit Court in *Vinson V. Taylor*,[15] and the District Court for Alaska (*Jeppsen v. Wunnike*[16]). When the Supreme Court of the United States agreed to hear an appeal of *Vinson v. Taylor*, advocates for both employees and employers hoped the Court would clarify the confusion about the standard of liability for an employer.

Reviewed under the name *Meritor Savings Bank v. Vinson*,[17] the case established important precedent for the proposition that an offensive work environment constitutes sexual harassment where the offensiveness is severe and pervasive. *Meritor* did not, however, clearly resolve the important question of which theory of employer liability should apply. Writing for the majority, Chief Justice Rehnquist said that "general principles of agency" should apply.

He first explained that in a *quid pro quo* case involving a supervisor, the supervisor exercises authority given him by the employer when he makes or threatens to make decisions concerning the employment circumstances of the harassment victim. His actions are thus properly charged to the employer, resulting in automatic employer liability. Rehnquist went on to say that Title VII should not be read to hold employers to this same standard in offensive environment cases where the employer is typically unaware of the harassing conduct. It cannot be assumed that the harassing employee is acting with the authority of the employer when he engages in the harassing behavior which creates the hostile environment, but is unrelated to tangible job benefits. The Court seemed to indicate that the employer should not be liable unless the victim could show that the harassing employee was acting in this role as agent of the employer.

Because *Meritor* is the only Supreme Court decision to date on sexual harassment, lower courts, both state and federal, deciding cases of sexual harassment will undoubtedly glean whatever guidance they can from the decision. Three aspects of the opinion are particularly important.

In-house grievance procedures: While the automatic standard was discarded, the Court did indicate that the employer is not "insulated" from liability by the mere existence of a procedure, a policy against discrimination, and the failure of the harassed employee to come forward. In his opinion, Rehnquist implied that if the employer's procedure properly informs employees that it will promptly investigate and resolve sexual harassment complaints, and if the procedures encourage victims to come forward, then an employer *might* avoid liability for offensive environment sexual harassment.

EEOC Guidelines: The Court concluded unanimously that both *quid pro quo* and offensive environment harassment constitute illegal sex discrimination under Title VII, citing with approval the definitions in the EEOC Guidelines. That the Court has given its blessing to these definitions increases the likelihood that they will be used in deciding other cases of sexual harassment, whether they arise under Title VII, under one of the state statutes addressing sexual harassment, or under Title IX.

Evidence on the issue of welcomeness: There is an emphasis in the EEOC definitions of harassment on whether the behavior of the harasser is "welcome." The Circuit Court in the *Meritor* case had ruled that evidence of the victim's provocative dress and sexual fantasies were not relevant to the question of welcomeness. Unfortunately, the Supreme Court disagreed, stating expressly that in a hostile environment case, there must be an evaluation of the totality of the circumstances, including evidence concerning the victim's dress, speech, and actions. This aspect of the decision is reminiscent of a not-long-bygone day when victims of rape were accused of inviting attack by their behavior and dress. The Court's indication that the harasser and his employer may present such evidence will surely discourage victims of harassment from coming forward.

Title VII and the law of sexual harassment in the work place apply to almost all institutions of higher education. Thus, after *Meritor*, administrators and managers who have supervisory roles *vis a vis* other institutional employees expose their institutions to automatic liability if they engage in *quid pro quo* harassing activities. It is less clear that liability would result where the administrator or manager is responsible for creating a hostile work environment, though if he were in some way acting as agent of the institution in his harassing activity, the institution would be liable.

One area in which the Court has left us without direct guidance is harassment by a co-worker. An employee would have a difficult time making a case of *quid pro quo* harassment, because a co-worker is not typically in a position of power, and therefore not in a position to offer the bargain in an expressed or implied way. In that more commonly encountered situation where the offensive work environment is created by a co-worker, no automatic institutional liability attaches; a court deciding such a case would probably look to the institution's knowledge of the existence of the harassing situation and find the institution liable for offensive environment harassment if the offensive behavior were pervasive and sustained over a period of time, such that the institution must have been aware of it. At the least, Rehnquist in *Meritor* gives clear instruction that colleges and universities as employers cannot avoid liability by ignoring the problem. The absence of clear, effective and well-publicized procedures which encourage victims to report harassment, as well as grievance procedures for following up on reported instances of harassment may lead to institutional liability.

Under Title VII a victim of sexual harassment can recover economic damages, such as back pay, lost wages and benefits, and may also be accorded injunctive relief, *i.e.*, a court order that the offensive behavior stop. Damages are problematic in an offensive environment case where, by definition, the victim suffers no loss of job benefit. Injunctive relief which could address the need for the institution to bring grievance procedures into line with the suggestions Rehnquist made in the *Meritor* case may be the most significant remedy.

One type of remedy not available in sexual harassment cases is monetary damages for mental suffering and emotional upset. Title VII sexual harassment cases often, therefore, combine an action under the federal statue with an action under state common law in the tort area, which would allow for these damages.

THE UNIVERSITY AS EMPLOYER: LIABILITY UNDER TITLE IX FOR SEXUAL HARASSMENT

Title IX as a remedy for discrimination of an employee of an institution of higher education has a mixed history. As the law stands today, Title IX is not an acceptable mechanism to provide relief to most educational employees.

Title IX of the Education Amendments of 1972[18] was passed to prohibit sex discrimination in higher education. Enforced by the Office for Civil Rights (OCR) of the U.S. Department of Education, Title IX states that "no person in the United States shall, on the basis of sex, be excluded from participation in, be denied the benefits of, or be subjected to discrimination under any educational program or activity receiving Federal financial assistance . . ." The sanction threatened against an institution found in violation of Title IX is withdrawal of federal funds.

Under Title IX regulations, institutions receiving federal funds must establish a procedure through which victims of sex discrimination can complain, but the victim may also go directly to the OCR, if she prefers, with no obligation first to work through to completion the institutional process. The OCR may seek termination of the institution's federal funding if the complaint is valid and cannot be resolved informally.

In 1979, the Supreme Court held that an individual could also bring a private law suit directly against an educational institution for violation of Title IX (*Cannon v. University of Chicago*[19]). In 1982 in *North Haven Board of Education v. Bell*,[20] the Court approved regulations promulgated under the Act which indicated that Title IX protects not only students, but also employees of educational institutions. Combined, these two cases should have enabled educational employees to sue their institutions directly for sex discrimination in employment, which would have included, presumably, sexual harassment. The OCR has no regulations like the EEOC Title VII Guidelines which define sexual harassment, but by that time, *Alexander v. Yale*[21] had been decided, holding that the definition of sex discrimination under Title IX includes sexual harassment.

In 1984 however, the Court decided *Grove City College v. Bell*,[22] which had the effect of narrowing the interpretation of Title IX so that its prohibitions were deemed "program specific." In *Walters v. President and Fellows of Harvard College*,[23] the District Court for Massachusetts, following the *Grove City College* precedent, held that a custodial worker could not recover for sexual harassment under Title IX. Although Title IX does protect employees from sex discrimination, including sexual harassment, the position held by the employee was not directly enough related to the delivery of educational services and was not in a *specific* educational program or activity receiving federal funds.

The U.S. District Court for the Western District of Wisconsin in *Storey v. Board of Regents of the University of Wisconsin System*[24] also found a way to limit the applicability of Title IX in employment situations. The plaintiff in a Title IX lawsuit need not exhaust administrative remedies or follow elaborate procedures. There are no mandatory conciliation requirements and no time limitations. By contrast, Title VII, although the most comprehensive anti-discrimination statue applicable to employment, requires a plaintiff to pursue remedies through other forums before suing in federal court. Filing a complaint with the EEOC and state agencies, and the follow-up procedures which may be necessary, along with strict time limits for pursuing complaints, make Title VII a cumbersome and time consuming way to redress complaints of harassment. In *Storey*, the court held that an educational employee who has recourse to a remedial statute, such as Title VII, may not circumvent the elaborate administrative and procedural structures designed to apply in such situations by bringing suit under Title IX.

The Civil Rights Restoration Act, passed in March, 1988,[25] overrules the "program specific" requirements of *Grove City College*. But even if the Act eliminates the problem experienced by the custodial worker in *Walters*, other limitations remain: the principle of the *Storey* case, for example, would be left in place.

Two other Supreme Court cases interpreting laws with wording similar to Title IX, *Atascadero State Hospital v. Scanlon*[26] and *Guardians Association v. Civil Service Commission*,[27] construing the Rehabilitation Act of 1973[28] and Title VI of the Civil Rights Act of 1964,[29] respectively, potentially limit the reach of Title IX.

In *Atascadero*, the Supreme Court held that a private suit could not be filed against a state institution unless the state expressly waived its immunity from suit granted by the eleventh amendment of the U.S. Constitution. Because of the similarity between the Rehabilitation Act and Title IX, this case could be used to prevent employees working at state-funded institutions of higher education from bringing suit against those institutions under Title IX for sex discrimination, including harassment. Given the significant number of state-funded institutions, this poses a real barrier to many institutional employees.

Another case, *Guardians Association v. Civil Service Commission*, may require intent to discriminate on the part of the employer before an employee can recover under Title IX. *Guardians* is a Title VI case, but again, similarity of language makes it probable that it would be relevant precedent in a Title IX case. Unlike Title VII, Title IX is not reinforced by regulations which would permit recovery based on discriminatory impact alone. It is therefore possible that under Title IX, the employee victim of sexual harassment in an educational institution would have to show intent to discriminate in both quid pro quo and hostile environment cases.

Assuming an employee suing under Title IX for harassment is able to overcome the limitations of *Atascadero* (not an employee of a state institution) and *Guardians* (able to allege discriminatory intent, not just discriminatory impact), and convince a court to ignore *Storey* (Title VII the preferred statute under which an employee addresses sex discrimination on the job), what remedy is available? The only remedy specified by Title IX is withdrawal of federal funding from the institution, which may seem inadequate compensation for an individual plaintiff. As under Title VII, no monetary damages for emotional distress are recoverable. Title IX does not even allow for the equitable relief of back pay available under Title VII. The only individual incentive for pursuing private litigation under Title IX is that the winning plaintiff may be awarded attorney's fees by the court.[30]

In the final analysis, because of the many possible limitations, Title IX is an unsuitable vehicle for addressing sexual harassment of an employee of an educational institution.

THE UNIVERSITY AS EDUCATOR: LIABILITY UNDER TITLE IX FOR SEXUAL HARASSMENT OF STUDENTS

Although Title IX holds little promise for educational employees, for students who experience sexual harassment, Title IX provides the only federal remedy. Few students have brought actions under Title IX, probably for reasons having to do both with the student circumstance and with the nature of relief available. Students are transient members of the institutional community; they have little to gain personally by reform. Further, litigation takes a long time; it is not unusual for a student's case to be moot because she graduated before it was heard. Students are also inhibited by the perception that the institution will defend the accused harasser. Reprisals may come from peers; sexual harassment is somewhat like rape in that the victim may find herself stigmatized because she brought the charge.[31]

The relief available provides no counter incentive: Under Title IX, the remedy is withdrawal of federal funds from the institution; there is no monetary remedy for mental suffering and emotional distress caused by the harassment situation.

Despite this discouraging picture, some few Title IX cases articulate the law with respect to harassment of students. Further, now that the Supreme Court has decided the *Meritor Savings Bank* case, the principles articulated there give hints about how sexual harassment of students might be treated in the future.

In *Alexander v. Yale*,[32] the District Court of Connecticut approved the action of a student victim of *quid pro quo* harassment. The student alleged that she received a low grade in a course because she rejected her professor's proposition for an "A" in exchange for "sexual demands." The court cited a Title VII case (*Barnes v. Costle*[33]) for the principle that conditioning academic advancement on sexual demands is sex discrimination, just as is conditioning employment advancement on such demands.

The same court, however, dismissed claims by a male faculty member that he was unable to teach in the atmosphere of distrust created by faculty harassing women students. The court also dismissed the claim of a student that she suffered distress because of harassing activity directed toward another woman student. None of the plaintiffs in *Alexander v. Yale* tried to make a claim of hostile environment sexual harassment.

In 1985, the Pennsylvania District Court decided *Moire v. Temple University School of Medicine*,[34] a case in which a medical student did make such a claim. Although the Court found that the student did not prove her particular case, it recognized that an "abusive" environment is sexual harassment under Title IX. The Court accepted the EEOC Title VII Guidelines as "equally applicable" to Title IX, and said that "[h]arassment from abusive environment occurs where multiple incidents of offensive conduct lead to an environment violative of a victim's civil rights."

Now that the Supreme Court in the *Meritor* case has approved the EEOC Guidelines' definitions of both *quid pro quo* and offensive environment harassment, it is even more likely that these definitions will be translated to the higher education setting when a student victim alleges harassment by a faculty member, or by any other member of the institutional community.

There is little doubt that, after *Meritor*, an educational institution would be held automatically liable for *quid pro quo* harassment of a student where the harasser was a faculty member or administrator in a position of influence as to that student's future.

As courts develop the standard of liability of the educational institution for offensive environment harassment, the special nature of the enterprise should be considered. A student expects her college or university to provide an environment that promotes learning, or at least one that does not hinder it. The student is relatively powerless in almost every relationship she experiences with faculty, teaching assistants, and administrators. Because sexual harassment occurs "in the context of relationship of unequal power,"[35] the student is especially vulnerable. Given the damaging effect harassment can have on the educational environment, it would not be unreasonable for courts to hold institutions of higher education to a more demanding standard of liability in a case where the victim of harassment is a student, rather than an employee. Thus, while in *Meritor*, the court stopped short of holding the employer automatically liable to an employee in a Title VII offensive environment case, it might be argued that automatic liability of the institution is appropriate in a Title IX offensive environment case where the victim was a student harassed by a member of the faculty or staff in a position to influence that student's future.

There are few legal guideposts where a student is sexually harassed by another student. However, Rehnquist's comments concerning policies and procedures may enlighten the area somewhat. While institutional liability would not be automatic, no college or university can safely ignore any complaint of harassment whether by faculty, staff, or fellow students. If the institution knows of the harassment and does nothing, the possibility of liability increases. Strong policies and effective grievance procedures, both well publicized to encourage students to report instances or patterns of harassment, are crucial.

Two remaining issues arise which institutions must address to deal effectively with the sexual harassment of students.

It is unrealistic, unfair, and probably counter to Rehnquist's admonishments about effective procedures which encourage victims to come forward, to expect the student victim to represent herself in the grievance proceedings or to hire a private attorney to represent her and prosecute the case. On the other hand, if the institution vigorously prosecutes those accused of harassment through the in-house grievance channels and makes a good argument on behalf of the victim against the accused, might not the student victim use that very same argument against the institution in a federal lawsuit under Title IX? The answer is yes, though the institution should be able to avoid liability by showing that, as soon as it learned of the harassment, it investigated and punished the offending individual.[36]

The second issue concerns whether "welcomeness" is a defense to offensive environment harassment and whether consent on the part of the student victim is a defense to *quid pro quo* harassment.[37] As mentioned above, the *Meritor* opinion instructs lower courts hearing charges of sexual harassment to permit evidence of the victim's behavior and dress to determine whether, given the totality of the circumstances, an offensive environment existed.

Courts should seriously question whether a student by her behavior and dresses expresses any degree of "welcomeness" to the sexually-oriented harassing behavior of a faculty member or administrator. Likewise there is serious doubt that a student in a *quid pro quo* situation "consents" to the sexual demands in any manner. Even though in both situations the student's behavior may not be physically coerced, the unequal power of the student and the faculty member make it unlikely that her behavior voluntary, in the sense of freely agreed to.

STATE LAWS AND THE EQUAL PROTECTION CLAUSE

State laws and the equal protection clause (fourteenth amendment, U.S. Constitution) should also be mentioned as providing alternative theories for relief of victims of sexual harassment. State tort law is where employee and student victims must look for monetary damages for the mental suffering and emotional distress associated with sexual harassment. Two examples of cases are *Howard University v. Best*[38] and *Micari v. Mann.*[39] Success with this theory depends on the common law of each state concerning damages for intentional infliction of emotional distress.

There are also cases that recognize sexual harassment as discrimination prohibited by the equal protection clause. The Court of Appeals for the Seventh Circuit in *Bohen v. City of East Chicago*[40] approved the use of the equal protection clause, and said that the victim only needed to prove intentional discriminatory treatment, not that the harassment altered the terms or conditions of employment.

Notes

1. 42 U.S.C. §§ 2000e et seq. (1982).

2. 20 U.S.C. § 1681 (1982).

3. 413 F. Supp. 654 (D.D.C. 1976), rev'd on other grounds as *Williams v. Bell*, 587 F.2d 1240 (D.C. Cir. 1978).

4. 13 F.E.P. Cases 123, (D.D.C. 1974) rev'd as *Barnes v. Costle*, 561 F.2d 983 (D.C. Cir. 1977) (ultimately finding discrimination).

5. 390 F. Supp. 161 (D. Ariz. 1975), vacated without opinion, 562 F.2d 211 (9th Cir. 1977).

6. 418 F. Supp. 233 (N.D. Cal. 1976) rev'd on other grounds, 600 F.2d 211 (9th Cir. 1979).

7. 422 F. Supp. 553 (D.N.J. 1976) rev'd, 568 F.2d 1044 (3d Cir. 1977) (ultimately finding actionable harassment).

8. 29 C.F.R. § 1604.11 (1986).

9. 561. F.2d 983 (D.C. Cir. 1977).

10. 477 U.S. 57 (1986).

11. 641 F.2d 934 (D.C. Cir. 1981).

12. 29 C.F.R. § 1604.11 (1986).

13. 682 F.2d 897 (11th Cir. 1982).

14. 709 F.2d 251 (4th Cir. 1983).

15. 753 F.2d 141 (D.C. Cir. 1985), rev'd and remanded as *Meritor Savings Bank, FSB v. Vinson*, 477 U.S. 57 (1986).

16. 611 F. Supp. 78 (D.C. Alaska 1985).

17. 477 U.S. 57 (1986).

18. 20 U.S.C. § 1681 (1982).

19. 441 U.S. 677 (1978).

20. 456 U.S. 512 (1982).

21. 459 F. Supp. 1 (D. Conn. 1977), 631 F.2d 178 (2nd Cir. 1980).

22. 465 U.S. 555 (1984).

23. 601 F. Supp. 867 (D. Mass. 1985).

24. 604 F. Supp. 838 (W.D. Wis. 1985).

25. P.L. 100-259 [s.557]; Mr.22, 1988.

26. 473 U.S. 234 (1985).

27. 463 U.S. 582 (1983).

28. 29 U.S.C. § 794 (1982).

29. 42 U.S.C. § 2000(d).

30. Civil Rights Attorney's Fees Award Act of 1976, 42 U.S.C. §§ 1988 (1982).

31. R. Schneider, *Sexual Harassment and Higher Education*, 65 TEX. L. Rev. 525 (1987).

32. 631 F.2d 178 (2nd Cir. 1980), aff'g 459 F. Supp. 1 (D. Conn. 1977).

33. 561 F.2d 983 (D.C. Cir. 1977).

34. 613 F. Supp. 1360 (E.D. Pa. 1985).

35. MacKinnon, SEXUAL HARASSMENT OF WORKING WOMEN, 1979.

36. R. Schneider, *Sexual Harassment and Higher Education*, 65 TEX. L. Rev. 525 (1987).

37. E.D. Ingulli, *Sexual Harassment in Education*, 18 RUTGERS L.J. 281 (1987).

38. 484 A.2d 958 (D.C. App. 1984).

39. 481 N.Y.S. 2d 967 (Sup. 1984).

40. 799 F.2d 1180 (1986).

References

Dziech and Weiner, The Lecherous professor: Sexual Harassment on Campus 1984.

Korf v. Ball State University, 762 F.2d 1222 (7th Cir. 1984).

Cole, *Recent Legal Developments in Sexual Harassment* 13 J.C.U.L. 267-284 (Winter 1986).

Crocker and Simon, *Sexual Harassment in Education* 10 CAP. U.L. REV. 541-84 (1981).

McCarthy, The Developing Law Pertaining to Sexual Harassment 36 *Educ. L. Rep.* 7-14 (1987).

Appendix

V

Sample Listing of References on Sexual Harassment on Campus

Suzanne Siegel and *Michele A. Paludi*

Articles on the topic of sexual harassment began to appear in professional journals in the mid-1970s and have been increasing in number since then. Finding this literature isnot difficult, but requires searching across many academic disciplines. Two good general guides to the literature on sexual harassment can be found in a publication by M. Dawn McCaghy: *Sexual harassment: A guide to resources.* (Boston, G.K. Hall, 1985) and in a publication by Phyllis Crocker: *Annotated bibliography on sexual harassment in education* (Women's Rights Reporter, 7, 91-106).

Three resources of special interest to those doing research on sexual harassment in particular and on women's issues in general are:

Women's Studies Abstracts: This is a basic indexing and abstracting source for research on the study of women. It covers not only feminist and women's studies sources, but selectively covers articles of 1,000 words or more in journals in many other fields. It began publication in 1972 and is published quarterly. It is available in printed format only.

Studies on Women Abstracts: This index has been published bimonthly since 1985. It is international in scope, scanning major journals and books. It includes journal articles, books and book chapters. It, too, is available in printed format only.

Catalyst Resource on the Workforce and Women: This database, available online only, is produced by the Catalyst Information Center (250 Park Avenue, New York City). It covers many aspects of women's issues, focusing on those which relate to career and work areas. There is no printed index, but accessions lists are published and the collection is open to the public by appointment.

In addition to these three specialized sources, the following databases all provide useful information:

ERIC *(Educational Resources Information Center):* The online version covers the years 1966 on. It is available in printed form as *Current Index to Journals in Education* (1969-) which indexes articles from over 700 major education and education related journals, and *Resources in Education* (1966-), which indexes education related documents.

Sociological Abstracts: Available online (1963-) and in printed format (1952-). This index scans over 1200 journals and other serial publications to cover the world's literature in sociology and related areas in social and behavioral sciences.

Psychological Abstracts: Available online as *PsychInfo* (1967-) and in printed form (1927-). This is an international service which covers over 1300 journals and other publications in psychology and behavioral sciences.

ABI/INFORM: Available online (1971-). Almost 700 publications in business and related fields are scanned. The database contains much useful information on women, focusing on career and workforce issues. A somewhat comparable printed resource is *Business Periodicals Index* (1958-) which is itself available online and covers approximately 300 sources.

Legal Resources Index: Available online (1980-). The database covers over 750 key law journals and six law newspapers, plus legal monographs. It provides a legal perspective on women's issues. A useful printed index is the *Index to Legal Periodicals* (1908-), which is also available online.

Index of Economic Articles: Available online as *Economic Literature Index* (1969-) and in printed form (1886-). This covers approximately 260 economic journals and 200 monographs. It is valuable for the economic perspective it provides on women's issues.

For more general, less scholarly material there is:

National Newspaper Index: Available online and in microfiche (1979-) which covers the *New York Times, Christian Science Monitor, Wall Street Journal, Washington Post,* and *Los Angeles Times.*

Magazine Index: Available online and in microfiche (1959-) which indexes more than 430 popular magazines. Comparable printed resources are *Reader's Guide to Periodical Literature* (1900-) which indexes about 200 general interest magazines, and *Access* (1975-) which indexes national general interest publications not covered in Reader's Guide.

Alternative Press Index: Available in printed format only (1969-). This index covers close to 200 leftist and radical opinion journals and newspapers from the English speaking world.

A useful and interesting resource is the *Social Sciences Citation Index* (1971-), available online as *Social SciSearch* (1972-). In addition to conventional research by title words, author, journal names, it is possible to search an author's cited references in this source. Beginning with a single useful source article, one can trace other authors who are citing that source and who presumably are researching the same or related areas.

What follows is a selective bibliography of material concerning sexual harassment in the academy. This material was gathered by searching many of the above mentioned resources.

INDIVIDUAL, LEGAL, AND INSTITUTIONAL RESPONSES TO SEXUAL HARASSMENT

Beauvais, K. (1986). Workshops to combat sexual harassment: A case study of changing attitudes. *Signs, 12*, 130-145.

Betts, N. and Newman, G. (1982). Defining the issues: sexual harassment in college and university life. *Contemporary Education, 54*, 48-52.

Brandenburg, J. (1982). Sexual harassment in the university: Guidelines for establishing a grievance procedure. *Signs, 8*, 320-336.

Crocker, P. (1983). An analysis of university definitions of sexual harassment. *Signs, 8*, 696-707.

Hoffman, F. (1986). Sexual harassment in academia: Feminist theory and institutional practice. *Harvard Educational Review, 56*, 105-121.

Hughes, J., and Sandler, B. (1986). *In case of sexual harassment: A guide for women students. We hope it doesn't happen to you, but if it does . . .* Washington, D.C.: Association of American Colleges.

Ingulli, E.D. (1987). Sexual harassment in education. *Rutgers Law Journal, 18*, 281-342.

Jackson, P.I. (1985). Defining the nature of professional relationships: Campus sexual harassment policies and the professional status of women. Paper presented at the Society for the Study of Social Problems.

Henig, S., and Ryan, J. (1986). Sex differences in levels of tolerance and attribution of blame for sexual harassment on a university campus. *Sex Roles, 15,* 535-549.

Honstead, M.L. (1988). Correlates of coping methods of sexually harassed college students. Dissertation Abstracts International, Vol. 48 (8A), 1987.

Lebrato, M.T. (Ed.) (1986). *Help yourself: A manual for dealing with sexual harassment.* Sacramento: California State Commission on the Status of Women.

Markunas, P., and Joyce-Brady, J. (1987). Underutilization of sexual harassment grievance procedures. *Journal of the National Association of Women Deans, Administrators, and Counselors, 50,* 27-32.

Northwest Women's Law Center (1986). *Sexual harassment in the schools: A statewide project for secondary and vocational schools.* Washington, D.C.: Women's Educational Equity Act.

Padgitt, S., and Padgitt, J.S. (1986). Cognitive structure of sexual harassment: Implications for university policy. *Journal of College Student Personnel, 27,* 34-39.

Powell, G.N. (1986). Effects of sex role identity and sex on definitions of sexual harassment. *Sex Roles, 14,* 9-19.

Roark, M.L. (1987). Preventing violence on college campuses. Special Issue: *Counseling and Violence, 65,* 367-371.

Schneider, B. (1987). Graduate women, sexual harassment, and university policy. *Journal of Higher Education, 58,* 46-65.

Somers, A. (1982). Sexual harassment in academe: Legal issues and definitions. *The Journal of Social Issues, 38,* 23-32.

Stewart, L. (1982, October). Sexual harassment as discrimination: Guidelines for effective responses. Paper presented at the Annual Meeting of the Communication, Language, and Gender Conference, Athens, OH.

Strauss, S. (1988). Sexual harassment in the school: Legal implications for principals. *NASSP Bulletin, 72,* 93-97.

Thomann, D.A., and Wiener, R.L. (1987). Physical and psychological causality as determinants of culpability in sexual harassment cases. *Sex Roles, 17,* 573-591.

Welzenbach, L. (Ed.) (1986). *Sexual harassment: Issues and answers. A guide for: Education, Business, Industry.* Washington, D.C.: College and University Personnel Association.

Winks, P.L. (1982). Legal implications of sexual contact between teacher and student. *Journal of Law and Education*, 11, 437-477.

INCIDENCE OF SEXUAL HARASSMENT ON CAMPUS

Adams, J., Kottke, J., and Padgitt, J. (1983). Sexual harassment of university students. *Journal of College Student Personnel*, 24, 484-490.

Benson, D., and Thompson, G. (1982). Sexual harassment on a university campus: The confluence of authority relations, sexual interest and gender stratification. *Social Problems*, 29, 236-251.

Cammaert, L. (1985). How widespread is sexual harassment on campus? Special Issue: Women in groups and aggression against women. *International Journal of Women's Studies*, 8, 388-397.

Coleman, M. (1987). A study of sexual harassment of female students in academia. *Dissertation Abstracts International*, 47, 2815.

Crocker, P.L., and Simon, A. (1981). Sexual harassment in education. *Capitol University Law Review*, 10, 541-584.

Dziech, B., and Weiner, L. (1984). *The lecherous professor*. Boston: Beacon Press.

Fitzgerald, L., Shullman, S., Bailey, N., Richards, M., Swecker, J., Gold, Y., Ormerod, M., and Weitzman, L. (1988). The incidence and dimensions of sexual harassment in academia and the workplace. *Journal of Vocational Behavior*, 22, 152-175.

Fitzgerald, L.F., Gold, Y., Ormerod, M., and Weitzman, L. (1988). Academic harassment: Sex and denial in scholarly garb. *Psychology of Women Quarterly*, 12, 329-340.

Franklin, P., Moglin, H., Zatling-Boring, P., and Angress, R. (1981). *Sexual and gender harassment in the academy*. New York: Modern Language Association.

Fuehrer, A., and Schilling, K. (1987, May). Sexual harassment of women graduate students: The impact of institutional factors. Paper presented at the Midwestern Psychological Association, Chicago.

Gartland, P. (Ed.) (1983). Sexual harassment on campus. *Journal of NAWDAC*, 46, 3-50.

Glaser, R., and Thorpe, J. (1986). Unethical intimacy: A survey of sexual contact and advances between psychology educators and female graduate students. *American Psychologist*, 41, 43-51.

Kraus, L., and Wilson, K. (1980). Coercion in the college classroom: A study of sexual harassment. Paper presented at the Southern Sociological Society.

Lott, B. (1982). Sexual assault and harassment: A campus community case study. *Signs*, 8, 296-319.

McCormack, A. (1985). The sexual harassment of students by teachers: The case of students in science. *Sex Roles*, *13*, 21-32.

Pickrell, J. (1987). Academic sexual harassment: Sexual harassment of students. *Dissertation Abstracts International*, *47* (8A), 2808.

Popovich, P., Licata, B., Nokovich, D., and Martelli, T. (1986). Assessing the incidence and perceptions of sexual harassment behaviors among American undergraduates. *Journal of Psychology*, *120*, 387-396.

Pryor, J., and Day, J. (1988). Interpretation of sexual harassment: An attributional analysis. *Sex Roles*, *18*, 405-417.

Reilly, M., Lott, B., and Gallogly, S. (1986). Sexual harassment of university students. *Sex Roles*, *15*, 333-358.

Rossi, P., and Webber-Burdin, E. (1983). Sexual harassment on the campus. *Social Science Research*, *12*, 131-158.

Sandler, B. (1981). Sexual harassment: A hidden problem. *Educational Record*, *62*, 52-57.

Schneider, B. (1987). Graduate women, sexual harassment, and university policy. *Journal of Higher Education*, *58*, 46-65.

Sigal, J. (1987, August). Sexual harassment on three college campuses. Paper presented at the American Psychological Association, New York.

Till, F. (1980). *Sexual harassment: A report on the sexual harassment of students*. Washington, D.C.: National Advisory Council on Women's Educational Programs.

Tuana, N. (1985). Sexual harassment in academe. *College Teaching*, *33*, 53-64.

Vance, S. (1981). Sexual harassment of women students. *New Directions for Higher Education*, *9*, 29-40.

Whitmore, R. (1983). *Sexual harassment at UC Davis*. Davis: Women's Resources and Research Center.

Organizations Concerned with Sexual Harassment on Campus

Carole Ann Scott

The following is a list of organizations dealing with sexual and gender harassment. Additional information may be obtained by contacting the Project on the Status and Education of Women of the Association of American Colleges, 1818 R St., NW, Washington, D.C. 20009.

Alliance Against Sexual Coercion
P.O. Box 1
Cambridge, MA 02139

American Association of University Professors
1 Dupont Circle
Washington, D.C. 20036

American Council on Education
Office of Women in Higher Education
Washington, D.C. 20036

American Psychological Association
1200 17th St. NW
Washington, D.C. 20036

Cleveland Women Working
1258 Euclid Avenue
Cleveland, OH 44115

Equal Employment Opportunity Commission
2401 E St., NW
Washington, D.C. 20507

Institute for Women and Work
    Cornell University
    15 East 26th St.
    New York, NY 10010

National Association for Women Deans, Administrators,
    and Counselors
    1625 1st St., NW
    Washington, D.C. 20006

New York Women Against Rape
    666 Broadway
    New York, NY 10012

9 to 5
    YWCA
    140 Clarendon St.
    Boston, MA 02116

Stop Sexual Abuse of Students
Chicago Public Education Project
American Friends Service Committee
    407 South Dearborn St.
    Chicago, IL 60605

U.S. Commission on Civil Rights
    New England Office
    55 Summer St.
    Boston, MA 02110

U.S. Department of Education
    Office for Civil Rights
    Washington, D.C. 20202

Vocations for Social Change
    353 Broadway
    Cambridge, MA 02139

Audiovisual Material on Sexual Harassment on Campus

Michele A. Paludi

Sexual Harassment in Higher Education
University of California, Irvine
Office of Affirmative Action and Equal Opportunity
714-856-5594

Your Right to Fight: Stopping Sexual Harassment on Campus
State University of New York, Albany
Affirmative Action
Administration 301
Albany, NY 12222
518-442-5415

Tell Someone
University of Michigan
Affirmative Action Office
Ann Arbor, MI 48109
313-764-3423

You Are the Game: Sexual Harassment on Campus
Indiana University
Audio Visual Center
Bloomington, IN 47405
812-332-0211

Sexual Harassment on Campus: Current Concerns and Considerations
Old Dominion University
Center for Instructional Services
Norfolk, VA 23529
804-683-3181

Sample Workshop Materials for Training Faculty about Sexual Harassment

Michele A. Paludi and *Richard Barickman*

OUTLINE OF WORKSHOP TOPICS FOR FACULTY
AND ADMINISTRATORS[a]

Workshop I: Sexual and Gender Harassment: Definitions, Incidence, and
the Implications for Women's Career Development

Case Studies Dealing with Definitions of Harassment
Discussion of Case Studies
Presentation on Incidence Rates of Sexual and Gender Harassment
Discussion of Incidence Rates
Conclusion to Session
Sharing Initial Reactions to Information Presented
Stereotypes versus Realities

Workshop II: Sexual and Gender Harassment: Individual, Institutional,
and Legal Remedies

Presentation by Sexual Harassment Panel of College
Presentation by Legal Counsel
Presentation by Employee Assistance Program
Presentation by National Consultant on Sexual Harassment
Conclusion to Session
Discussion of Remedies of Harassment

Workshop III: Gender Harassment: Tarnishing the Ivory Tower

Presentation on Gender Harassment
Discussion of Nonsexist Alternatives to Sexist Verbal and Nonverbal
Communications

Discussion of Perceptual Differences in Verbal and Nonverbal
   Communications
Conclusion to Session
Discussion of Gender Harassment

Workshop IV: Sexual and Gender Harassment: Strategies for Change

Presentation of Power Issues Involved in the Academy
General Discussion of Power, Gender, and Harassment
Conclusion to Session
Discussion of Workshops

CASE STUDIES ILLUSTRATING LEVELS OF SEXUAL HARASSMENT [b]

*   Pretend you just arrive to your first faculty position after completing
your Ph.D. You are eager to enter this next stage of your career
development. Upon your arrival to the department, you are met by a full
professor in the same department who shows considerable interest in your
research and teaching skills. You are quite flattered by his interest and agree
to discuss your research over lunch in the faculty dining room a few times
during the first month you are at this job. After a few months you find he is
touching you, rubbing his hand over your back and chest and patting you
on the bottom. He starts asking you to meet him for early dinners/late
lunches off campus. He starts to make seductive remarks about your body.
You start to feel that you are subtly being bribed with some sort of reward
to engage in sexual behavior with this full professor, who also happens to be
on the Promotions and Tenure Committee in your department. After
several weeks of this behavior, your colleague makes unwanted attempts to
have sexual intercourse with you that resulted in your crying, pleading, and
physically struggling with him.
*   Professor Jane McKay is walking down the hall in her department.
Professor John Smith, Jane's department chair, walks up from behind. As
John passes Jane, he pats her on the bottom and says, "Hurry up—you'll
never get to your class on time."
*   At a faculty meeting, Professor Martinez comments that the course on
women's literature doesn't have to be offered the next semester since it is
not an important course in the curriculum.
*   Maria, a senior in college, goes to Professor Nelson's office to discuss a
paper. He pats her hair, kisses her on the head, and attempts to kiss her on
the lips.
*   In her introductory psychology class, Ramona notices that her profes-

sor stares at her while she is taking tests and comments about her looks as a greeting each morning.

* Dee, a junior biology major, arrives 15 minutes late to her summer school class because of traffic. As she enters the lecture hall, Dee is whistled at by her professor and a few of the male students in the class. The men also laugh among themselves and comment on Dee's outfit—shorts and a tee shirt.

Notes

a. Copies of specific exercises, articles, and handouts may be obtained from Michele Paludi, Department of Psychology, Hunter College, 695 Park Avenue, New York, NY 10021.

b. These case studies were developed by Richard Barickman and Michele Paludi, Co-Coordinators, Hunter College Sexual Harassment Panel, 1988. Additional information may be obtained from Richard Barickman, Department of English and Michele Paludi, Department of Psychology, Hunter College, 695 Park Avenue, New York, NY 10021.

The Student in the Back Row:
Avoiding Sexual Harassment in the Classroom

Sexual Harassment Panel of Hunter College

The student in the back row may feel sexually harassed even though the professor has never made any advance or even a direct personal remark. The student may feel humiliated, embarassed, or angry.

> IF the professor regularly tells jokes that present women as sex objects;
> OR habitually uses "he" or "his" to refer to students (even though 75 percent of Hunter's students are women);
> OR listens intently when a male student talks and responds to his remarks, but only smiles politely when a female student talks;
> OR makes derogatory remarks about gays and lesbians.

This kind of behavior may seem harmless or trivial to some people; and the professors who engage in it may have no intent to hurt or embarrass any student. But according to Title IX of the 1972 Federal Education Amendments, sexual harassment includes "objectionable emphasis on the sexuality or sexual identity of a student . . . when the intent or effect of the objectionable acts is to create an intimidating, hostile, or offensive academic environment for the members of one sex." The U.S. Department of Education Office of Civil Rights, the American Council on Education, and the CUNY Board of Trustees official policy on sexual harassment support this concern with sexual stereotyping.

Studies of students' reactions to this sort of classroom behavior (such as the 1980 Report on Sexual Harassment of the National Advisory Council on Women's Educational Programs) strongly indicate that many students do feel uncomfortable or abused when sexual discrimination sets the tone of a classroom. Though it obviously cannot be equated with attempts at seduction or sexual coercion, this sort of discriminatory behavior, called "gender harassment" is the most widespread form of sexual harassment in the classroom. According to recent studies, 70 percent of women college students experience gender harassment during their college years.[1]

The Hunter College Panel on Sexual Harassment has prepared this pamphlet in order to increase awareness among Hunter faculty of this form of sexual harassment. It is a step in our effort to promote discussion of the problem of sexual harassment—and of ways to remedy it—among students, faculty, and staff at Hunter. The following discussion is adapted from a pamphlet, *Avoiding Sexual Discrimination in the Classroom*, produced at California State University, Northridge, by the Women's Studies Program Committee, with joint sponsorship from the Counseling Center and School of Humanities.

> When the professor lectured, he directed it to the men in the class. They usually sat in a group together, and you could tell where the professor focused his eyes and directed his voice. . . . The professor continually told sexually derogatory jokes about women during class. Most of the women in the class went along with him and laughed at his jokes. I didn't. . . . One time he commented that Ms. M_____ didn't have a sense of humor. I felt a lot of pressure, because I wanted to speak up, but I felt my grade would suffer.[2]

This student is describing her experience with sexual discrimination in the classroom. Discrimination on the basis of gender or sexual orientation, however inadvertent, can discourage students from taking full advantage of their academic experiences. Ideally, the University classroom is a place where information and knowledge are shared equally among all students. However, research at a number of institutions—including Barnard, Berkeley, Dartmouth, Harvard, Oberlin, Wisconsin, and Yale— indicates that some male and female instructors behave in ways that demean women or exclude them from full participation in their courses.

Much discriminatory behavior towards students is not deliberate, since most teachers consciously intend to treat all students justly and fairly. Yet faculty have the power to control many events and interactions in the classroom, and in doing so they convey attitudes and values as well as ideas and information. Teachers who make disparaging remarks about, or implicitly devalue women, gays, or lesbians can undermine students' self-confidence and enthusiasm for learning. This negative experience in the classroom can create serious obstacles to students' academic, professional, and personal growth. The impact is similar to the effects of discrimination based on race, religion, age or other physical or cultural characteristics. Thus, a useful test for determining whether behavior is sexist is to imagine addressing similar kinds of behavior to members of a racial minority.

Examples of this kind of sexual stereotyping include the following:

* Explicit use of derogatory terms or stereotypic generalizations, such as "older women don't belong in college"; "Women have trouble with calculus"; or "Homosexuals engage in self-destructive life styles."

* Use of "humorous" images or statements that demean or trivialize people because of gender or sexual orientation, such as jokes about "dumb blonds," "gay hairdressers," or "lesbian feminists." In many instances women are portrayed primarily as sexual objects, as when slides of *Playboy* centerfolds are used to illustrate lectures in an anatomy class. Women who do not laugh at such jokes may be told (and may believe) that they lack a sense of humor. This accusation ignores the fact that such humor is directed at women.

* Reinforcing sexist stereotypes through subtle, often unintentional means, such as using classroom examples in which professional people, such as psychologists, managers, or politicians, are always referred to as men (even though many women students plan to enter these fields). Similarly, gays and lesbians may be habitually associated only with certain professions.

* Continual use of generic masculine terms such as "he" or "man" or "mankind" to refer to people of both sexes. Research indicates that these terms evoke masculine images in students' minds and effectively eliminate women as subjects of discourse, even though there may be no intent to do so.[4] References may also be made to men and women as *necessarily heterosexual* ("When you get married and have kids . . .").

Examples of discrimination against women as individuals or part of a group may incude the following:

* Habitually recognizing and calling on men more often than women in class discussions.

* Interrupting women more often than men, or allowing others in the class to do so.

* Addressing the class as if no women were present by using statements such as "When you were boys . . ." or "Ask your wives. . . ."

* Listening more attentively and responding more extensively to comments made by men than to those made by women.[5]

* Treating women who ask extensive questions and challenge grades as troublemakers when men are not treated this way. Women returning to

college report that some professors seem to feel threatened by their presence since they are more likely to challenge and question than younger women.

The fact that much sexual discrimination is intangible or unconscious permits some well-meaning teachers to dismiss or ignore it. However, there is little doubt that this behavior puts its victims at a distinct educational disadvantage and may have other lasting effects. In particular, such actions can discourage students from participating in class and from seeking help outside of class, can cause them to avoid or drop classes or to change majors, and can undermine their scholarly and career aspirations.

Certainly it would be a mistake to believe that all or most sexual discrimination is intentional. Teachers, like all other people, reflect and transmit unexamined cultural assumptions which may include the belief that women are less intellectually committed than men and that their work is less competent and important than men's work.[6] These assumptions are not confined to men; women faculty also can discriminate against women in the classroom. And, again, gay men and lesbians may also be the victims of similar stereotypic assumptions. Racial and ethnic biases may also reveal themselves in sexual discrimination.

Even small acts of discrimination are significant because they are part of a pervasive and cumulative pattern of social inequality. Teachers can begin to challenge that pattern first by carefully examining their own feelings and preconceptions about the roles of women and men in society, and then by becoming alert to overt and subtle differences in their interactions with men and women in the classroom.

A number of specific techniques are available for helping to eliminate sexual discrimination in the classroom. These include the following:

* When making general statements about women (or any other group), be sure that they are based on accurate information. Universal generalizations about any social group, such as "Women don't think geographically," are likely, at best, to represent uncritical oversimplifications of selected norms.

* Avoid "humor" or gratuitous remarks that demean or belittle people because of gender or sexual orientation, just as you would avoid remarks that demean or belittle people because of their race, religion, or physical characteristic. Respect the dignity of all students.

* Avoid using generic masculine terms to refer to people of both sexes. Although the effort to do this may involve some initial discomfort, it will result in more precise communication and understanding.

* When using illustrative examples, avoid stereotypes, such as making all authority figures men and all subordinates women.

* Try to monitor your behavior toward men and women in the classroom. (You might ask a friend to observe your classes.) Ask, for example:

— Do you give more time to men than to women students?

— Do you treat men more seriously than women students?

— Are you systematically more attentive to questions, observations, and responses made by men?

— Do you direct more of your own questions, observations, and responses to men than to women?

— Do you assume a heterosexual model when referring to human behavior?

* Encourage your department to add a question concerning discriminatory behavior in the classroom to teaching evaluations.

* Choose course material which does not perpetuate sexual stereotypes.

* Become better informed about sexual discrimination in the classroom. Useful sources on this subject include:

Phyllis Franklin et al., *Sexual and Gender Harassment in the Academy: A Guide for Faculty, Students, and Administrators* (New York: Commission on the Status of Women in the Professions, The Modern Language Association of America, 1981). Available for $3.50 and $1.00 postage from MLA, 62 Fifth Avenue, New York, NY 10011.

Guide to Nonsexist Language (Project on the Status and Education of Women, Association of American Colleges, 1818 R St., NW, Washington, D.C. 20009). Available for $2.00.

Roberta M. Hall and Bernice R. Sandler, *The Classroom Climate: A Chilly One for Women?* (Washington, D.C.: Project on the Status and Education of Women, Association of American Colleges, 1818 R Street, NW, Washington, D.C. 20009.

Myra P. Sadker and David M. Sadker, *Sex Equity Handbook for Schools* (New York: Logman, Inc., 1982).

Increased understanding and awareness can lead to important changes in behavior. The long-term professional rewards of these changes include better communication with students, improved teaching effectiveness, and eventual realization of equal educational opportunity for all students.

Notes

1.   Billie Dzeich and Linda Weiner, *The Lecherous Professor: Sexual Harassment on Campus* (Boston: Beacon Press, 1984).

2.   This quote is taken from one of several reports from students in the California State University, Northridge, Women's Studies minor who described their experience with sexual discrimination in the classroom in Spring 1983.

3.   Roberta M. Hall and Bernice R. Sandler, *The Classroom Climate: A Chilly One for Women?* (Washington, D.C.: Project on the Status and Education of Women, Association of American Colleges, 1982), 2.

4.   See Hall and Sandler, 1982.

5.   Characteristic patterns of speech in women may predispose some teachers to treat them less seriously than men. Men's speech often is more assertive, couched in terms of impersonal abstractions and tough, "devil's advocate" exchanges. Women's speech often is more tentative, hesitant, polite and deferential. Styles of speech are correlated with gender, and a teacher unconsciously may react more to the style than to the content of a student's utterances. See Hall and Sandler, 9-10.

6.   See Veronic F. Nieva and Barbara A. Gutek, "Sex Effects on Evaluations," *The Academy of Management Review*, Vol. 5, No. 2, 1980, 267-276.

Training for Faculty in Issues Relating to Sexual Harassment on Campus: A Resource Manual

K.C. Wagner

The following material was developed for a seminar for faculty who were designated as sexual harassment "support counselors" for students on their college campus.

The material describes two participatory sessions which followed a film and group discussion. These materials were used for purposes of discussion and reference. They were presented as examples to be adapted, revised, or changed according to the philosophy and purposes of the committee and the institution.

All of these materials were adapted from Working Women's Institute counseling program and represent eleven years of collective experience and refinement. The materials, files, and resources from Working Women's Institute are available from:

Center for Research on Women
101 Barnard Hall
3009 Broadway
New York, NY 10027
212-280-2067

I thank my colleagues for developing and refining the following materials: Peggy Crull, Julie Goldscheid, Karen Sauvigne, Katy Taylor, Joan Vermeulen.

Sample Workshop Agenda

Session 2

I. Introduction
    A. What is a support counselor?
       1. qualities
       2. functions
       3. expectations
    B. Policy of college
       1. EEOC Guidelines and Supreme Court decision in Vinson-Meritor case
       2. Alexander versus Yale case
    C. Record keeping
       1. philosophy
       2. logistics
          a. release form
          b. intake form
          c. referrals inside and outside campus
II. Sexual Harassment on Campus
    A. The definition of sexual harassment on campus
       1. Scope and range
          a. attitude (*i.e.*, voice, tone, non-verbal behavior)
          b. environment (*i.e.*, innuendoes, language, cartoons, posters)
          c. patterns of incidents
    B. The Lecherous Professor
       1. The Roles they Assume: "Everyone knows that's just his style"
       2. The Reasons: "Balancing the 'blame the victim' scenario"
       3. The Context: "Surveying the land"
    C. The College Women as Target of Harassment
       1. Acknowledging the biases
       2. Vulnerabilities
       3. Attempts at coping
III. The Initial Interview
    A. Principles
    B. Group exercise
    C. Feedback
IV. Problem Solving and Interview Techniques
    A. Purpose
    B. Sequence

C. Outcome

V. Questions and Answers

Session 3

VI. Developing Options
    A.   The Next Steps
        1.   philosophy
        2.   small group problem solving
    B.   Role Play Presentations
    C.   Feedback
VII. The Follow Up
    A.   Time frame
        1.   crisis intervention
        2.   short term options
        3.   long term options
    B.   Educational Function
        1.   forums
        2.   faculty meetings
        3.   curriculum
VIII. Questions and Answers

Group Exercises

Situation

A college student has made an appointment with you to "check out" the Sexual Harassment Task Force. You have no other information about who the student is or the nature of the situation. This is your first meeting together.

Group Goal

The goal for the group is to fully explore the problem with the student, discuss the stress impact of the situation (emotional, physical, school related), ideally how the student would like to see the situation resolved and, if appropriate, some coping strategies. This is to be done as if you were the same support counselor. What this means is that there is to be a flow, a process, a logical progression of exploration. Consequently, it is essential that you listen to each other while following up on ideas in order to create this movement.

Method

Each person in the group will have the opportunity to ask two questions of this student. It is perfectly okay to follow the same topic or line of probing of the person before you. But remember, the goal is to explore all the issues.

Notes:

Sexual Harassment Committee
Support Counselor Manual

Contents: Draft Intake Form, Draft Release Form, Initial
Interview, Interview Techniques, Defining the Role of the
Support Counselor, Thoughts on Options, and Group Exercise

Draft Intake Form

CONFIDENTIAL

Date of call   Counselor   Case No.

_____   _____   _____

Name _____   Sexual Harassment

_____ current

_____ past

Address: _____   Other _____

_____

_____

_____

Telephone (H) _____

(W) _____

Draft Intake Form (continued)

Appointment Date _____

Follow up:

Description of sexual harassment problem—student status, nature of incident, description of harasser, school related consequences.

Stress Reactions—emotional, physical, school related.

Counselor Impressions—personal, options, strategies to pursue. Be aware that you may have to show these records to others; avoid any statements that could be used against the student. Example: vague and potentially harmful: "student was hysterical." Safer comment: "student displayed anxiety as is a typical reaction to this type of behavior."

Other critical facts:

Strategies	Done to Date/Outcome	Discussed/Will Do
Contact with other students		
Verbal objection		
Written objection		
Keeping log		

Strategies	Done to Date/Outcome	Discussed/Will Do

Complaints (Check)
— to harasser
— chair of department
— dean
— Sexual Harassment
   committee
— Affirmative Action
— other

Consult(ed) with MD,
   Attorney, Therapist

Status of Parental
   Involvement

Other:

Follow Up Contacts:

Date	Who Called	Content	Counselor

Draft Release Form

I have contacted the Sexual Harassment Task Force Committee of _____
College for information regarding my rights and options as a student.
I fully understand that the Sexual Harassment Task Force Committee of _____
College and the Task Force member I spoke with are *not* responsible for any decision
I may make regarding my academic situation or the results of any such decision.
I understand that I am most familiar with the circumstances firsthand, and I must
finally make a choice about what course(s) of action to take.

_____

Name

Draft Release Form (continued)

Date

Member

Initial Interview

Introduce Committee/Task Force, its name, and affiliation within college community:

> its philosophy—its role—discuss extent of confidentiality and your role as support counselor.

Establish guidelines for the contact:

> type and nature of contacts;
> goal of meetings;
> student's responsibility regarding decisions.

Conduct meeting:

> process to explore situation, provide information and options; initiate exploration (what, when, where, how); explore stress impact (personal and school related); non-judgmental, active and observant listening; guided movement (ventilation, validation, clarification, partialize, practice); establish short and long term goals; summarize status of situation to date; schedule folow up.

Follow up:

> contact with student;
> explore other referral sources, if appropriate;
> contact with support counselor network;
> contact with other administrative supports;

Interview Techniques

Individual Into Group Context as Student

> "The stress that you have described is, of course, very debilitating but it is a common feature of sexual harassment."

> "Although each individual is unique in terms of how they respond to stress, there are some common symptoms shared by those who experience sexual harassment."

"Some common stresses experienced by women dealing with sexual harassment are. . . ."

Clarification Statements

"Let me see if I understand the situation, you are saying that. . . ."
"It sounds like. . . ."
"Are you saying that you want to get the harassment to stop but you are afraid to jeopardize your grade?"

Reality Statements

"It's not an easy choice to make but research shows that ignoring sexual harassment doesn't make it go away."
"It's really up to you to decide on a strategy since you have to follow through with it."
"My role is to provide you with information on the issue, on your rights and options as a college student."
"We all have expectations of how the situation should be resolved, but to be most effective it's important for you to use the steps that the college has put into place."

Supportive Statements

"You have been under much stress and you have handled it the best you could."
"I know how frightening it is to make a decision without having any guarantees."
"You are in the best position to make judgments about your situation, trust your instincts."
"I know how overwhelming it feels to face the entire situation; let's break it down into parts."

Action-Oriented Statements

"Let's brainstorm about all the possible things you could say to express your objections."
"A suggestion would be to list the low and high risk strategies with the possible consequences of each."
"Let's move to a discussion of your rights and options as a student."

Defining the Role of the Support Counselor

Counselor Involvement

The Next Step. Using your case situation, each group should decide on a next step (assume that this was a collaborative decision with the student), designate characters for a role play, have a brief rehearsal and then present it to the group.

The student will deal directly with the professor on a one-to-one basis. (SCENE: The professor will be defensive and try to blame the student.)

OR

An informal, more personal approach to the professor is utilized by the counselor without the student present.

(SCENE: The counselor tries to mediate a solution, which is difficult given the conflicting points of view which emerge from the discussion.)

A meeting with the professor is considered inappropriate; another strategy is developed which involves bringing this to the attention of an administrator or affirmative action.

(SCENE: The counselor is trying to protect the identity of the student while trying to get a sense of the administrator's response.)

OR

Other:

Which issues should be addressed? What kinds of documentation are needed or should be used to illustrate points? What kinds of solutions should be suggested? How would the counselor or the student go about opening the meeting or initiate the discussion? How should it be structured?

Thoughts on Options

There is no one best option for any situation; what will work depends on the:

> individual (her/his personal profile and interpretation of the problem);
> situation (what seems possible, given the setting).

Every strategy has potential risks and benefits. It is a good idea to have each student spell out what s/he thinks s/he might gain/lose when considering an option.

Often a student will be reluctant or fearful to act. Unless s/he is in physical danger there is usually time to carefully think through the strategy that makes most sense. Try to facilitate how to define the situation on her/his own terms. A good first step is almost always to encourage a written log, to get a clear sense of what exactly has happened, as well as to develop documentation that may be helpful. Identify other students, past and present with similar problems.

Develop a series of coping strategies to enable the student to deflect remarks.

Role play verbal responses with students to give them confidence that they can object to the behavior (*i.e.*, change subject, avoid one-to-one contact, social events, take another student along).

Encourage a log to keep dated records of incidents and attempts to deal with the situation. This log should include names of witnesses, copies of pictures, notes, etc.

Legitimize stress reactions by defining typical patterns.

When in the middle of the problem, it is hard to see the supports that may exist. Students should be encouraged to think about supportive students who would be available to them during class or the school day. Or, groups of students who would get together and let a professor know about his offensive behavior.

Timing is an important factor in discussing options. A letter objecting to the harassment may be seen as inflammatory if it comes out of the blue, but may effectively show that you're serious if it follows a discussion.

It is not uncommon for related issues (*i.e.*, sexual assault, the need for long term counseling, etc.) to surface in the course of a discussion of options. If appropriate, make referrals to campus or community groups.

Group Exercise

Instructions: One member assume student's role, later should give group feedback on counseling approaches. Remaining group members should each have two interactions with "student;" remember, you are to act as if you are the same support counselor.

Student—Female

You are very frightened of telling anyone about a series of incidents with your professor that made you feel uncomfortable. This included stares during class, comments about your looks as a greeting each morning and touching you under the chin as you were asking him a question after class one afternoon. While you were alone in his office discussing your term project, he suggested that you go out for coffee "sometime." You have not given any verbal response but have demonstrated your objections by moving away or blushing. You feel very guilty since you felt flattered by his attention at first. However, the incident in his office made you think there were strings attached. It's mid-way through the term and you just want to get this to stop. You are very anxious about being alone with him and you are afraid you grade will be negatively affected by this.

Student—Male

You are very angry about the fact that the "girls" in your lab seem to get favorable treatment by your professor who is always flirting with them. You feel that his flirtation with them in class takes time away from your questions. You think that the C you received on your lab project was proof that you didn't get your fair share of his attention. You have even seen the professor walk out with a group of girls in the class and have seen them talking in the parking lot. You want your grade changed and his behavior to stop. You think that all a girl has to do to get a good grade is to look pretty.

Student—Female

You say you are coming out of your concern for a friend, who is unwilling to come forward herself, but you are really talking about yourself. Call your friend Eileen and say that she has confided in you about a problem she is having with her math professor, Mr. Green. You recount the following story:

> Eileen was failing math and Mr. Green offered to work with her after class. At first they met in the library and then on two occasions met on a Saturday in his home. Eileen really appreciated his help since she planned to attend a 4 year college the following fall. After their last meeting Mr. Green suggested they go out for lunch to celebrate her progress. Eileen enthusiastically agreed to his idea and Mr. Green suggested that he drive his car there. Eileen expected to go to a nearby diner and was surprised that he drove to a small cafe in another town. While they were at lunch Mr. Green started touching her hand and speaking in low, romantic tones. Eileen successfully changed the topic and left feeling panic stricken. She missed her two classes the following week and had another student pretend to be her mother and say that she was ill. Eileen felt that Mr. Green was really nice to help her and didn't want to get him into trouble but felt sick about the situation and wondered if she had encouraged him without realizing it.

Finally you blurt out that you are talking about yourself and are terrified about facing him and unable to concentrate on studying for your finals.

Contributors

Richard Barickman, an Associate Professor of English at Hunter College, is co-author (with Susan MacDonald and Myra Stark) of *Corrupt Relations*, a study of sexuality and gender in Nineteenth-century British fiction. He is currently Co-Coordinator of the Hunter College Panel on Sexual Harassment, which he helped to found. He has written about sexual harassment, conducted workshops and participated in panels on sexual harassment in the college environment.

Mary Kay Biaggio obtained her Ph.D. from Utah State University and has served on the faculties of University of Idaho, Indiana State University, and Oregon Graduate School of Professional Psychology at Pacific University, where she is currently serving as Program Director. She has been a member of a research team examining various forms of sexual victimization, including sexual harassment. She has taught Feminist Therapy and the Psychology of Women, as well as taking an active role in university policies regarding sexual harassment and the status of women on university campuses.

Deborah Watts is a counseling psychologist at Indiana State University's Counseling Center and adjunct Assistant Professor with the Counseling Psychology doctoral program. She received her doctorate in counseling from the University of Maryland. Most of her clinical work is with survivors of interpersonal violence—incest, rape, battering, and sexual harassment. She also trains doctoral students in individual counseling with an emphasis on gender issues.

Arlene Brownell is Director of Research and Project Development with International Learning Systems, Inc., a management consulting company in Evergreen, Colorado. Previous to her work in private industry, she was Assistant Professor of Psychology at Indiana State University. After receiving her Ph.D. in Social Ecology at the University of California at Irvine, she completed an NIMH Postdoctoral Fellowship in Psychiatric Epidemiology at the School of Public Health, University of California at Los Angeles. Her research includes the study of the relationship between environmental stressors (*e.g.*, sexual victimization) and well-being, with an emphasis on the stressor-moderating effects of social support and coping.

Lela Demby completed her undergraduate degree at Princeton University, where she worked on establishing a peer support system for students who were victims of academic sexual harassment. She has been particularly interested in issues of academic sexual harassment that are unique to ethnic minority women.

Darlene C. DeFour received her undergraduate degree from Fisk University and her Ph.D. from the University of Illinois at Urbana-Champaign. She is an assistant professor of Psychology at Hunter College. She is an active member of the Association of Black Psychologists. Her current research interests include the study of the impact of networks and mentors on the career development of Black graduate students and professionals.

Louise F. Fitzgerald received her doctorate in psychology from the Ohio State University and is currently Associate Professor of Educational Psychology and Psychology at the University of Illinois at Champaign-Urbana. She is widely published in the area of women's career development, and is the co-author of *The Career Psychology of Women*, published by Academic Press. She is the co-author of the *Sexual Experiences Questionnaire*, and continues to conduct research on sexual harassment in academia. Her latest studies have to do with coping patterns of harassment victims. In addition to her research, Dr. Fitzgerald teaches graduate courses in the psychology of women and feminist psychotherapy.

Dorothy O. Helly earned degrees from Smith College, Radcliffe College, and Harvard University. She is a historian of Victorian England. At Hunter College she is a professor of history and has been an associate dean, coordinator of Women's Studies, and has co-chaired the Sexual Harassment Panel from 1984 to 1988. She was one of the first to raise the issue of sexual harassment at the college and helped write the panel's guidelines. She considers her work as a coauthor of *Women's Realities, Women's Choices: An Introduction to Women's Studies* (Oxford University Press, 1983) as central to her analysis of the issue and strategies to overcome it.

Sam Korn is a professor at Hunter College, City University of New York and Chair of the Department of Psychology. He has been part of the New York Longitudinal Study of the development of temperament and adjustment since 1960. He has also been president of the City University of New York Council of the American Association of University Professors, a member of the Board of Directors of the New York Civil Liberties Union, and was the Hunter College Ombudsperson from 1979 to 1985.

Mary P. Koss is a professor of psychiatry at the University of Arizona Medical School. For over ten years she has conducted research on hidden rape, that is, sexual aggression and victimization among the general population. One project, a national study of more than 6,000 college students, was the subject of the book, *I Never Called it Rape: The Ms. Report on Recognizing, Fighting, and Surviving Date and Acquaintance Rape*. Also recently completed was a study of the impact of victimization on health and medical services usage among working women. Under contract from the National Institute of Mental Health she prepared a mental health research agenda in the area of violence against women. In addition to many papers published in the scientific literature, Dr. Koss is the co-author of the book, *The Rape Victim: Clinical and Community Approaches to Treatment*. She is an associate editor of the journal, *Violence and Victims*, and is a member of the editorial boards of the *Journal of Consulting and Clinical Psychology* and *Psychology of Women Quarterly*. In 1986, Dr. Koss was recipient of a distinguished publication award from the Association of Women in Psychology.

Bernice Lott received her Ph.D. from UCLA in 1954 where she majored in Social Psychology and minored in Cultural Anthropology. Her interests have continued to be in socialization, interpersonal attitudes and behavior, and have more recently focused on the experiences of women and, in particular, on sexist discrimination in face-to-face situations. The Association for Women in Psychology twice honored her with its Distinguished Publication Award, and in 1988 she received an award for Excellence in Scholarship from the University of Rhode Island. Her most recent book (1987), published by Brooks/Cole, is *Women's Lives*.

Alayne Ormerod is a graduate student in counseling psychology at the University of Illinois at Urbana-Champaign. She earned an undergraduate degree in psychology from Westmont College in Santa Barbara, California, and a master's degree in counseling psychology from the University of California, Santa Barbara. Originally a native of the Philadelphia area, she lived in Santa Barbara for ten years prior to moving to Illinois. She is currently examining the relationship between women students' self-efficacy and coping behaviors with sexual harassment.

Lauren M. Weitzman is a graduate student in counseling psychology at the University of Illinois, Urbana-Champaign. A native of California, she earned an undergraduate degree in psychology and women's studies at the University of Utah, and a master's degree in counseling psychology at the University of California, Santa Barbara. Strongly committed to research and practice in areas relevant to women, she is currently working on an exploratory model examining factors involved in labelling the experience of sexual harassment.

Yael Gold is currently working on her doctorate in counseling psychology at the University of Illinois at Urbant-Champaign. Originally a native of New York, she received a B.A. from the University of Arizona and then went on to complete a Master's in counseling psychology at the University of California, Santa Barbara. She addresses a variety of issues related to women in both practice and research. She is presently conducting research aimed at examining the ways that women cope with sexual harassment and other forms of sexual exploitation.

Michele A. Paludi is a developmental psychologist who specializes in women's achievement and the career pathways they follow. She has studied mentoring and being mentored, fear of success, performance evaluation, attributions for success and failure, and recently, sexual and gender harassment of undergraduate women. She is currently investigating the incidence of harassment of women of color and re-entry women. She is the author of *Teaching the psychology of women: A manual of resources* (1990 by SUNY Press) and the coeditor of *Images of women in the academy: A feminist restructuring of the disciplines* (1990 by Haworth Press). At Hunter College she has been a member of the Sexual Harassment Panel and its co-coordinator since 1988. Michele facilitates the Hunter College Women's Career Development Research Collective, which includes as its participants, *Judi Dovan, Marc Grossman, Joni Kindermann, Brenda Lehrer, Susan Matula, Donna Mulcahy, Julie Ostwald,* and *Carole Ann Scott.*

Kathryn Quina is an Associate Professor of psychology and women's studies at the University of Rhode Island, and Psychology Coordinator at the URI College of Continuing Education. She has been active in research, crisis intervention, and public education about rape and harassment since 1975, and has coauthored *Rape, incest, and harassment: A guide to counseling survivors* (forthcoming by Praeger). She has been a Mellon Scholar in feminist curriculum transformation, and recently coedited *Toward a psychology of people: Integrating gender and cultural diversity into the psychology curriculum* (1988 by the American Psychological Association).

Vita C. Rabinowitz received her Ph.D. in social psychology from North-western University in 1978. She is currently an Associate Professor of Psychology at Hunter College. Her research interests focus on attributional processes in helping relationships, particularly in medical and psychothera-peutic settings, and coping with victimization.

Carole Ann Scott was a returning student at Hunter College, CUNY, after 12 years as a professional actress. She served on the Hunter College Sexual Harassment Panel and participated in the Hunter College Women's Career

Development Research Collective. She is pursuing her own research in the area of developmental psychology. She intends to go to law school.

Sandra Shullman is an organizational psychologist in private practice in Columbus, Ohio. In her role as Director of Organizational Horizons, Inc., she conducts training seminars and workshops on sexual harassment in businesses in the Columbus area. She was the co-author (with Louise Fitzgerald) of the Sexual Experiences Survey, an instrument used to obtain incidence data in national surveys of academic and workplace sexual harassment.

Barbara Watts is the Dean of the Law School at the University of Cincinnati. Her research and writing deals predominantly with issues of sex discrimination, including sexual harassment.

Bernice Sandler has been Director of the Project on the Status and Education of Women of the Association of American Colleges since its inception in 1971. The Project is the oldest national higher education project concerned with achieving equity for women students, faculty, and administrators. The Project has published over 100 original papers, including the first nationally distributed papers on sexual harassment in academe, and on the chilly classroom climate for women.

Suzanne Siegel is a reference librarian and Head of Computer Search Services at Hunter College Library.

Helen Remick is the Equal Employment Officer for the University of Washington. She is nationally recognized as an expert on comparable worth and has presented over 200 speeches and training sessions on comparable worth and sexual harassment.

Jan Salisbury is a psychotherapist in private practice and an organizational consultant in sexual harassment. She has served as an expert witness in many sexual harassment trials. She was senior author of "Counseling victims of sexual harassment" published in *Journal of Psychotherapy* with Helen Remick, Donna Stringer, and Angela Ginorio.

Donna Stringer is a social psychologist with 15 years' experience managing women's organizations. She is currently Deputy Director, Washington State Department of Licensing, and an organizational consultant with Andy Reynolds and Associates. She has conducted research, developed policies and procedures, and provided over 100 speeches and training sessions on sexual harassment.

Angela Ginorio is Director of both the Women's Information Center and the Northwest Center for Research on Women at the University of Wisconsin. She is a social psychologist who has published in the areas of ethnic relations, gender roles, and sexual harassment. She has served on American Psychological Association committees regarding ethnic minority concerns.

K.C. Wagner is a national consultant in the area of sexual harassment prevention within the work environment and academia. For eight years she worked at the Working Women's Institute in New York City, one of the leading organizations in the fight against sexual harassment. In her capacity as Counseling Director, K.C. provided individual advocacy or group workshops to over 500 women annually. As Director of the Institute, she conducted seminars at corporations and educational institutions across the country and was featured on national television and in the print media. In 1985, K.C. co-authored, with Peggy Crull, a survey report entitled "Gender bias and sexual harassment in the Federal Aviation Administration's Eastern Region."

Sue Rosenberg Zalk is the Director of the Center for the Study of Women and Society of the City University of New York. She is also Professor of Educational Foundations at Hunter College. Her research has concerned the development of gender role identity and also racial identity. She is one of the authors of *Women's realities, women's choices*, the first text written for the introductory course in women's studies. Sue's work on expectant fathers is considered to be classic in the fields of parenting and sexuality. She is the recent past president of the Women's Division of the New York State Psychological Association.

Index